Android

App Distribution

By Fuad Kamal & Evana Margain Puig

Android App Distribution

By Fuad Kamal & Evana Margain Puig

Notice of Rights

Notice of Liability

Trademarks

ISBN: 978-1-950325-23-8

Table of Contents

Book License

By purchasing *Android App Distribution*, you have the following license:

- You are allowed to use and/or modify the source code in *Android App Distribution* in as many apps as you want, with no attribution required.
- You are allowed to use and/or modify all art, images and designs that are included in *Android App Distribution* in as many apps as you want, but must include this attribution line somewhere inside your app: "Artwork/images/designs: from *Android App Distribution*, available at www.raywenderlich.com".
- The source code included in *Android App Distribution* is for your personal use only. You are NOT allowed to distribute or sell the source code in *Android App Distribution* without prior authorization.
- This book is for your personal use only. You are NOT allowed to sell this book without prior authorization, or distribute it to friends, coworkers or students; they would need to purchase their own copies.

All materials provided with this book are provided on an "as is" basis, without warranty of any kind, express or implied, including but not limited to the warranties of merchantability, fitness for a particular purpose and noninfringement. In no event shall the authors or copyright holders be liable for any claim, damages or other liability, whether in an action of contract, tort or otherwise, arising from, out of or in connection with the software or the use or other dealings in the software.

All trademarks and registered trademarks appearing in this guide are the properties of their respective owners.

Before You Begin

This section tells you a few things you need to know before you get started, such as what you'll need for hardware and software, where to find the project files for this book, and more.

What You Need

To follow along with this book, you'll need:

- **Kotlin 1.5.** This book uses Kotlin 1.5 throughout. The examples may work with an earlier version of Kotlin, but they're untested.
- **Android Studio Bumblebee or later.** Android Studio is the main development tool for Android. You'll need Android Studio Bumblebee or later for the tasks in this book. You can download the latest version of Android Studio from Android's developer site here: https://developer.android.com/studio.
- **A Github Account**. Some examples in this book use Github. You can set up an account here: https://www.github.com.
- **A Google Play Developer Account**. Many examples in this book use the Google Play Developer console. If you don't have a Google Play developer account, you can set one up here: https://play.google.com/console/u/0/signup.

If you haven't installed the latest version of Android Studio, be sure to do so before continuing with the book. The code covered in this book depends on Android 12, Kotlin 1.5 and Android Studio Bumblebee. You may run into problems if you try to work with an older version.

Book Source Code & Forums

Where to download the materials for this book

The materials for this book can be cloned or downloaded from the GitHub book materials repository:

- https://github.com/raywenderlich/paps-materials/tree/editions/1.0

Forums

We've also set up an official forum for the book at https://forums.raywenderlich.com/c/books/android-app-distribution. This is a great place to ask questions about the book or to submit any errors you may find.

"In loving memory of my wife, Huma. Not every warrior carries a sword."

— Fuad Kamal

"To my partner Miguel, who has pushed my career by helping me see beyond my mental limitations and has been by my side as I achieve what I never thought I would. To my mom and sister, who support me unconditionally and help me every day to stay on track and find new strategies to become a better version of myself. To my grandma and grandpa, who were by my side when I was growing up. To my friends, who are always there for me to hear my craziest ideas and give fun to my days. To Ray Wenderlich and each of the members of the team for giving me this great opportunity to write my first book and to explore the great world of teaching what I love the most."

— Evana Margain

"To my parents, friends and colleagues, who have always supported me and pushed me to achieve more. This book wouldn't have been possible without them."

— Subhrajyoti Sen

About the Authors

Evana Margain Puig is one of the authors of this book. She's an expert in mobile development and architecture in native Android and iOS. She has helped build apps for many companies and devices. She likes the integration of her job with iOT, which has made her develop apps for smart devices like TVs, cars and appliances. She's also into video games and has made great friends across the world through this hobby. She is @evanamp on Twitter and you can find her personal website at evanamargain.com.

Fuad Kamal is one of the authors of this book. He provides mobile strategy, architecture and development for the Health, Fitness and Telematics markets. If you've ever been to an airport, you've likely seen his work — the flight arrival and departure screens are a Flash 7 interface he wrote towards the beginning of the millennium. He's also into photography. He can be contacted through anaara.com. He's @FlexRonin on Twitter and Instagram.

About the Editors

Lance Gleason is the final pass editor of this book. Over the years, he has worked in everything from server side development, IoT and wearables to mobile development. He has been an Android fan ever since he pre-ordered the G1 in 2008. After a few years of being an Android fan, he finally took the plunge into Android development when he became a Google Glass Explorer in 2013. He's had a chance to work on projects for organizations ranging from small startups to large companies with millions of users. When he isn't writing code, you can find him traveling to interesting places, wine tasting, scuba diving or exploring a new hobby or interest. You can find him on Twitter at @lgleasain.

Eric Crawford is a tech editor of this book. He's a Senior Software Developer at John Deere, where he bounces between iOS and Android development. Before coming to Deere, he did freelance mobile development and server-side web development utilizing Java. In his free time, he likes to dabble into other platforms like IOT and cloud computing

Subhrajyoti Sen is a tech editor of this book. He's a Google Developer Expert for Android and an Android Engineer at KeepTruckin, where he develops apps to improve the trucking industry. Before this, he also worked on apps to improve the experience of Indian investors. He believes in the power of Open Source and communities and actively tries to give back. When not writing code, you can find him binge-watching anime, reading up on public policy or playing Rocket League.

April Rames is the editor for this book. She is a former high school English and theatre teacher and director. When not volunteering at her daughters' schools, she usually spends her time being asked to pretend to be a unicorn, zombie princess or super hero. In her spare time, she enjoys reading, making pasta and exploring the Gulf Coast with her family.

Introduction

If you're creating a consumer Android app, you'll need to publish it to the Google Play store. When Android first came out, publishing an app was a fairly simple process. As the platform has matured, however, extra required steps have been added to the publishing process. To successfully publish your app, you'll need to know how to navigate this process.

Furthermore, there are many app publishing tools and techniques that can make the difference between a successful app release and one that has issues. While Android developers of all experience levels will find the information in this book useful, there are two groups that will benefit the most from this book:

1. New Android developers.
2. Experienced Android developers that have not worked on consumer apps or who haven't been directly involved in the app release process.

How to read this book

This book is divided into four sections. If you're new to the consumer release process, reading the book in a linear fashion might be the best approach. On the other hand, if you're more experienced or need a reference for a looming deadline, you can choose to skip around and use each chapter as a standalone tutorial.

This book is split into four main sections:

Section I: App Store Quick Start

You need some fundamental knowledge to publish an app to the app store. For example, you need to know the nuts and bolts of building and publishing the app along with some key concepts surrounding test tracks — including beta and alpha releases — and release strategies. Taken together, these concepts are what we like to call **minimal viable product**, or **MVP**, for publishing an app to the app store.

Section II: Security & Optimization

A secure and streamlined app can be the difference between a successful release and one with problems. This section will show you the various steps of developing apps that are secure, reasonably sized and optimized. The topics you'll cover in this section include app permissions, obfuscation and steps for hardening your app's security.

Dynamically deploying features allows you to do limited testing. Depending on the technique you use, it can also be a great way to reduce the app's size by only loading the features each user needs. You'll learn about that in Chapter 8, "Adding Features Dynamically".

You might also want to create a white label version of your app or build flavors for testing. Chapter 9, "Build Variants: Implementing Build Types," covers all of that to guide you through the process of creating build variants and flavors.

Section III: Automation — Continuous Integration & Delivery

Manually building and releasing your app is time-consuming and error-prone. Chapter 11, "Automation Tools for Your Local Environment" guides you through tools and steps to help automate the process.

It's also important to have reliable builds that can build on multiple machines — and that means constantly integrating code so releases don't become a big, error-prone merging event. Chapter 12, "Continuous Integration & Build Servers" shows you some tips and tricks to get CI set up for your project.

Section IV: Beyond Publication

In an ideal world, you could release an app and, without doing anything, have it be wildly successful and generate money while you relax in the tropics. However, in the real world, an app is a living thing that needs continuous care and feeding.

App ratings can make or break an app's success in the store. Chapter 13, "Getting Top Ratings & Avoiding Negative Reviews", talks about techniques for cultivating good reviews and addressing negative ones.

Finally, it's important that the app doesn't only perform well upon release, but in the future as well. Chapter 14, "Monitoring & Improving App Performance", will show you how to make sure that your app is continuing to delight users over its lifespan.

Section I: App Store Quick Start

You need some fundamental things to publish an app to the app store. For example, you need the nuts and bolts of building and getting the app published along with some key concepts surrounding test tracks, including beta and alpha releases, and release strategies. Taken together, these concepts are what we like to call **minimal viable product**, or **MVP**, for publishing an app to the app store.

Chapter 1: The Perfect Build

By Evana Margain Puig

Whether you're releasing an app for the first time or you've done it a hundred times, everyone wants a perfect build. In this book, you'll find the steps you need to get your build there.

Publishing your Android app is one of the most exciting moments in creating a mobile app. It's that great moment when you get to share your hard work with the world. This book will guide you through the process and help you deliver a great product. You can check specific chapters if you want to explore a topic in-depth, or go step-by-step to learn how to publish an app to the Google Play Console.

In this chapter, you'll get an overview of all the topics you'll learn about in this book. In short, you could say this chapter will help you assemble all the ingredients of a perfect build and deployment system for Android apps.

You'll also download and explore *PodPlay*, the fully finished sample project used throughout the book. It's the final project in the "Android Apprentice" book. You'll use the app to learn the process of publishing apps to the Google Play Console as well as all the best practices, tips and tricks about the publishing process.

You'll also cover many of the terms and concepts you'll use throughout the book. Don't worry if you don't understand them all right away. Follow along as the chapters dive deep into each concept, and when you finish, you'll know exactly what each term means.

What to expect from the release process

The first expectation of any delivery process is to make your app available to users. This process can have many steps. In this book, we've divided the process into four sections:

1. *App Store Quick Start*: This is the section you're reading right now. You'll learn the bare minimum needed to get your app in the Google Play Console. If you're on a tight timeline, don't worry. This first section will help you get your app out for your users in no time.
2. *Security and Optimization*: Of course, you can release your app with the basics, but at some point, you'll want to add more features, such as optimizing your app size and offering your users advanced security. In this section, you'll learn more intermediate topics like permissions, security, making your app smaller, delivering features on-demand and build variants and types. While that might sound like a lot of information, you'll learn how to add each feature to your app one chapter at a time. In the end, both your users and the development team will thank you for adding these features.
3. *Automation: Continuous Integration and Delivery*: In this section, you'll learn about the concept known as **mobile dev ops**. When you're done, you'll understand the ins and outs of continuous integration and continuous deployment and delivery (CI/CD). You'll use Fastlane and GitHub actions, so you won't have to purchase anything to learn the process. Most of the knowledge you get from those two tools is easily portable to any other commercial tool.
4. *Beyond Publication*: The development process doesn't end once your app is in the Google Play Console. Bugs will appear, users will give feedback and you'll need hotfixes. This section will help you with the things that you'll need to take care of *after* you release your app. You'll learn how to manage user feedback, get analytics and crash reports as well as other key ways to market your app.

After going through the app's four sections, you'll have a good deal of experience with publishing apps in the Google Play Console. Since each chapter is about a specific topic you can come back to each of them when you're ready to take your app to the next level. Time to get started!

Tools for Release

At this point, you might be wondering what tools you need to release your app. There are three that you will need:

1. *A Google Developer Account*, which requires a one time-fee of $25 USD.
2. A finished app you want to upload. The app doesn't have to be production-ready, as you'll learn how to make releases for testing purposes to help you iterate on your development process. In this book, you'll use a sample app that's fully functional so you can follow along even if you don't have your own app yet.
3. *Android Studio* for generating certificates and adding configurations to your app.

The next chapter will give you step-by-step instructions for setting these up.

In an ideal world, what would "the perfect build" look like?

If you wanted to make a list of the characteristics of a "perfect build", it would be as unique as the app you're about to release. But in general, "the perfect build" would include:

- Separate versions for each of your environments.
- Separate versions for each of your app versions: For example, paid vs. free vs. premium.
- Groups of people who function as pre-release testers.
- Clear documentation with your app information.
- A repository with all your app *secrets*, which is a fancy way of saying all the keys, certificates and passwords required for your app release process.
- Reliable CI/CD tools that ensure code quality, run tests and do other heavy lifting.
- An easy and predictable way to release your app.
- Tools to get information from crashes, analytics and any other data you need.
- Clear communication paths with your final users so they have a great experience and want to use your app.

While this list could go on and on, these are the essential parts of a "Perfect Build".

Releasing pain points

If you ask any developer who has released an app in the past, particularly if it was a long time ago, they'll likely have a funny story about how much suffering they went through.

Fortunately, you have this book to help you avoid most of these pain points. Here are a few common ones you're likely to encounter in your build and delivery process:

Payment process

One of the most discouraging things for new developers is paying a fee to upload your apps. Unfortunately, going through online payment systems isn't as easy as it should be.

Moreover, in a company or corporate environment, the choice of "who's paying" for the account can become bureaucratic. Look at the next chapter for a step-by-step walkthrough of the payment process.

Filling out the Google Play console forms

Developing an app is a complex and multidisciplinary process, so when the time comes to release it, you'll expect the process to be fast and easy since you've already put in several hours of work. Let me warn you that the Google Play Console will require a lot of information, and many times you'll find you don't know the information, or hadn't even thought about some of it.

They'll also request some legal compliances you may not be aware of so you'll have to do some research to understand the terminology. Don't worry: This book has you covered. In the following chapters, you'll learn most of this process so that you don't have to make guesses while filling out the forms.

Saving the app certificate

When you release your app for the first time, you'll create a unique certificate that's valid for the app's lifetime. It's often hard to understand that you can't regenerate or recover this file if you lose it. Fortunately, in this book you'll learn some strategies to avoid losing the certificate.

CI / CD

Continuous integration and *continuous delivery* are widely discussed topics in the developer community. It's particularly interesting in the mobile area since you don't own the server where you deploy your app. Hence, you have to adhere to the guidelines and changes from the Google Play Console or whichever store you deploy to. CI/CD tools are powerful allies in your deployment process, and, with correct implementation, they'll make your life easier.

Concepts & Terminology

As you go through this book, you'll find terminology that may be new to you. You'll learn each term when it's needed, so be patient and follow along. If you don't find it, maybe it's a topic you'll see later in the book. To start, let's introduce some terms that are often confusing and may need some clarification.

Manual release

A *manual release* is when a person publishes an app by doing every step manually, and with as few tools as possible, except for basic ones like the Google Play Console and Android Studio. Examples of manual processes include not using any CI/CD tools, triggering tests whenever you want and exporting analytics information directly on the Google Play Console. In this book, you'll learn this approach first because you need to understand how they work manually before you can automate them.

Continuous integration

This term doesn't refer to the tool itself, but instead refers to the practice of triggering a build every time you make a change to your app, which also runs tests and linters.

The idea of continuous integration comes from many of the best software development practices and provides early bug detection. Basically, you want to avoid breaking your app when introducing new features. You'll learn about Continuous Integration in this book.

Continuous deployment

If you already have a continuous integration workflow and add continuous deployment, every change you make will automatically be released to production. This is more common in web apps, since you can usually release it directly to the server. But you can perform continuous deployment in Android by deploying to your beta testers through apps that send a built APK to them every time you make a change to the app.

> **Note**: The term deployment doesn't necessarily mean releasing to the end-user. You can have your app in production, say uploaded to the Google Play Console, but only released through alpha or beta channels without the production end-user having access to it. You'll learn about the options for doing this later in the book.

Continuous delivery

Although the terms delivery and deployment are sometimes used interchangeably, delivery in this case refers to the end-user, not the distribution platform of your choice. With continuous delivery, you release every change you make in a fixed time frame to the end-user. Since this requires a highly organized and committed team, usually only very large companies do this.

Getting the sample project

After all this theory, you now have a general idea of what you'll learn in this book. To dive into the release process, you'll work with a sample project called *PodPlay*, a podcast app built as the final project of Android Apprentice. It's a fully functional app that's ready for uploading to the Google Play Console.

This section is *optional*: If you don't know how to open a project in Android Studio, follow along. If you already know how to open a project, feel free to skip to *Running the Sample Project*.

Ensure you've downloaded or cloned the materials for this book. and go to the Chapter 1 materials folder. Go to **Android Studio ▸ Open an existing Android Studio Project**, and navigate to the location where you have the starter project for this chapter.

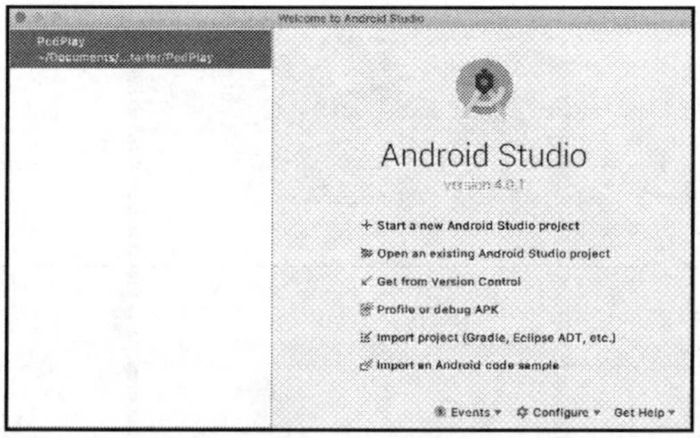

At the moment, you're not going to make any changes to the project. Instead, simply Look at what the project includes so you're familiar with what you're going to work on throughout the book.

The first time you open the project, a fresh Gradle build will run. You can check the status on the bottom right of the Android Studio status bar. Wait for it to say "Gradle sync finished" as in the image below.

It may take some time as it'll download all the dependencies you don't have yet. Don't worry. It's an automatic process, so you don't need to know which dependencies are missing.

Running the sample project

Once the Gradle Build finishes, try running the project with the buttons at the top right of Android Studio.

> **Note**: Make sure you have an emulator setup or a device connected to the computer so you can see what you'll work with.

The build process may take a while since it runs the Gradle build again. The amount of time depends greatly on your machine specs.

The first screen you'll see is an empty white screen with the title **Subscribed** and a search button.

Now click the search button and search for your favorite podcast by typing **Ray Wenderlich** in the search box.

Afterward, you'll see a list of podcasts that match your search. Click one of them.

You'll see the description of the podcast and a list of episodes. You can even click an episode and start playing it right away.

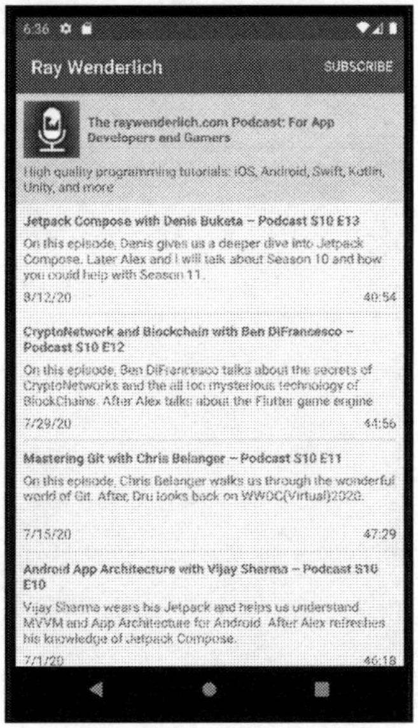

Click subscribe so you have that podcast in your subscribed list on the first screen. Then go back to this first screen.

Repeat the same process a couple of times if you want to add more podcasts. Also try playing an episode and listen to the podcast through the app. As you may notice, even though it's a simple app, it's functional and ready for you to publish to the Google Play Console.

Looking at PodPlay's code

Now that you understand the app you'll deploy, take a quick look at the code.

> **Note**: For this book, you don't necessarily have to understand the code. Many DevOps profiles do amazing things without understanding the language of the app they're releasing.

This project has a *package by layer* structure, which means you'll find a package for each layer of the app's architecture.

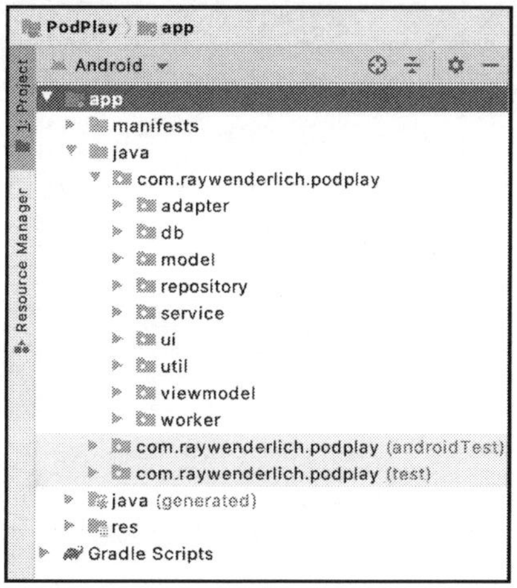

Look at the **ui** package to get a high-level understanding of the app structure. You'll find one Activity called **PodcastActivity** that takes care of searching for and displaying episodes. You will also find two Fragments:

1. **EpisodePlayerFragment** appears whenever you want to play a specific episode.
2. **PodcastDetailsFragment** appears when you check the details.

There's also an **adapter** package that displays the lists of podcasts and episodes as a helper to the UI.

Next, you'll look at **model**, which contains two classes:

1. Episode
2. Podcast

These classes are objects that represent the episodes and podcasts and have keys for persisting the information.

Then look at the **viewmodel** package and notice you have two View Model classes.

1. **PodcastViewModel** takes care of everything related to a podcast: Retrieving them, saving them, modeling the data of both the full podcast and the episodes.
2. **SearchViewmodel** takes care of the podcast searches and brings them back whenever you search for something.

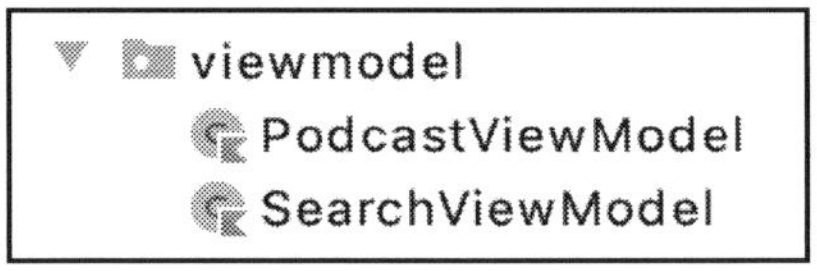

The **service** package takes care of all the backend communication. Anything related to network calls and responses happens there.

Besides that, there's also a persistency layer with a **repository** package and a **db** for persisting the data the next time you start the app.

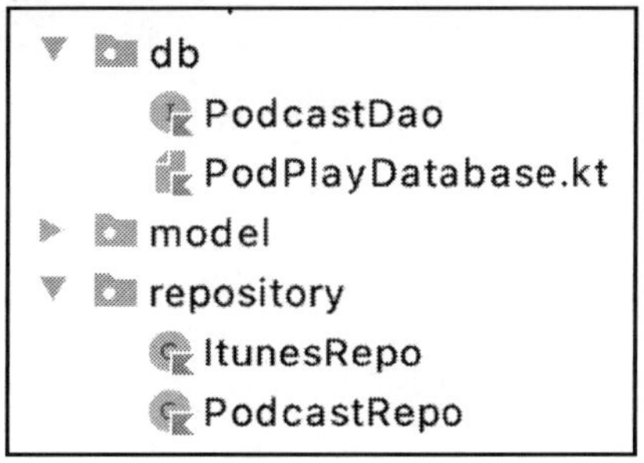

This is a general overview of the app structure. But again, you don't need to understand the code to release it to the Google Play Console.

Now you're ready to learn how to manually release the app!

Key points

- Releasing to the Google Play Console can involve many different practices but you don't have to do everything from the beginning.
- Google Play Console requests a series of forms that you need to fill out, including information and images from your app.
- You should keep your app's **certificate** in a safe place.
- **Security** and **Optimization** are essential points to consider when releasing an app.
- A good release workflow helps you get your app in front of testers before releasing it to the final user.
- Several tools can help make your release process easier and help you automate it.
- CI and CD can seem daunting and complicated initially, but if you release often, the effort saved will outweigh the learning curve. Plus, they aren't as tricky as they appear from the outside.
- PodPlay is a fully built app you'll use to learn how to release an app to the Google Play Console.
- There's no need to understand an app's code to release it to the console. One of your targets is to make the release process standalone, one that anyone in the team can perform.

Where to go from here?

This is just the beginning of your publishing journey. Now that you understand the process from a high level, move to Chapter 2, "App Store Quick Start". You'll get a hands-on approach by manually submitting the app to the Google Play Console and follow the happy path of the release process.

Chapter 2: App Store Quick Start

By Fuad Kamal

So you've finally built that app you've been dreaming about. Now it's time to share it with the world! But where do you start?

By the end of this chapter, you'll have the essentials you need to deploy your app to the Google Play Store. Later in this book you'll explore in greater depth many of the topics you'll touch on briefly in this chapter. Although this chapter focuses primarily on preparing the app for the Google Play Store, most of the steps apply regardless of the publishing platform.

Here's a quick overview of each step:

- Clean up any debugging code you may have in the source.
- Check the app version information.
- Create a release version of the app with the correct signing key.
- Test the release version on as many devices as possible.
- Create a Google Play Console developer account.
- Create screenshots, promotional graphics and videos.
- Fill out the app details on the Google Play Console.

Now you're ready to walk through these items in detail.

Code cleanup

First, make sure your project and code are ready for release. Here are a few items to consider:

Choosing a good package name

Once you submit an app to the store, you can't change the package name. The package name is embedded in **AndroidManifest.xml**, but you can set it in the app's **build.gradle**.

The package name must be unique from all other apps in the Play Store. One of the best ways to ensure your name is unique is to use a reverse naming convention based on your own domain name. For example, **PodPlay** published by **raywenderlich.com** has the package name **com.raywenderlich.podplay**. You can view your app's package name in your app-level **build.gradle**, as shown below.

```
defaultConfig {
  applicationId "com.raywenderlich.podplay"
  ...
}
```

> Note: For more information on how to use the package name and how it differs from the application ID, see the Android developer documentation:https://developer.android.com/studio/build/application-id .

Turning off debugging for release builds

By default, Android Studio creates debug and release build types for new projects.

For the release build type, Android Studio disables debugging by default. You can verify this by looking at the **buildTypes** section in the app **build.gradle**. If you have a `debuggable true` line in the release build type, remove it.

In the starter project for this chapter, open **app build.gradle**. Notice the `buildTypes` section:

```
buildTypes {
  release {
    minifyEnabled false
    proguardFiles getDefaultProguardFile('proguard-
android.txt'),    'proguard-rules.pro'
```

```
  }
}
```

There are two things of note here. First, when you make a new Android project in Android Studio, it sets `minifyEnabled` to `false`. Generally, you want to set `minifyEnabled` to `true`. However, setting it to `true` can have consequences, especially in more complex apps, so test your release build to make sure it works properly.

`minifyEnabled` allows code shrinking, obfuscation and optimization for your project's release build type but also increases build times. If you're unfamiliar with `minifyEnabled`, it can be a source of hard to track down bugs, which is another reason to test your release build thoroughly.

The second thing of note is the name of the Proguard file referenced, **proguard-android.txt**. You'll learn more about Proguard rules later. For now, know that the above reference is there because the sample app was made with an earlier version of Android Studio. As of Android Studio version 4.0.1, new projects reference **proguard-android-optimize.txt** by default. This change provides additional optimizations for your release build.

Change the `buildTypes` section to:

```
buildTypes {
  release {
    // Enables code shrinking, obfuscation, and optimization for
    // only your project's release build type.
    minifyEnabled true

    // Enables resource shrinking, which is performed by the
    // Android Gradle plugin.
    shrinkResources true

    // Includes the default ProGuard rules files that are
    // packaged with the Android Gradle plugin.
    proguardFiles getDefaultProguardFile(
      'proguard-android-optimize.txt'),
      'proguard-rules.pro'
  }
}
```

Removing logging

For your app's security, you should remove debugging log messages from your app's published version. Remove logging by deleting **Log** calls in the code.

Alternatively, you can let something called **R8** remove the calls during the release build. You'll learn more about R8 later. For now, know that to have R8 remove the logs, you need to add the following lines to **proguard-rules.pro** in the root of your project:

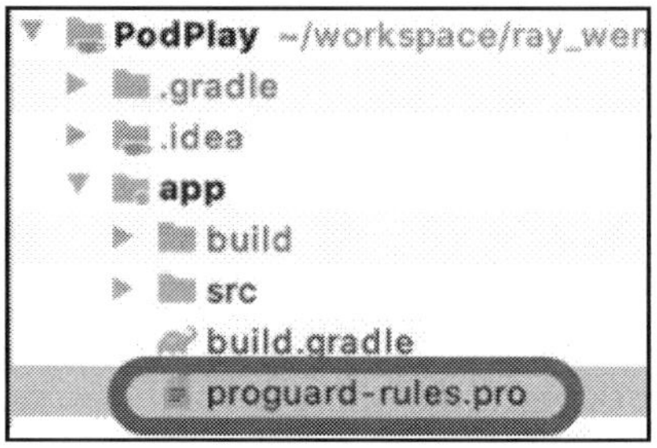


```
-assumenosideeffects class android.util.Log {
  public static boolean isLoggable(java.lang.String, int);
  public static int v(...);
  public static int d(...);
  public static int i(...);
}
```

This code removes verbose, debug and information log calls but leaves warnings and errors. Make sure any remaining warning or error messages don't log personal data.

Verifying production settings

If your app communicates with external services, has update URLs, API keys or other configuration items that are different during development, change them to the proper production settings.

Removing unused Resources

Run the *Remove unused Resources* command in the Refactor menu. Then check for stray files in your project. Look inside **src** to make sure it contains only source files. Check **assets** and **res** for outdated raw files, drawables, layouts and other items. If found, remove them from the project.

Localizing

Perform any final localization tasks, such as translating your string files to other languages. You can broaden your app's appeal with this simple yet often overlooked step.

Versioning

Before releasing the app, make sure you have a strong versioning strategy. It's critical to maintaining the app and keeping a handle on support issues that may arise.
Users should be able to identify the version number and trace it back to a specific source code snapshot. This ability to trace helps with debugging.

The **app.gradle** build file is the best place to specify your app version. Two primary settings control versioning: **versionCode** and **versionName**. Typically, you'll find these settings in the **defaultConfig** section, as show here:

```
defaultConfig {
  applicationId "com.raywenderlich.podplay"
  minSdkVersion 23
  targetSdkVersion 30
  versionCode 1
  versionName "1.0"
  testInstrumentationRunner
"android.support.test.runner.AndroidJUnitRunner"
}
```

- **versionCode**: This is the internal version number, which the user can't see. It's an integer value, and you should increase it with each new build you upload to the Play Store. The Play Store uses this number to determine if one build is older than another. It won't allow installs that downgrade to an older version.
- **versionName**: This is the external version number visible to the user. You have full control over how it's formatted. Most apps use a *major.minor.point* release format for `versionName`. The key is to have a consistent formatting convention. Remember to update the string with each new release.

> **Note**: Developers often refer to the major.minor.point release scheme as Semantic Versioning. For more information on this scheme, check out https://semver.org/.

Building a release version

Each time you build and run your app during development, Android Studio produces an APK file and installs it on the emulator or device. This APK file contains your app's executable code as well as all of its resources.

When using the default debug build type, Android Studio automatically generates an APK and signs it with a debug key. This debug APK also has a special **debuggable** flag set and includes extra information to make debugging easier.

Google won't let you submit an APK built for debugging to the Play Store. You also shouldn't distribute it directly to users.

To make sure the **debuggable** flag isn't set, and to have Android Studio build an optimized **release** version of the APK, use the `release` build type. Like the debug version, you must sign the release APK. But in this case, you should sign it with your private signing key.

Creating a signing key

To build a release version you first need to generate the signing key you'll use to sign the app. The key stores in a keystore file. You must sign any future versions of the same app with the same key.

This key is critical to the security of your app. You should always keep it private and in a safe place. If you lose the keystore, you won't be able to release a new version of your app under the same package name!

> **Note**: Google has a Google Play App Signing feature. This service lets Google manage your signing key, giving you some options if your key is lost or compromised. When using this method, you'll sign the app with an **Upload Key**. Then Google will resign the app with your actual app signing key.
>
> The next chapter will cover this in more detail, but you can learn more here: https://developer.android.com/studio/publish/app-signing.html#google-play-app-signing.

In Android Studio, use the following steps to create your signing key:

1. Click **Build ▸ Generate signed Bundle / APK...** from the menu.

2. An Android App Bundle is a format that includes all of your app's compiled code and resources but defers APK generation and signing to Google Play. Google Play then uses your app bundle to generate and serve optimized APKs for each user's device configuration, so users only download the code and resources they need to run your app. Select **Android App Bundle** and click **Next**.

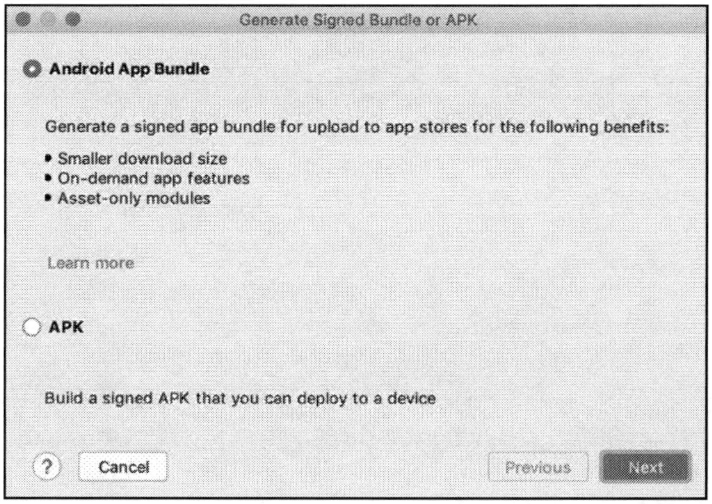

3. Select **Create new...** to create a new keystore. A keystore can hold multiple signing keys, each of which is referred to by an alias name.

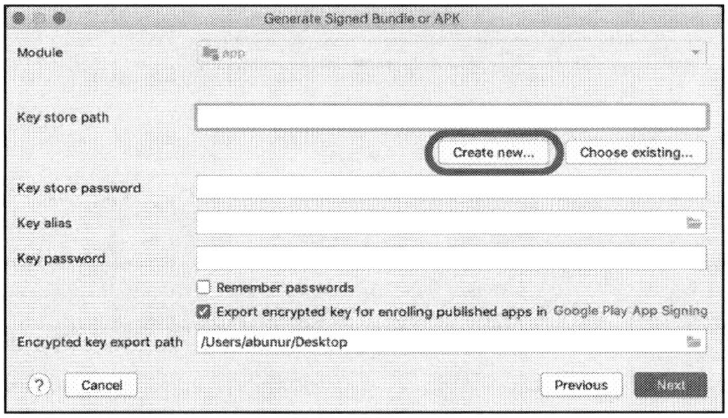

4. The New Key Store dialog appears.

5. Select the **Key store path** where you want to store the file. You must use a specific extension, such as **.jks**. Otherwise, the Google Play console may throw an error when you try to upload the APK.

6. Fill in the keystore **Password** and repeat it in the **Confirm** field. Make sure you store this password safely because you'll need it whenever you access the keystore.

7. Fill in the following items for the **Key**:

   Alias: Enter a name for the key, usually the name of your app.

   Password: Enter a password for this alias.

   Confirm: Repeat your password.

   Validity (years): Leave this at 25 years. The key expires after this time.

   Certificate: Enter your personal information in these fields. The user won't see your data, but it's part of the signing certificate in the APK file.

8. Click **OK**. The original dialog, with the values already populated, appears.

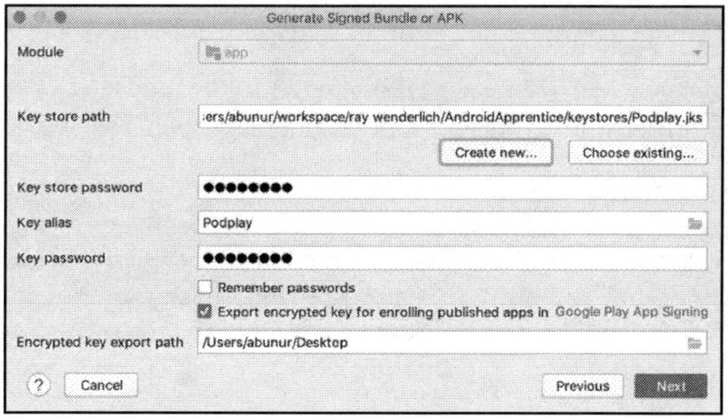

9. If you don't want to enter passwords each time you build a release version, check **Remember passwords**.
10. To take advantage of Google Play App Signing, check **Export encrypted key for enrolling published apps in Google Play App Signing** and choose a destination folder to save the encrypted key. This key is encrypted for transfer to Google Play.
11. Click **Next**.
12. Fill in the **Destination Folder**. Typically, this a folder outside of your main project folder.

    Under **Build Variants**, ensure you've selected **release**.

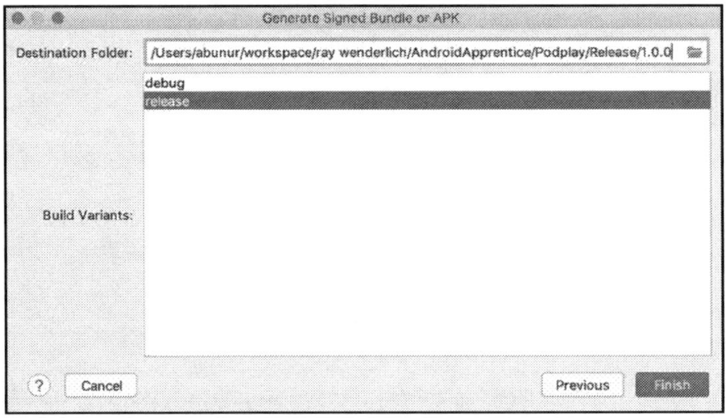

13. Click **Finish**.

    Android Studio builds and signs the release Android App Bundle file and places it in the destination folder. A popup appears at the bottom right corner of Android Studio when the build is complete.

    Android Studio names the final output file **app-release.aab**.

You'll follow these same steps each time you build a release version. However, you can skip steps three through seven since you already created the keystore and key.

> **Note**: It's worth mentioning again that you must keep your release keystore and password secure! If someone gets ahold of your key, they can do all sorts of damage, including distributing malicious apps under your identity.

Checking your file size

Check the size of the app bundle file. If it's over 500MB, you won't be able to publish it as-is to the Play Store. You can get around this limitation by using dynamic feature modules.

While this isn't an issue for most apps, if you find yourself with a large bundle file, check out this guide to using app bundles and dynamic feature modules: https://developer.android.com/guide/app-bundle/. You'll learn more about dynamic feature modules in future chapters.

Release testing

Test the release file on as many devices as you possibly can. Subtle bugs can show up when running the release versus debug versions of your app, especially when running on different hardware devices. At a minimum, test on at least one phone and one tablet.

You can test your Android App Bundle using **bundletool** to generate APKs from your app bundle and deploy them to a connected device. You can find details about downloading and using bundletool here: https://developer.android.com/studio/command-line/bundletool

Alternatively, you can use the Play Store to deploy to devices to test your release build. You'll learn how in the following sections.

Nothing beats testing your app on a real device, so it's a good idea to have at least one around. Interacting with your app on an actual device provides immediate feedback on many aspects of your app's user experience, including gestures, touch targets and inconsistencies you might not notice on the emulator.

You should also test your app on a variety of device types from different manufacturers, as well as screen sizes and resolutions. Most of us don't have the luxury of a vast library of hardware. That's where the Firebase Test Lab can come in handy. It lets you test your app on a wide variety of devices and Android versions. For more information on Firebase Test Lab, refer to the documentation here: https://firebase.google.com/docs/test-lab/

Creating your Google Play Store listing

Now that your release APK is ready, it's time to review the steps to create a Google Play Store listing.

Google Play Console signup

First, sign up for a **Google Play Console** account. The Google Play Console is your gateway to managing and publishing your apps on the Google Play Store.

Go here to sign up for a new Google Play Console account or sign in if you already have one:

https://play.google.com/apps/publish/

First, verify that you're signed in with the correct account. Read and agree to the developer agreement. Then click **CONTINUE TO PAYMENT**. The current one-time registration fee is $25.

After you finish paying, you'll go to the Developer Profile screen. Make sure you pick a good **Developer name** as it's shown in the Play Store below the name of your app.

The main console

Once you finish with signup, you'll move to the main console.

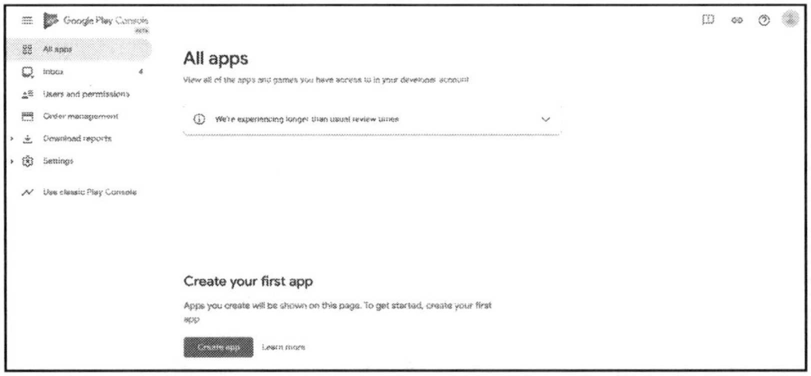

In the menu on the left, you have several options:

- **All apps** is where you add new apps or manage existing ones.
- **Inbox** is where you'll find messages from Google Play.
- **Users and permissions** is where you can add additional users to your account and manage what those users can do and see under your account.
- **Order Management** lets you manage orders, including giving refunds, for paid apps or in-app purchases.
- **Download Reports** provides various reports, including crashes, reviews, statistics, user acquisition and financial records.

And finally, **Settings** provides several sub-sections:

- **Developer account**: You can manage profile settings, control API access and set up payment options. In this section, you'll find **Developer page**, where you can configure how your developer page looks in the Play Store. Your developer page won't be available until you publish your first app.
- **Preferences**: This is where you set notification preferences and control privacy settings.
- **Email lists**: You can manage alpha and beta testers from this section. Note that you can only use Gmail addresses for your tester distribution lists.
- **License testing** is where you test your licensing and in-app billing integrations. You can set up testers to make in-app purchases without getting charged anything.
- **Manage game projects** provides additional features for games. You can find more info here: https://developers.google.com/games/services/.
- **Pricing templates**: You can use pricing templates to set up or manage the same set of prices for multiple paid apps and in-app products.

Creating your first app

Click **Create app** on the main console screen.

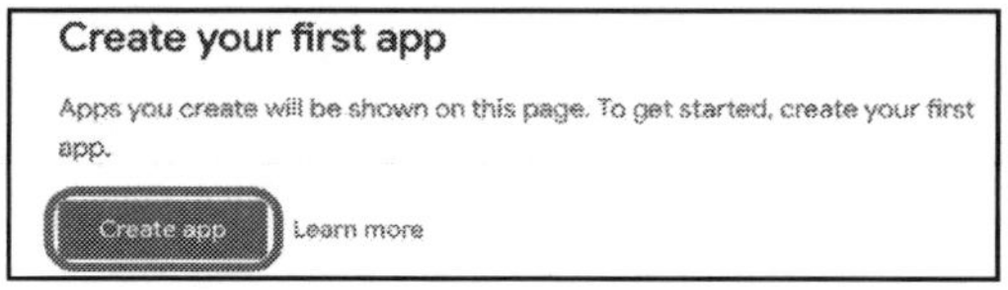

In the future, when you have other published apps, you'll use the **Create app** button at the top of your list of apps instead:

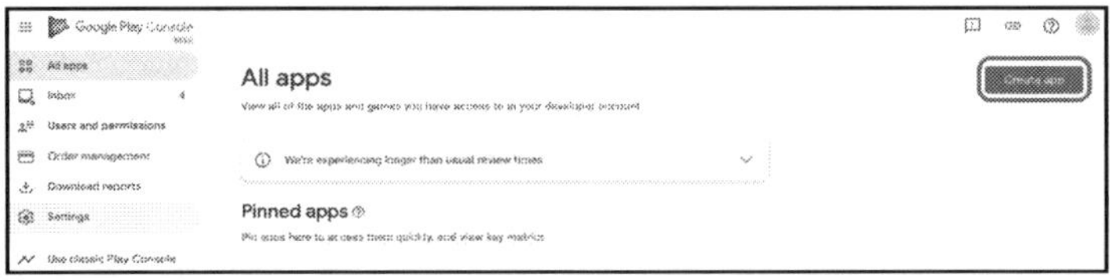

Note: At this point, you're only preparing the store listing and creating a draft version of the app. You won't publish anything until you use the Publish step.

Fill out the **Create app** form:

1. First, fill in the title of your app.

2. Then choose the default language for your app.

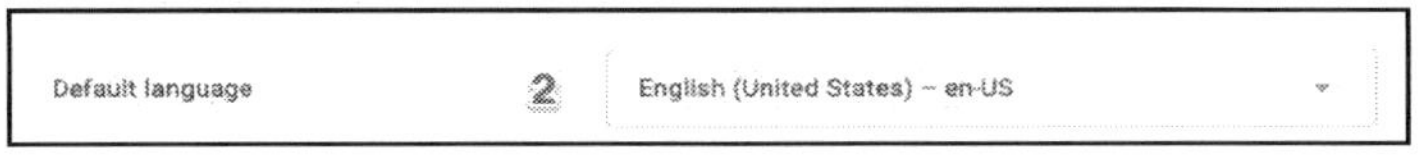

3. Select whether it's an app or a game.

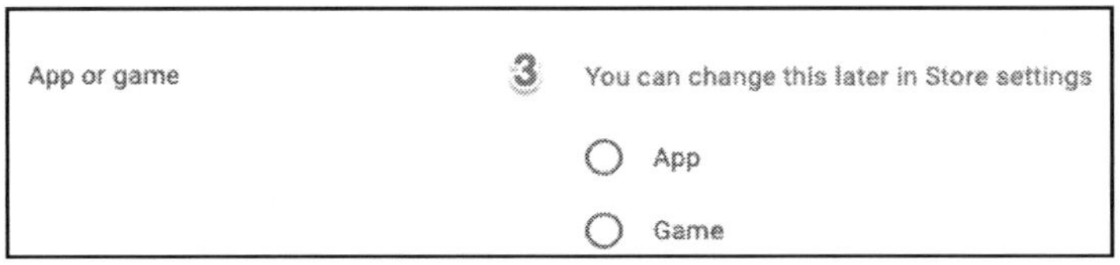

4. Then select whether your app is paid or free. If you choose free, you can only change this up until the app publishes. After that, free apps can never convert to paid apps.

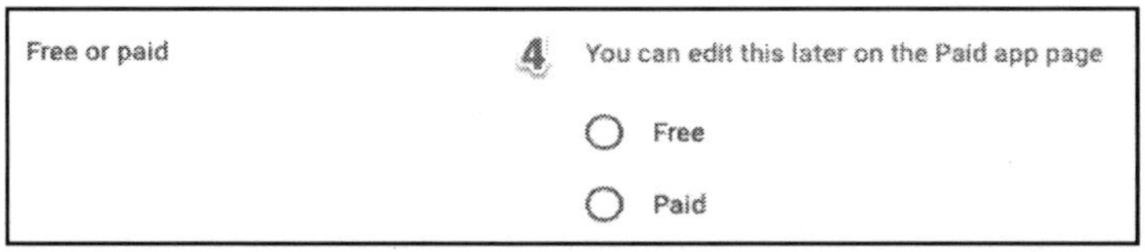

5. Check the legal declarations.

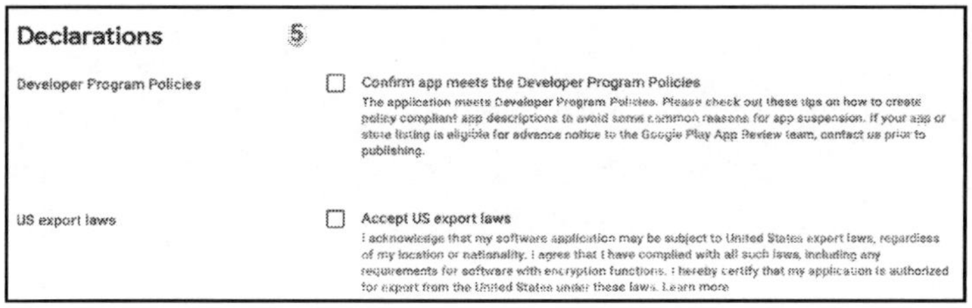

6. Finally, click **Create app**.

After that, you return to the dashboard page. You're not quite done yet. You still need to fill out a bunch of information about your app and upload the app bundle you created earlier. But now the dashboard presents a wizard listing the remaining steps and what you need to do:

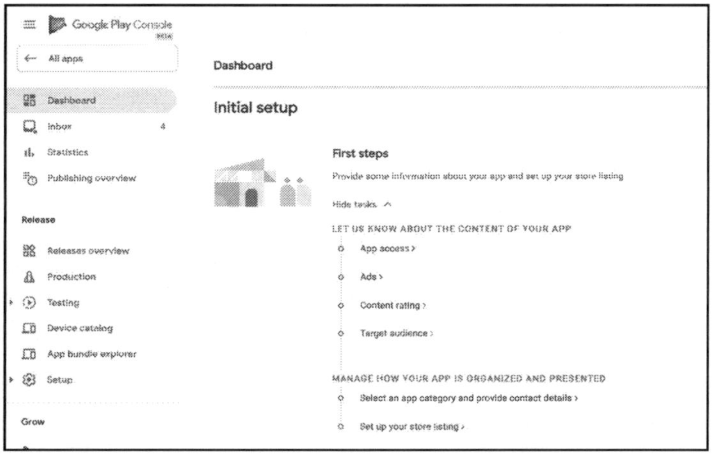

It might seem like a lot of steps, but it's not too bad. Fill out all the required information under the **First steps** task. As you finish each section, a checkmark appears next to that section to show it's complete:

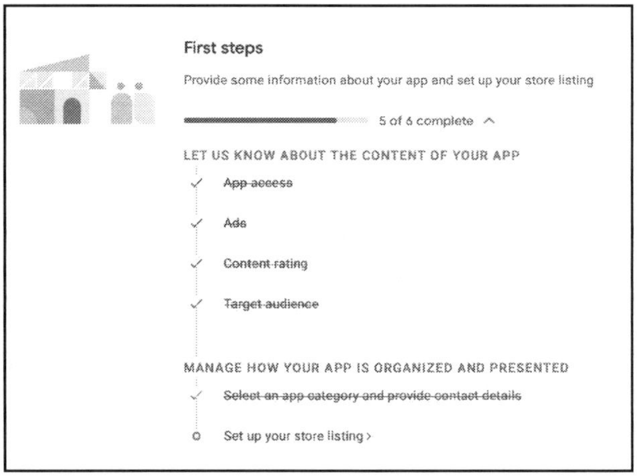

You can't skip this step. The **Release your app** task has a lock icon, and you can't access it until you complete this.

> **Note**: At this point, you're only preparing the store listing and creating a draft version of the app. You won't publish anything until you complete the **Release your app** step.

Go back to the **All apps** section and see your new app listed there with **App status** set to draft:

Click your app's name to go back to the dashboard and setup steps. The majority of the steps gather information so the Play Store can categorize your app properly. However, the final step, **Set up your store listing**, asks you to upload some graphic assets. Setting up your store listing is critical since it defines how potential users find and perceive your app.

Main store listing

Click **Set up your store listing** to view the sub-tasks there. App name is already complete. Fill out the short and full description fields.

Store graphic assets

Your app needs the following graphic assets:

- **App icon**: This icon only shows up in the Play Store. Your app's launcher icon still shows on the user's device. **Apply Pixels** is an excellent resource for easily creating app icons and other assets required by the Play Store: https://applypixels.com.
- **Featured graphic**: You'll find the featured graphic at the top of your app listing.
- **Screenshots**: You're required to upload at least two screenshots, although you can have up to eight per device type. You can upload portrait or landscape orientation screenshots.

> **Note**: You can create screenshots from the emulator using the camera icon on the emulator toolbar.

For specifics on the image dimensions and more, see the descriptions in the Play Store Console.

- **Video**: While not required, it's highly recommended you provide a video demo of your app. A video is a great way to capture potential users' attention. You'll get into this more later in the book.

Once you complete the **First Steps** section, your app title and icon will appear on the dashboard. The **Release your app** section is now unlocked.

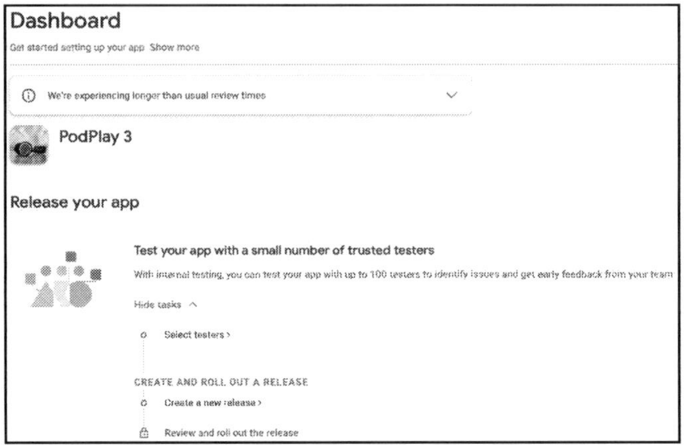

Releasing your app

Click **Select testers** to go to the **Internal testing** page. You'll learn about the different release types in the next chapter. For now, create a quick email list in this section with a list of testers who will test your first app release. If you don't have any testers, list your email address so you can deploy builds to your device through the Play Store. You also have the option to provide a feedback URL or email address for testers to provide feedback.

Once you create one or more test group email lists, select one and click **Save changes** on the bottom right.

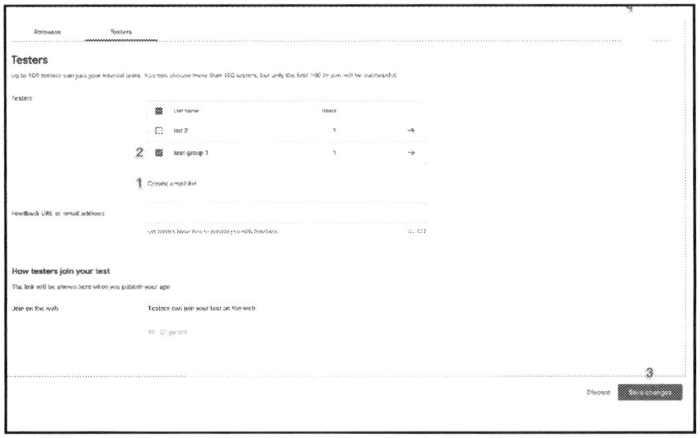

Finally, click **Create new release** in the upper right corner. You'll go to the page where you upload your app bundle and make the app available to testers.

You'll see a note reminding you Google will manage the signing key for you. Click **Continue**. Then drag and drop **app-release.aab**, the app bundle you created earlier, onto the section titled **App bundles and APKs** to upload your release.

When your app bundle uploads successfully, you'll see it listed beneath the upload section with details about the build:

File type	Version	API levels	Target SDK	Screen layouts	ABIs	Required features
Android App Bundle	1 (1.0)	23+	30	4	All	1

Next, provide a name for the release under **Release details**. If you haven't already thought about a release naming strategy, now would be a good time to do so. You want to be able to distinguish each release to avoid confusion and address bugs as they appear.

Finally, fill out the release notes section and click **Save**. Then click **Review release** at the bottom.

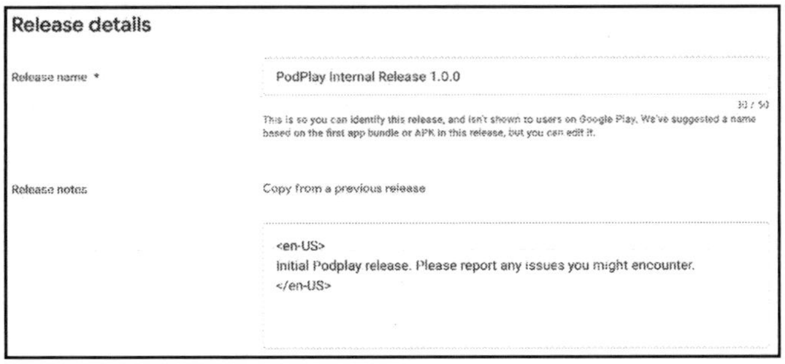

If there are any issues with your release, they'll appear on the next screen. You can **Edit release** to address them.

If you have no errors, click **Start rollout to internal testing** at the bottom of the screen. You'll see a confirmation dialog. Click **Rollout** to release your app.

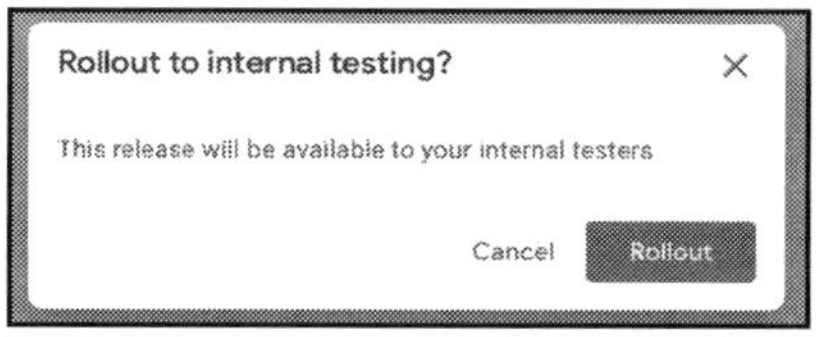

Congratulations! You've released your app to the Google Play Store!

Note: It may take a little time for your app to appear published on the Google Play Console. You also might need to refresh the Google Play Console page to see the publication status update. If you included your own Gmail address in the selected tester list, you can search for and install your app using the **Google Play** app on your Android device.

Once your release shows as published, click **Testing -> Internal testing** in the Google Play Console to see the release under the **Releases** tab.

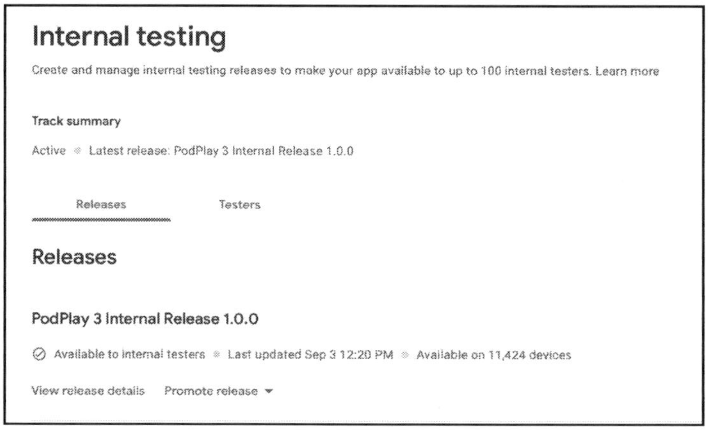

Click the **Testers** tab. You'll also see a **Copy link** button at the bottom. You can use it to get a URL your testers can use to install the app.

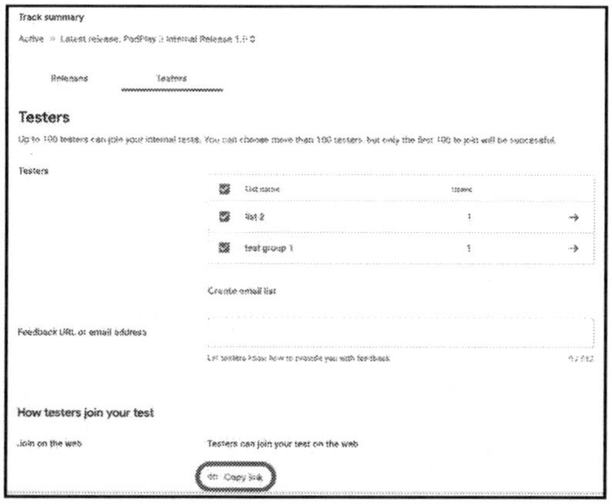

Key points

- A **keystore** stores your signing key details. Keep track of the passwords and store them in a safe place, or you won't be able to continue releasing your app under the same name.
- **R8** provides a mechanism for optimizing and obfuscating your app. Choose your options wisely and test thoroughly to avoid bugs.
- The **Google Play Console** provides a dashboard through which you can manage your app releases, testers and much more.

Where to go from here?

Take some time to go through all of the menu items on the Google Play Console. You'll discover Google provides developers with several tools to help apps succeed once they're in the Play Store.

You should also check out the YouTube video "Use Android Vitals in the Google Play Console to Understand and Improve Your App's Performance" (https://www.youtube.com/watch?v=vj3Y8L5HLdg) from Google I/O 2017. Members of the Google Play team go over some of the fantastic tools available to developers.

You've released your app to the Google Play Store, but there's much more to creating a successful app. The rest of this book will dive deep into these topics.

Chapter 3: Preparing for Release: Test Tracks

By Fuad Kamal

In the previous chapter, you created an **Alpha release** through the **Closed testing** release track. In this chapter, you'll dive deeper into the app publishing process and discover various ways to test and distribute your app within your team. You'll also go through the Alpha and Beta testing process to make sure your app is ready to share with the world. In the next chapter, you'll learn how to make your app go *live* to the general public and the issues around production releases.

> **Note**: You don't have to release your app through Alpha and Beta channels. You're free to take your initial release straight to production!

Play Console overview

Developing and publishing your app is just the beginning. In 2020, Google launched a completely revised Play Console for better managing and deploying apps. The new Play Console introduced a major UX facelift, improved team management, a modern interface using Google Material design language and a new menu structure.

As you saw briefly in the previous chapter, the Play Console is grouped into several main areas by function: **Release**, **Grow**, **Quality**, **Monetize** and **Policy**. In this chapter, you'll get an overview of the entire Play Console. You'll deep dive into some of these sections in this and the next chapter.

Google Play Console gives you the power to scale with access to billions of users. It also gives you the tools to acquire them, like the ability to test the text and graphics of your store listing to drive more installs.

The Play Console gives you the power to iterate. **Testing tools** and **pre-launch reports** help you identify issues before they affect your users so you can release with confidence. It lets your users beta test new features and then roll them out in stages to ensure a safe launch.

The Play Console lets you make data-driven decisions with access to insights about your app, such as **metrics**, and what your users are saying through **reviews** and ratings. With the Play Console, you can monitor your app's policy status so you can stay compliant.

Grow

Grow contains everything you need to supercharge your user acquisitions, from pre-registration to store listing experiments. It also features **acquisition reporting**.

Quality

Google designed the Quality section for QAs and team leads. It contains all the signals and features that tell you how your app performs in the wild, including both its technical performance with Android vitals and how people feel about it through ratings and reviews.

Monetize

Monetize brings together Play Console setup, reporting and optimization tools to help you grow your business through in-app purchases and subscriptions.

Policy

Policy helps you release confidently on Google Play. At the time of this writing, the author experienced multiple Play Console rejections on internal releases due to **Google Policy** compliance issues. The reasons you provide for various app permissions *matter*, and Google has become increasingly strict about Policy reviews. For more information about Google Policy, see https://play.google.com/console/about/policystatus/.

Release

Designed with Release managers in mind, **Release** collects all Google's tools to upload and distribute you apps, review your testing and production tracks and check how your latest updates perform.

Releases overview

The **Releases overview** shows you an up-to-date snapshot of your testing and production tracks to quickly see which versions are being tested, by how many users and in which countries.

Private vs public apps

There are two main types of mobile apps, regardless of the platform. The most common type is **public apps**, which are generally available to everyone. Developers typically distribute these through an app store, such as Google Play or Amazon Appstore.

The other type of apps are **private apps**. These are also known as **enterprise apps** or **Enterprise Mobility Managed**, or EMM, apps. While this book mainly focuses on public apps, everything you learn here is also applicable to EMM.

You can use the Play Console to manage both your EMM and public apps. For more information on EMM in the Android ecosystem, as well as the **Google Play EMM API**, refer to the **Android Enterprise** documentation page for integration with your CI/CD toolchain found here: https://developers.google.com/android/work/overview. You'll learn more about continuous integration and delivery in section three of this book.

Test tracks

Before you publish your app to the world, it's important to test it with a small group of users. Testing not only catches bugs but also helps with scaling and rolling out updates faster.

The key is to distribute a test version of your app to a small group of trusted users. This group could be your wider team, product managers, a QA team or whoever can give you early feedback.

You *could* directly email or otherwise share an APK with the testers, but that can be cumbersome and places an undue burden on them. Also, you lose the benefits of using an app bundle: APKs need to be universal for all the supported devices. Therefore, the installation package is much larger than if the users receive only the files they need for their particular installation through an app bundle on the Play Console.

A track is a way to define a group of users to whom you can publish your app. Google provides three different tracks: **Internal**, **Closed** and **Open**. Additionally, Google designates two **release types**: **Alpha** and **Beta**. The Closed track only has the Alpha release type while the Open test track only has the Beta release type.

The Alpha and Beta release types provide an excellent way to get feedback to make sure your final release is as polished and stable as possible. The only requirement for testers is a physical Android device and a **@gmail**, **G Suite** or **Google** account.

Alpha and Beta release types are designed for testing at scale, with potentially millions of users. Because of this, they're also a bit more involved and tedious to deploy.

For fast, iterative testing Google introduced the **Internal test track**.

Internal test track

The Internal test track is for direct distribution to your quality assurance, or QA, team. Deployment is much faster than the other tracks. The first time you deploy, it may take up to 48 hours. However, after that your builds will be available to your testers within a few minutes.

With the Internal test track, you can have up to 100 testers, which you organize by email address. There are no country limitations for distribution. While they can install Paid apps for free, testers still must pay for in-app purchases unless you add them to a **license testers list**. Any device exclusion rules you define for your app won't apply to internal testers.

When Google first introduced the Internal test track, they said it wouldn't be subject to **Play Policy** or security reviews, but later they reversed their stand on this. Beware as this might change in the future since the goal behind internal testing was to make it fast and easy to deploy to your most trusted testers.

Testers don't need a special app or permissions to install your test builds with the internal test track. All they need is a link, which you'll find in the Play Console's **App bundle explorer**.

The updates for internal testers are also different than they are for Alpha and Beta testers. Users can be *either* alpha/ beta testers **or** internal testers: They must opt-out of one to join the other.

The **Play Console publisher API** and many Play Console publisher plug-ins support the Internal test track. That means you can easily automate publishing to the internal test track from your existing toolchains and workflows.

The internal test track is great for quick iteration during development, catching bugs early, getting fast feedback from your team and testing Play integration. Because your app is still published through Play, it supports all the Play features: LVL testing (https://developer.android.com/google/play/licensing/setting-up) (https://developer.android.com/google/play/licensing/setting-up), in-app purchases, the Android app bundle and dynamic developer features.

Exploring the internal test track

In the previous chapter, you deployed a build of your app to the Play Console using an Internal Test Track. Go to the Play Console now and select **All apps** from the menu. You'll see a list of apps under a title heading, which includes the number of apps you currently have in the Play Console.

You may have only one app at this time, but as the number of apps in your Play Console grows, you can highlight the most important ones by pinning them. Click the pin icon in your app listing to add it to the **Pinned apps** list:

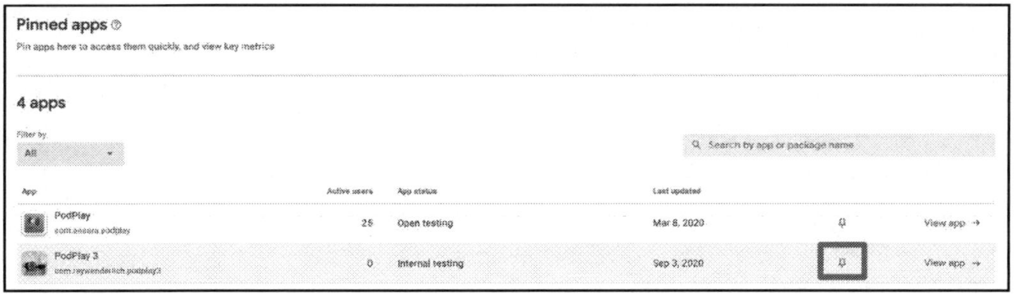

When you have multiple pinned apps, you can drag and drop them to arrange their order. You can see summary KPIs for pinned apps without going into the dashboard for each app.

Click **View app** to go to the dashboard for your app. Then click **App bundle explorer** from the Play Console menu on the left to go into the App bundle explorer.

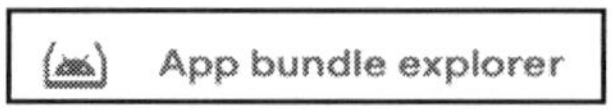

In the App bundle explorer, you can see all the deployment details for your current app bundle. Spend some time exploring and become familiar with all the information here. Some things of particular note are:

- The permissions that your app lists in its manifest.
- Which API levels your app is compatible with.
- The number of Android devices, specifically which devices your app should work on.
- How many active releases you have.
- Which types of releases you have.

You can also see the size of the download for your users to install the app.

Next, click the **Downloads** tab in the App bundle explorer. Here you'll find the link you can share with your testers to install the internal test build.

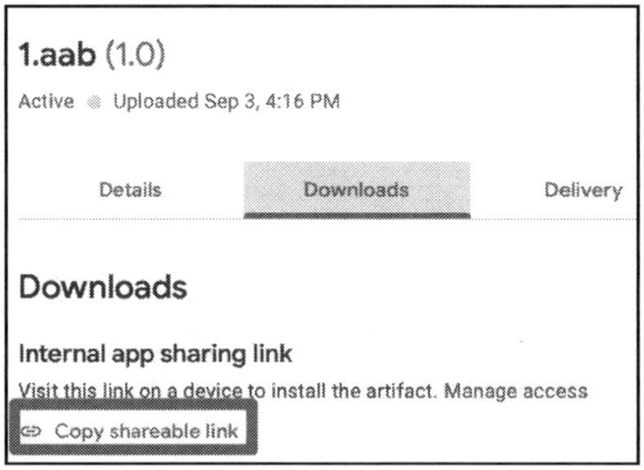

Installing an internal test track build

So you've deployed your build to the internal test track, and you sent out the shareable link to your testers. You check with your testers to see how it's going, only to find out they weren't able to install it.

Some of them say they got a 404 Error when they clicked the link. Others say when they click the link on their device, they get a popup message that says *Internal app sharing is turned off....* What have you done wrong?

Actually, you haven't done anything wrong. It turns out there are some extra steps your testers need to take to install builds from the internal test track.

First, if you restricted the testers to only people on your selected email lists, they must sign in to their Google account with the respective email address *on the device* on which they are trying to install the build. If they aren't signed in with the correct email address, they may get a 404 server error on their web browser when they tap the install link.

Alternatively, you can open up testing to anyone who has the link. You can check this in the Play Console under **Release -> Setup -> Internal app sharing**.

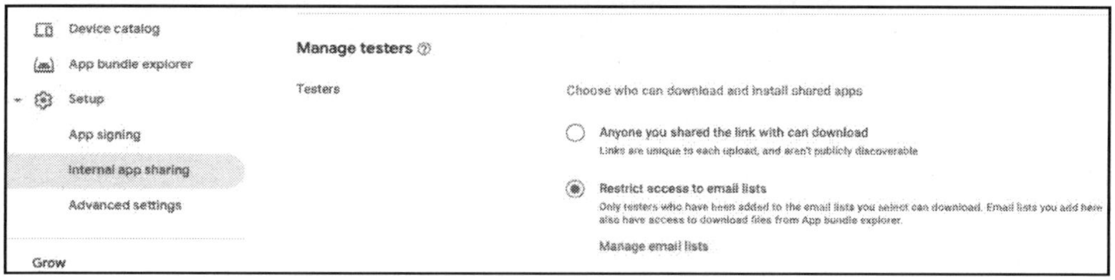

Second, the testers need to perform a bit of black magic, similar to what developers do before they can debug on a device. That's why they got the popup message.

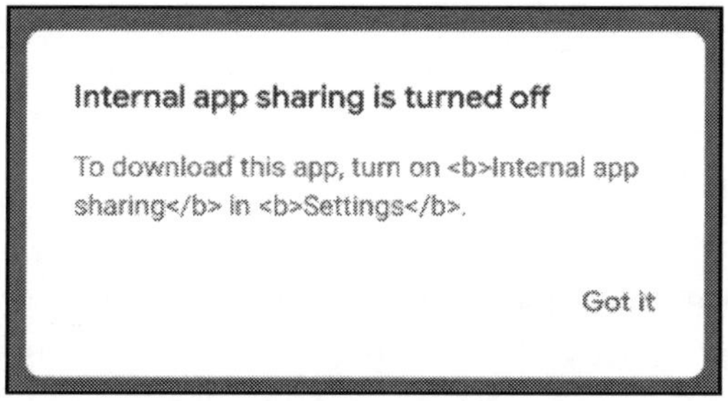

In the google play app, the tester should click the menu in the navigation drawer, then **Settings**.

Then they should **Enable Developer Options.** This is similar to enabling Developer Options within the Android Settings app. Tap seven times on the **Play Store Version**.

Once they get the **You are now a developer!** prompt, they'll see the **Internal App Sharing** option pop up on their device. Enabling **internal app sharing** will display a warning regarding the internal test nature of the apps they can now download.

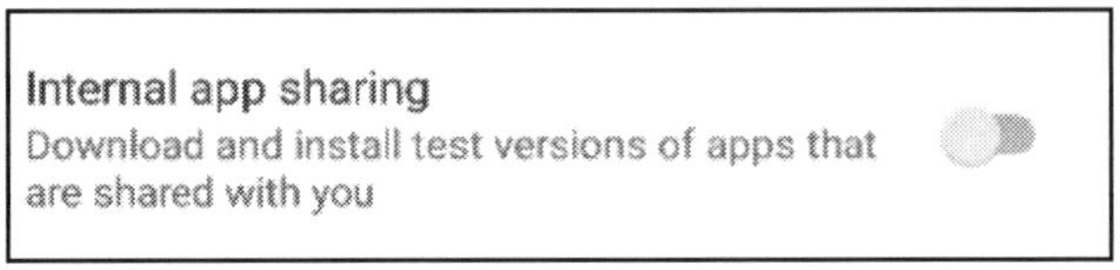

Once they've enabled internal app sharing they can click the download link again and see your internal test build available to install.

Closed test track

Once you have your app tested internally with up to 100 users on the internal test track, you're ready to have your app tested by real-world users. Typically, however, you're not yet ready to open up to everyone. For example, you might be looking for trusted feedback on a confidential set of features.

Closed testing lets you scale well with various testing scenarios. For example, what if you would like to test your app with a track for each feature branch? Or what if you would like to create a new track for each new milestone?

With Closed testing, you can create multiple closed tracks. You can have one production track, one open testing track and any number of closed testing tracks, plus an internal test track.

You can choose any name for the test track, and that same name is used in the Play Console publisher API. This is great for user studies, country-specific variants, feature branches and testing in incrementally larger groups. These are a few examples of the many ways you can use closed testing tracks.

In the Closed test track, there are only Alpha builds: There is no Beta. Beta is only for the Open test track, which you'll learn more about in the next chapter. You can promote your existing Internal test track build to an Alpha build in the Closed test track or upload a new app bundle to the Closed test track.

You'll try the former approach next.

Promote your internal build

In the Google Play Console menu, under **Release**, click **Testing -> Internal Testing**. Under the **Releases** tab, click **Promote Release -> Closed Testing -> Alpha**.

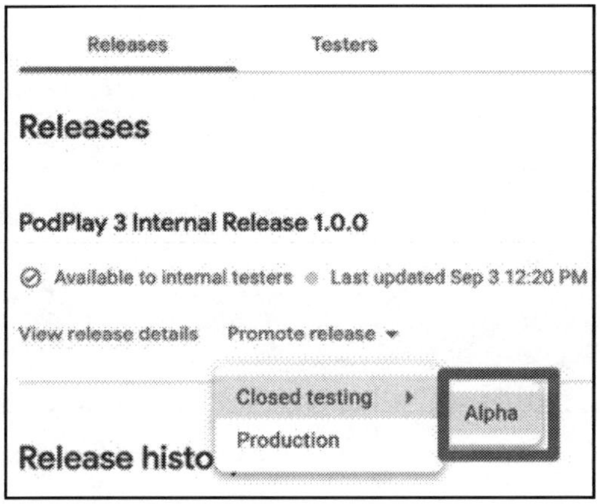

On the next screen, click **Review release**.

Note the warning and error messages displayed, and that the **Start rollout to Alpha** button is grayed out.

Since you're creating a new test track, you need to select the users who will test this track and the countries or regions where it'll be available. Remember that while tests for the Internal test track can be in any region, Closed and Open test tracks testers must be from the regions you specify.

If you click **Edit release** to add these details, you go back to the previous screen where you can only edit the release name, the release notes and upload new app bundles. There's no obvious way on this screen to add the countries or testers. Hopefully, this is a UX oversight Android will fix in a future update to the Play Console! But for now, take a look at where to update this information.

In the Play Console menu, click **Closed testing**. Note under **Active tracks** there is a heading for **Alpha** that says *There is no release on this track*. To the right of that, click **Manage track**.

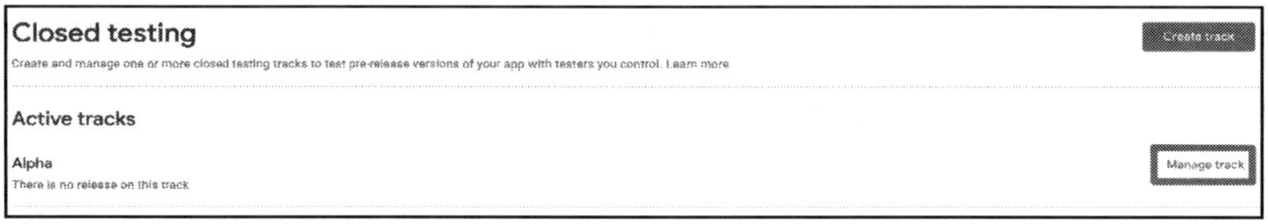

Here, at last, you'll find the **Countries/regions** tab and **Testers tab**, where you can edit this information.

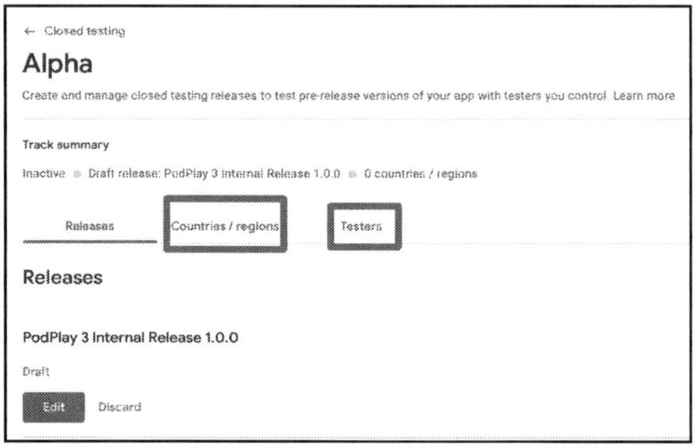

Click each tab and update those sections for your Alpha build. If you want to add all countries and regions click the check box in the first row titled **Country/region**.

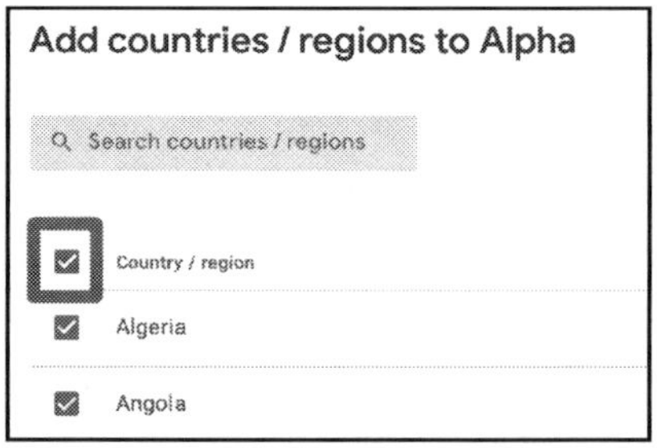

When you finish adding testers and countries, click **Save changes** at the bottom of the Testers tab. Note that you'll also find the links you can share with your testers to join the test group and download the builds at the bottom of the tab.

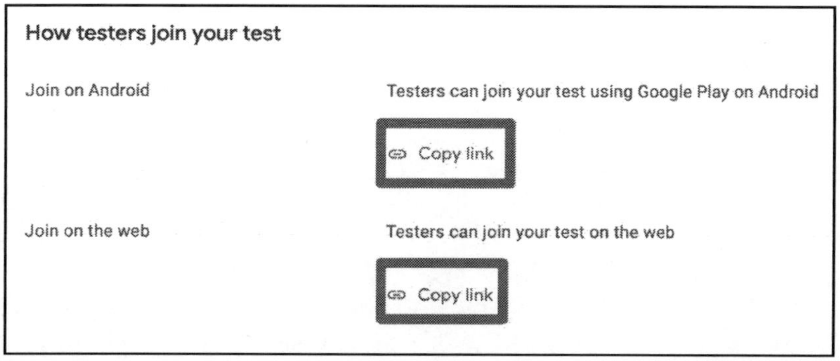

Again, unlike the Internal test track, you deploy your Closed and Open tracks through Google Play. However, with the Closed track, Alpha builds are only visible to people in your test group, while with the Open track, Beta builds are visible to the general public.

On the same page, click the **Releases** tab. Then click **Edit** for your Alpha release.

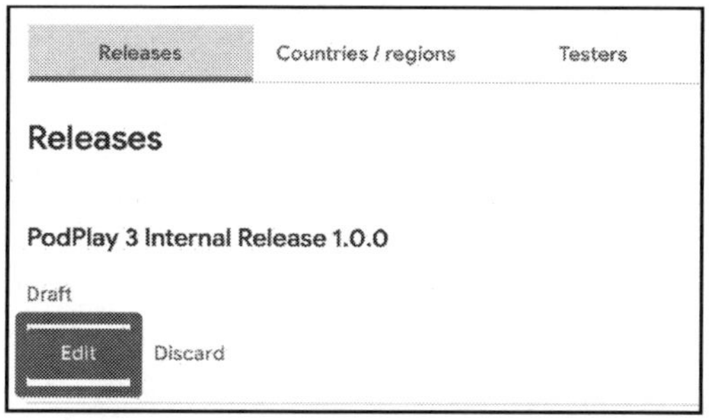

This brings you back to the page title **Create closed testing release**. Click **Review release** again. This time, you get rid of the warnings and errors and enable the **Start rollout to Alpha** button. Click it and you'll see a confirmation dialogue:

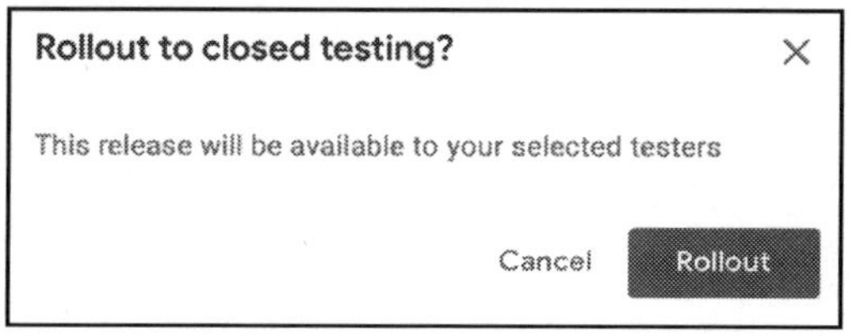

Click **Rollout** to launch your first Alpha release.

Congratulations! Your release now appears under the list of Alpha releases in the Closed track. Note that it may appear listed as *under review* until Google completes the app review for your release.

If you go back to the Internal track on the Play Console, you'll see your Internal release is also still available. It might be exactly the same build as the Alpha release, but the two are treated as separate and distinct by way of the test tracks.

Create multiple closed tracks

The process to create additional closed tracks is quite similar.

1. Select **Create track**.
2. Select whether you want to manage testers by email or Google Groups.
3. Copy the *Opt-in URL* to share with your testers.
4. Next to *Feedback channel*, add an email address or URL to collect feedback from testers. Testers will see your app's feedback channel on your tester opt-in page.

Country targeting for testing tracks

With country targeting, you can control the availability for each track individually. You can use this for both open and closed testing. It also lets you run a test in a different set of countries than those in which your production app is live.

Key points

Whew! You've covered quite a bit in this chapter! Here's a quick recap of some of the salient points:

- You can use **Play Console** to manage and deploy both enterprise and public-facing apps.
- Play Console has several sections to help you through all the stages of app deployment, from testing, release and monitoring, to debugging issues, monetization, license management and Google Policy compliance.
- You can have multiple **closed tests**, a single **open test** and a single **internal test**, concurrently.
- Internal testers can't access open or closed tests at the same time. They must opt-out of one to access the other.

Where to go from here?

For more information about closed testing, refer to the Play Store documentation: https://play.google.com/console/about/closed-testing/. In the next chapter, you'll learn more about open testing, deployment strategies for teams of all sizes and automated device testing.

Chapter 4: Strategies for Release

By Fuad Kamal

In the previous chapter, you learned how to distribute your app internally to your team and expand your distribution through Closed tracks or Alpha testing. In this chapter, you'll complete the app publishing process and discover additional ways to distribute your app. You'll also go through the Beta testing process to make sure your app is ready to share with the world, and finally, release your app to production.

Version codes

Before moving on to Beta testing, take a quick look at using version codes through the different release phases. Typically, you want your Internal release to have the highest version code since it should be testing the most recent changes. Your Alpha release will have the next highest version code, followed by Beta release. Production will have the lowest version code.

Note that some users may be in the Alpha group only, Beta group only or in both tester groups.

Here's a typical lifecycle an app might follow through the first few releases:

1. Release version 1 to internal testing.
2. Internal testers install version 1 and complete testing.
3. Promote version 1 to Alpha.
4. Alpha testers install version 1 and complete testing.
5. Promote version 1 to Beta.
6. Beta testers install version 1 and find some issues.
7. Address issues in version 2.
8. Release version 2 either to internal track or directly to Alpha.
9. Beta only testers continue with version 1. Alpha testers update to version 2.
10. Version 2 testing is complete.
11. Promote version 2 to Beta. Beta testers update to version 2.
12. Release version 2 to Production, which means users can download it from the Play Store.

13. Release version 3 to internal track.
14. Internal testers update to version 3. Alpha, Beta only testers and the general public remain on version 2.

Open test track

As you've seen, closed testing is great for when you want to test your app with a set of trusted testers. But typically, the problem with those users is they're not representative of the population of production users. Production users have a wider set of devices, but they might not be as motivated as trusted testers and may engage with a different set of features on your app. When you want to have broad coverage of your code, find technical issues or get more relevant business metrics, you can use **Open testing**.

Releasing to open testing allows any user to discover and join your testing community directly from the Google Play Store app on their device. These users can provide private feedback you can review in the Play Console. This type of feedback won't affect your public app ratings.

Opening testing is a great way to scale up and make sure the new version of your app provides a great experience to users before you launch it to the world.

You can cap the number of testers or users that can join the open testing program to keep things manageable.

Launch your beta release

In the last chapter, you promoted your internal release to a closed track Alpha release. Optionally, you might have also posted new builds or created multiple closed tracks. Now you can promote one of your alpha releases to the open test track as a Beta release, or post a new app bundle into a new open test track. Try the former.

In the Play Console menu, click **Closed testing**. For one of your Alpha releases, click **Manage Release**. Then click the **Promote release** link and examine the available options:

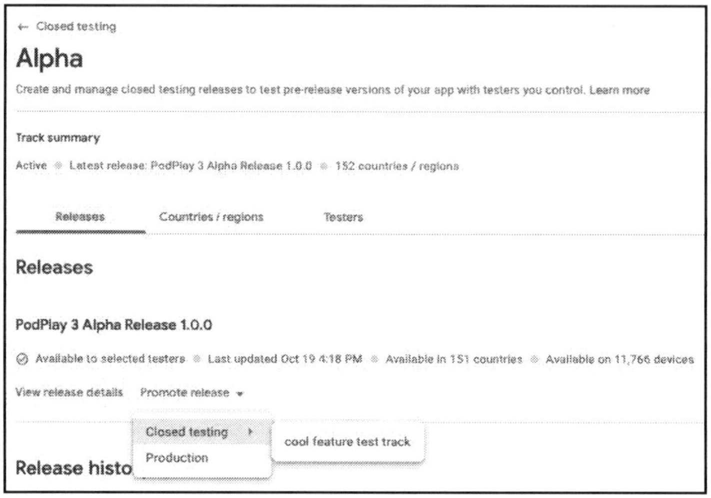

In the example above, you can promote the closed test build **PodPlay 3 Alpha Release 1.0.0** either to another available closed track or directly to production. However, there isn't an option to promote it to an open test track yet. That's because you need to create the test track before you can promote an existing build to it.

In the Play Console menu, click **Open testing**. Then click the **Start track** link to the right of the **Beta track summary**.

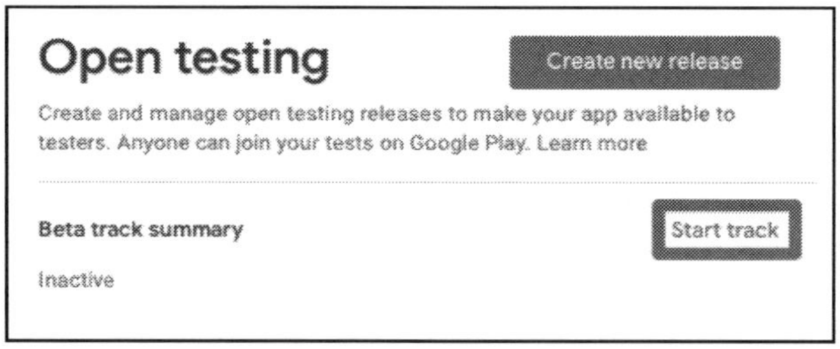

Go back to the Alpha track from the previous step. Now you can promote the release to **Open testing** in addition to other **Closed Testing** tracks and **Production**. Click **Open testing** from the options.

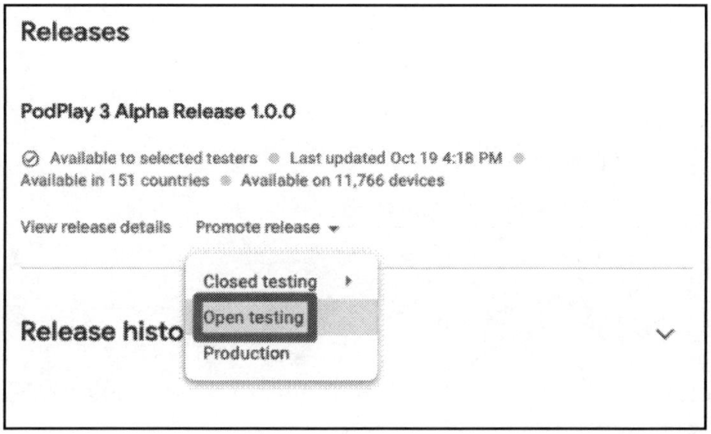

You're taken to the **Create open testing release** page. The process is similar to creating the Closed release. Like before, you need to select countries and regions where your release can be tested. However, now you don't need to select any test groups since the Beta will be available to the general public via the Google Play Store.

In the **Testers** tab, you can select **Unlimited** testers or limit the number of testers, where the minimum number of testers is 1,000. Fill in those details and provid a feedback email address for the testers. Now click the **Start rollout to Open testing** button. Play Console presents you with a confirmation dialogue, warning you *anyone* can now test your Beta release.

Click **Rollout** to release your Beta. Congratulations! Once it passes review, your app will be publicly available to test in Beta.

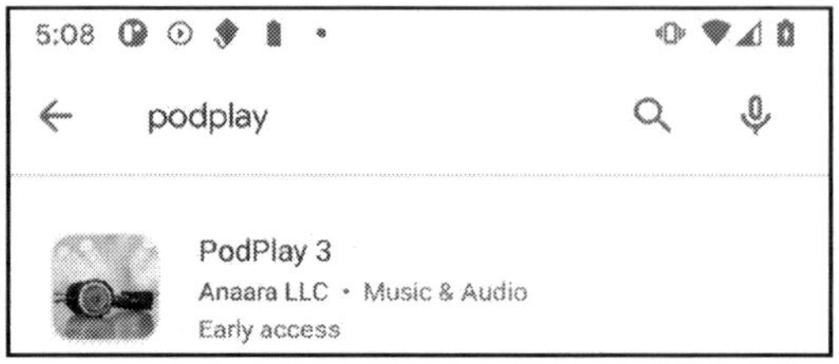

PodPlay 3 Beta listing on Google Play app

Pre-launch report

Before promoting one of your test builds to Production, you should take some time to review the pre-launch report.

The pre-launch report takes the app builds you publish to the Play Console and installs them on up to ten different devices. It runs your app for five minutes at a time with **robo** for nearly an hour of testing in total. It shows crash reports, performance issues and security vulnerabilities.

In the Play Console menu, click **Pre-launch report -> Overview**.

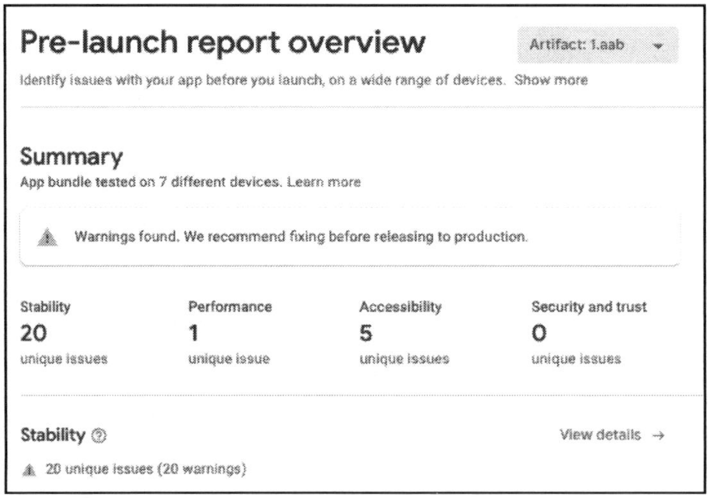

Pre-launch report overview

In the Overview section, you'll see a summary of all the issues in your app, divided into categories for **stability**, **performance**, **accessibility** and **security and trust**. From there, or in the **Details** section, you can dive into the details of each report.

Under **Pre-launch report -> Settings** you can set credentials for testing your app, deep links from which to test your app and which languages to test your app in. The **Settings** section Pre-launch report also has options to control the way your app is crawled, such as **robocall** scripts and demo loops for games. For more information about this, see the Google I/O 2018 video on Pre-launch: https://youtu.be/zTy-ur1Wnq4

The pre-launch reports can provide valuable information about how your app is performing on real devices. You can see screenshots of your app running on a large variety of devices, security scan results as well as performance and crash reports.

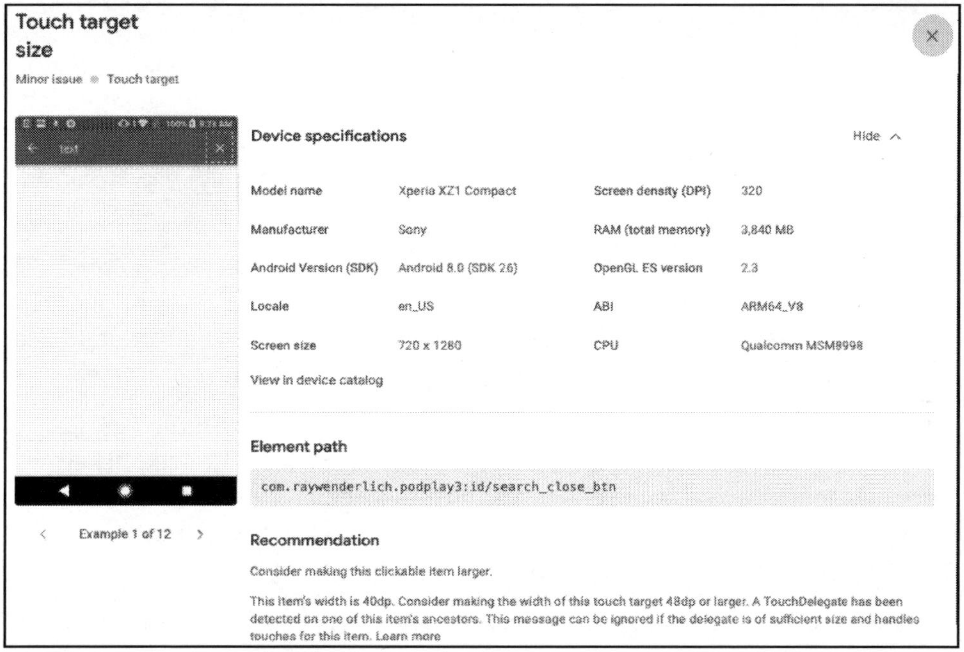

Accessibility issues revealed in Pre-launch

The Pre-launch section can provide valuable insights into how your app runs on actual hardware devices even before testers download it. To automate testing your app on more than ten devices, and for more options than are available in the Pre-launch section, you can leverage **Firebase Test Lab**. You can also integrate Firebase test lab with your CI/CD toolchain. For more information on Test Lab see *Beyond Pre-Launch Reports* in the Firebase documentation: https://firebase.google.com/docs/test-lab/android/test-lab-play

Rollout & quality

So you've tested internally, then in closed groups and finally, using open testing. You've polished the user experience, optimized business metrics and ironed out bugs and performance issues. You're confident this new release has it all. The only thing left to do is roll it out to the public.

At Google I/O 2017, Google announced the Android App Bundle. They also introduced the **Bundle Explorer** to the Play Console to help you understand your APK or bundle contents. It provides useful insight into the sizes of your APKs. Keeping your APKs as small as possible means users can download and install faster and have more free space left for other things on their devices.

On average, apps see a 20% size reduction by using Android App Bundle. The Bundle Explorer can show you the size savings you can achieve.

Google recommends using staged rollouts when releasing an app to production. As you've now seen, staged rollouts let you control the percentage of users eligible to update and gradually increases this as your confidence in the release grows. If something goes wrong, you can also halt the release so only a small percentage of users are affected.

You can further extend staged rollouts with the country targeted rollout option. This lets you rollout per country in addition to rollout by percentage. This option is useful for starting your release in a market that you have a deep understanding of. It also makes it easier to understand your business metrics as the rollout progresses.

Once your release is rolling out, you can use the **Quality** section in the Play Console to monitor key metrics, such as app ratings, as well as crashes and ANRs. These metrics help you evaluate your release and ensure it remains healthy as you proceed with the rollout. For more about ANRs, checkout the Android documentation: https://developer.android.com/topic/performance/vitals/anr

In the **Vitals** page you can check metrics like battery usage, jank, stuck wake locks and others. You may not have much data there now, but once you start testing your app, be sure to check out these features in the Play Console menu under **Android Vitals -> Performance**. For more on jank and stuck wake locks, checkout the Android documentation:

- https://developer.android.com/topic/performance/vitals/render
- https://developer.android.com/topic/performance/vitals/wakelock

Release to production

Once the Alpha and Beta testing are complete, you're ready for the final release to Production! This is as simple as promoting the final Beta version to Production.

To create your production release, click **Open Testing** in the Play Console menu. Then promote your release as before, only this time select **Production** from the **Promote Release** menu.

If you hit the **Create new release** button in the **Production** menu instead, you won't be able to promote your Open track release since you can only have one production release at a time. If you did that by mistake and wanted to promote your Open track release instead, simply discard the draft production release first.

Publishing API

For automating APK deployment with continuous integration systems or using Gradle plug-ins, Google has provided the **Publishing API**. Rolling out a release via the API uses the same release model you're now familiar with from the Play Console. This lets you name your release and more easily modify release notes. The APT also supports the testing tracks mentioned earlier. This is great for configuring your continuous integration system to push through your internal test track whenever you have a new build ready for QA.

It's possible to halt a release using the publishing API. This lets you fully automate your release process, including automatically responding to problems.

You can also manage draft releases via the API. So you can stage a draft release from your CI system and then have your product manager login, check that everything looks good and hit **confirm** and **Rollout**.

You can find the full API details and the associated client libraries here: https://developers.google.com/android-publisher.

Making use of the Google toolsets

There's great diversity in development team sizes, and user base sizes and app needs differ accordingly. Some apps have small developer teams, with maybe ten or fewer people, while others have hundreds or even thousands of developers. Smaller apps need ways to scale rapidly to a growing user base. Larger apps need ways to innovate safely and quickly. But all apps have a few needs in common:

1. Each app is constantly evolving.
2. Each app needs to add new and exciting features and adapt quickly to user feedback.
3. All app development teams would like to avoid bad updates and their implications.

There are some common tools and best practices that scale well from the smallest to the largest apps.

You need to ensure you can listen to your users and their feedback. You need to make sure you can maintain, validate and improve the key user and business metrics. And you need to optimize the technology to avoid bugs and performance issues while supporting incredibly diverse users and devices.

How do you scale? As a team grows in size and ambition, how do you continue to achieve good release attributes while still moving quickly?

There are a few strategies for creating a consistent process that scales well, even for deploying the largest apps. In this section, you'll learn some strategies to test new features and release your app's next versions.

Testing

You *could* test by always putting the raw, most bleeding-edge features into your Alpha track. This would ensure the team members could stay in tune with the latest and greatest features as the app progresses. However, as the team grows, this type of strategy can cause problems.

Teams need to be able to move quickly, experiment and occasionally break things. But product managers need fresh and *stable* builds to show off the latest features to upper management or other stakeholders. You may have a demo that has a lot of the new features. No one enjoys live demos that fail!

With multiple testing tracks, you can give individual teams their own builds where they can experiment independently of each other and the release process. They can deploy daily or even hourly if they wish, to share the latest features among themselves. You can also set the testing track's country availability to global to allow testers in any country to test your apps, even if the released product isn't globally available yet.

Multiple tracks also let you have a more thorough testing process at release time. By using individual team tracks, teams can test new features independently before you cut the final release. Once you're ready to release, you promote your build through multiple stages of testing, starting with a team-wide test of tens of people, to a company-wide test with thousands of users, and then a public, open beta with potentially millions of test users.

The open beta allows external users to try your latest and greatest features if they're willing to give you private feedback. Users can join directly from the store listing in the Play Store app. The open public Beta gives high volume, external feedback on a slew of device and platform combinations and real-world use cases.

Testing isn't just about mitigating the risk of bugs and crashes. It's also a chance to get feedback on features and ensure new features have the right impact on key performance indicators.

You might be wondering, why go through all these various stages of testing?

Why not go straight to open beta?

Well, you might want to test out some confidential new features before they're visible to external users.

Why have both a team-wide test and a company-wide test?

It's good to establish a tradition in your organization of dogfooding your apps. Dogfooding is the practice of a company or team uses its own products. You might not want to break the app for everyone in the company when you're testing out new features.

Why might you still need an open beta if you have a large company and do a company-wide test?

Even if a company-wide test can reach thousands of users, these users may tend to have a somewhat narrow set of Android devices, and they may have a narrow set of use cases or behaviors as compared to the general public. An open beta gives you much more scale and a device set that's more representative of your production users.

So, that's testing. You've validated your feature and your app update. Now, how do you roll out these updates and features to users? Read on to find out in the next section!

Feature rollout

A staged rollout is critically important to app development teams at large companies with mission-critical apps. Rather than updating billions of devices at once, you always want to start small and ramp up incrementally, keeping a close eye on business, user and crash metrics. At the first sign of any issues, you can always halt a release.

But how do you actually *manage* these releases?

One method for managing an app release is to wait until all the features scheduled for that release are ready, then cut and roll out the release. Does this sound familiar? This is how things work at quite a few large companies. It might *seem* to work most of the time, but unfortunately, features sometimes hit a snag, causing delays to all the other features scheduled for the release.

Soon, a January release can become a February release. And then you're pooling more and more features into that single release. More features lead to more testing, more bugs, more release candidates and more changes that make it hard to track down exactly what caused any particular bug or performance regression.

Additionally, since the next release might be a while away, developers scramble to get their features onto the release. Then in the meantime, you may discover you need to ship an urgent bug fix that can't wait. As the team scales, this cycle tends to spiral out of control.

However, you can avoid all the resulting stress from such situations.

Waiting for all the features to be ready slows down innovation and adds a lot of risk to the app release. So while it might seem counter-intuitive at first, releasing faster is *safer*. Keeping a continuous and predictable release cycle makes each release smaller, safer and easier to manage. And you can get those urgent bug fixes released quickly and painlessly.

Interestingly, when developers know the next release is only a few weeks away, they tend to avoid cramming their almost, but not quite, finished features into a given release.

So, this all sounds great, but how does it work in practice? How do you keep the release cycle running on time? And how do you ensure new features don't go live before they're ready?

Firebase Remote Config

You can use **flag-guarded feature development** to safely put out features in an app release. Google uses this technique internally for its app rollout cycles. Whenever possible, they try to avoid shipping new features directly with an app update. Google puts each feature behind a flag that can be toggled on and off from the server.

First, use the staged rollout to release the app update with all the flags turned off. By first deploying such a change neutral binary, it's easier and safer to get this update to all of your users. This also lets you evaluate the app binary itself, for things like stability and system health, as it installs on the user's device separately from the feature and how it's doing.

Once you deploy this change-neutral app update, you can then slowly enable each feature by turning on the flags. Carefully keep an eye on all important users, business and crash metrics to detect any issues. If you do detect any issues, you then can disable the feature by turning off the flag. This technique ensures an issue with one feature won't adversely affect all of the app update's other features.

One way to implement this type of technique is by using **Firebase Remote Config**.

Firebase Remote Config isn't limited to Android. So, your company could use it for both your iOS *and* your Android deployments. Firebase Remote Config moves much of the release cycle process you might typically go through with multiple app builds into the cloud. You can deploy changes to small, and then progressively larger, segments. Or you can perform A/B testing to evaluate if a change you're making is a good choice.

By circumventing the need to release multiple builds, it can enable you to roll out changes in minutes rather than days or weeks. You use Firebase Remote Config in conjunction with Firebase Analytics, formerly known as Google Analytics, to get real-time feedback on your rollouts.

For more information about Firebase Remote Config, see: https://firebase.google.com/products/remote-config.

Following the techniques outlined in this chapter and the previous one, Google maintains a bi-weekly release cycle for apps with user bases numbering in the billions of users.

Production release

Once the Alpha and Beta testing are complete, you're ready for the final release to Production! This is as simple as promoting the final Beta version to Production.

Go to the **App releases ▸ MANAGE BETA** section and click **RELEASE TO PRODUCTION**.

This creates a release in Production and displays the release screen to verify the details. As with the Alpha and Beta release, you need to review the release information before publishing it to the Play Store.

When you're ready, click **REVIEW**. If everything checks out, you'll see the **START ROLLOUT TO PRODUCTION** button.

For first-time app publishers, this can be both an exciting and stress-inducing moment. The app you've worked so hard on will finally be available for the public to enjoy.

Don't be nervous. Click **START ROLLOUT TO PRODUCTION**.

Pay attention to any warnings that may crop up. If everything looks good, click **CONFIRM**.

Within a short amount of time, your app will be live in the Play Store. Celebrate! Throw a launch party and spread the news about your first published app.

But don't party too long, because you haven't finished yet. Like a newborn child, you can't leave your production app on its own. It needs some tender loving care and attention to thrive!

Post-production

Here are some final tips to help keep your app in top shape.

- **Review your app stats on a regular basis**. The Play Console provides a wealth of information about the number and types of installs, number and frequency of crashes and overall ratings. Look for spikes or drops in any of these categories to stay on top of changes. Don't assume items will fix themselves: Be proactive and address issues as soon as they appear. See **Chapter 14** for a deep dive on this topic.

- **Check reviews and look for problem trends**. Even the best-made apps will inevitably get some negative reviews. Look for common threads in the reviews. If several users all complain about the same thing, that's an excellent hint to focus on that issue.

Positive reviews can also provide valuable feedback about what you're doing right and help drive future product development. You can also respond to user reviews using the Google Play Developer Reply to Reviews API, found here https://developers.google.com/android-publisher/reply-to-reviews, or in the Google Play Console.

See **Chapter 13** for a simple yet extremely effective strategy to generate positive reviews and get direct user feedback instead of negative reviews and the dreaded one-star ratings.

- **Be aware of new Android releases**. In some cases, a new Android OS release can impact how your existing app performs. Make sure to keep up with beta releases of the Android OS, and make sure your app performs as expected before the OS is released to the public.
- **List well-known issues**. If you have issues that are known and you can't fix them quickly, consider mentioning them in the Play store description along with a workaround if possible. It's better if users know about these issues rather than being surprised after they download the app.
- **Consider using staged rollouts**. You've covered staged rollouts and their benefits in-depth in this chapter. When using staged rollouts, you specify the percentage of users to update to the new release. You can also limit the update to specific countries. For the first release, you might consider rolling out to a single, smaller country before targeting your primary countries.

Other publishing methods

In some cases, you may need to distribute an app without going through the Play Store. It might be an enterprise app that will never go public, or it might be a side project you're distributing to friends and family.

There are a few ways to distribute an app directly.

Email distribution

Email requires the least amount of work on your part. All you do is attach the APK file to an email and have your users open the email on a compatible Android device.

Users will need to configure their devices to allow *unknown sources* before installing the APK. It's a good idea to include instructions in the email when sending out the APK.

If a user is running Android 8.0 or newer, they should look for the **Install unknown apps** section in the device settings.

If a user is running a version before Android 8.0, they should enable **Unknown sources** in the **Security** section of the device settings.

When the user opens an email with an APK attached, they can download the APK.

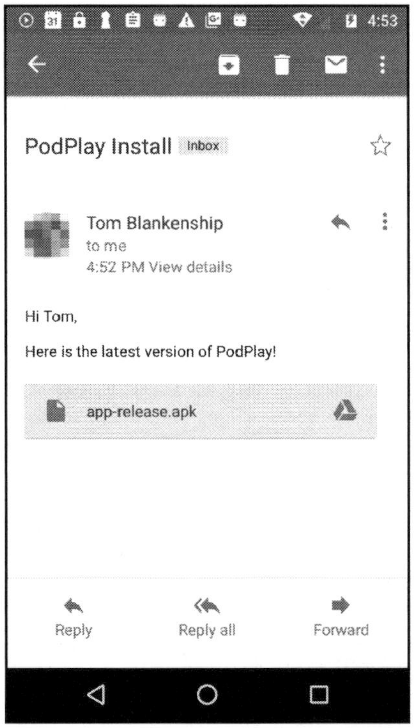

The user can then find the APK in their downloads app or by pulling down the notifications view. When they tap the APK file, they'll be prompted to install the app.

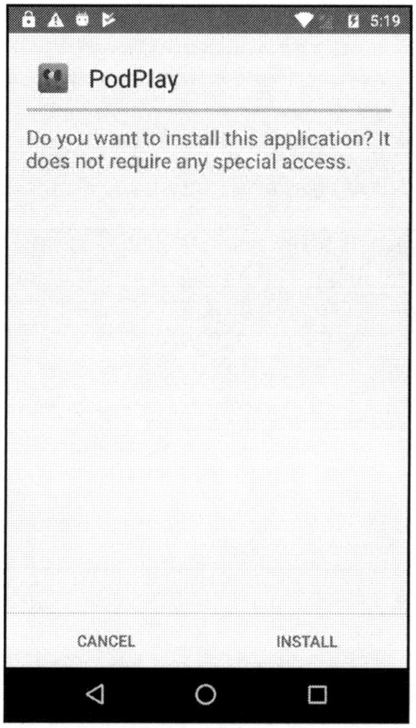

Website distribution

Another option is to host the APK file on your website or a cloud share service such as Dropbox, Google Drive or Slack. You can either send a link to the download location or point the users to the download page on your site. Whether the user taps the link from an email or the browser on the device, they'll be prompted to install the APK.

As with email distribution, the user must configure the device to allow unknown sources.

Other app stores

There are some other app stores available for publishing your app. You may want to take time to explore which options are available.

One of the most well-known stores is the **Amazon Appstore**. Amazon devices such as the **Fire TV** and **Fire Tablet** come with the Amazon Appstore by default. It contains apps made especially for Amazon products as well as many apps also found in the Google Play store. There's no registration fee for developers on the Amazon Appstore, and it also offers some unique monetization models.

There are some fundamental differences between Google and Amazon in the way apps are purchased and how in-app billing is handled. However, in both cases, you'll get 70% of the app earnings.

One big difference is that you can't switch a free app on Google Play to a paid one. You must make that decision during the initial rollout. Amazon lets you start your app as free and change to paid at any time. The Amazon App store process is a bit more involved and requires you to wrap your APK in their code.

You can always start by releasing to the Google Play store and then decide later if you also want to distribute the app to other app stores.

Key points

- You've seen why releasing is an exciting time and how to think about what constitutes a great release. A great release delights users, improves business metrics and is stable and performant.
- You took a look at the suite of tools the Google Play Console makes available to help you achieve efficient, well understood and low-risk app releases.
- You learned about the internal test track for fast, iterative testing with your team and testers.
- You looked at closed testing, where you get to control who can test your app. You saw how you can go beyond Alpha and Beta testing with multiple closed testing tracks.
- You learned how to best leverage open testing where any user can opt into testing your app directly from the Google Play Store. You've seen how this can bring massive scale to your app testing. You also looked at how to roll out your releases, the different areas of the Play Console, staged rollouts and a glimpse of the publishing API for automating your releases using Gradle and continuous integration tools.
- Finally, you saw an overview of Google's strategy for creating a consistent release process that scales from the smallest to the largest teams, and how to implement it yourself using Firebase Remote Config.

Where to go from here?

As mentioned earlier, developing and publishing your app is just the beginning. In the rest of this book, you'll dive deep into what lies beyond the app release.

In this and the previous chapter, you received a broad overview of the Play Console, a more in-depth look into Test Tracks and many of the things you need to pay attention to *before* releasing your app to production. Another aspect of Play Console is monitoring and promoting your app *after* releasing to production. This includes the **Grow** and **Quality** sections of Play Console and Play Store discovery. You'll learn more about that in section four of this book. You can also check out the *Google Play* playlist on YouTube: https://www.youtube.com/playlist?list=PLWz5rJ2EKKc9Kh-e9fhvc8EI16Avbifie

Section II: Security & Optimization

A secure and svelte app can be the difference between having a successful release and one with problems. This section will show you the various steps of developing apps that are secure, reasonably sized and optimized. Topics covered include app permissions, obfuscation and steps for hardening your app's security.

Dynamically deploying features allows you to do limited testing. Depending on the technique you use, it can also be a great way to keep the app smaller by only loading features that a user needs. You'll learn about that in chapter 8.

You also may want to create a white label version of your app or build flavors for testing. Chapter 9 covers all of that to help guide you through creating build variants and flavors.

Chapter 5: Permissions

By Fuad Kamal

In the previous section, you learned how to distribute and release your app. When you distribute your app, you may find one of your app's critical functionalities requires explicitly asking the user for permission to access certain hardware features. Furthermore, when you release your app into production, you need to ensure your users' data is secure. In this chapter, you'll learn about different types of **permissions**, how to gain access to features that rely on those permissions and how to secure your users' data.

Permissions

For security, you have to declare or request permission before using certain features on Android devices. Permissions protect access to **restricted data** and **restricted actions**. You declare permissions in the app manifest file. Certain types of permissions also require asking the user to actively grant them so your app can use them.

Permissions that only need to be declared in the app manifest and are granted automatically when your app is installed are called **install-time permissions**. The user sees a list of the install-time permissions your app requires on its app details page in the Play Store, but they won't get UI prompts from the app about them.

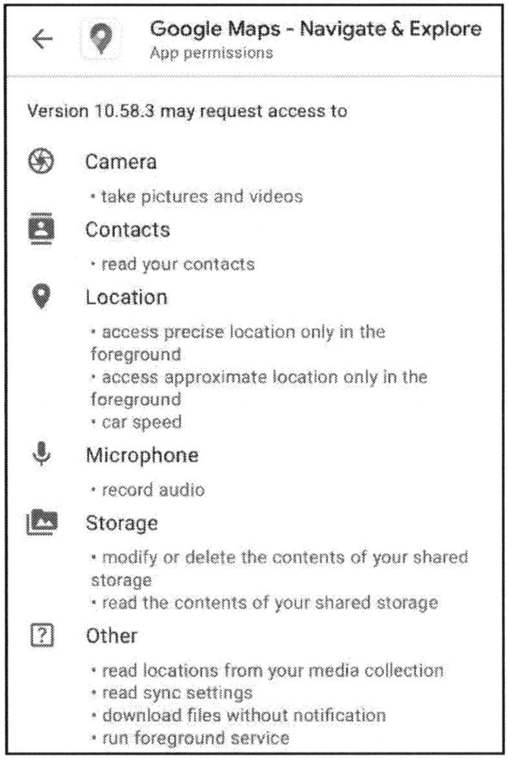

Play Store permissions listing for Google Maps.

Permissions that require authorization from the user at runtime are known as **runtime permissions**, or **dangerous permissions**. When you request a dangerous permission from the user, the system prompts them with a popup permission request.

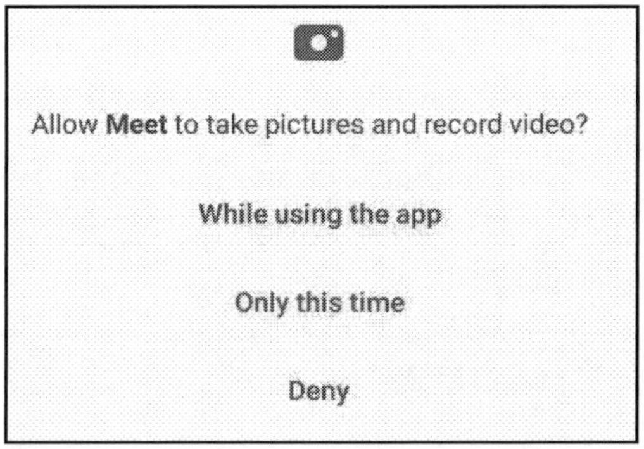

In-app permissions popup for Google Meets.

You need to keep some best practices and user experience design, or UXD, in mind when working with dangerous permissions. Also, while there are many types of permissions, the permissions ecosystem changes from version to version of Android OS. So, be sure to check the official documentation regularly.

Dangerous permissions

Android OS presents the user with a UI prompt whenever your app requests a runtime permission. You can ruin user experience by requesting permissions that don't make sense to the user or at the wrong time. So it's critical to follow Permissions best practices. To learn how, you'll update Podplay with some interesting features.

Until now, Podplay only searched for podcasts against the iTunes Store in the U.S. You review your app's analytics in the Play Console and realize your user base covers the globe. Wouldn't it be great if Podplay searched for podcasts in the user's country?

The app needs location permission, which is considered a dangerous permission, to search based on the user's location.

App manifest permissions

There are some common types of permissions your app might need to request. For a complete and current list of all Android app permissions, refer to the permissions API reference https://developer.android.com/guide/topics/permissions/overview.

Apps commonly need permissions such as access to the camera, microphone, location, networking information, Bluetooth access, various types of scoped storage and biometrics access. Also, be aware of permissions you need for any third-party libraries you use. For Podplay, you'll only need to add the **coarse location** permission.

Location permissions

Apps that need to know a user's location need location permissions. According to permissions best practices, you should minimize the data you collect from users.

You can request two levels of location accuracy: **coarse location** and **fine location**. If you don't require the user's precise location, you should request the course location permission. However, if you made an app that provided turn-by-turn directions, you'd need the fine location permission since you'd need to know the user's precise location to alert them to the next turn.

To access background location in your app, you must first obtain a foreground location permission: either `ACCESS_COARSE_LOCATION` or `ACCESS_FINE_LOCATION`. Otherwise, the system will throw an exception.

You'll get into how to ask the user for permission in a moment. But first, you need to list each of the permissions your app requires in the app manifest file.

Open **AndroidManifest.xml** for Podplay and add the following permission before the `application` tag:

```
<uses-permission
android:name="android.permission.ACCESS_COARSE_LOCATION" />
```

Since Android 11, you can't get background location permission from an in-app dialogue. Instead, you must explain the feature which requires the background location using an in-context UI.

If the user chooses to permit access, they're directed to the system settings to grant permission. The user can only choose the **Allow all the time** option for the location permission on this settings page, as shown below:

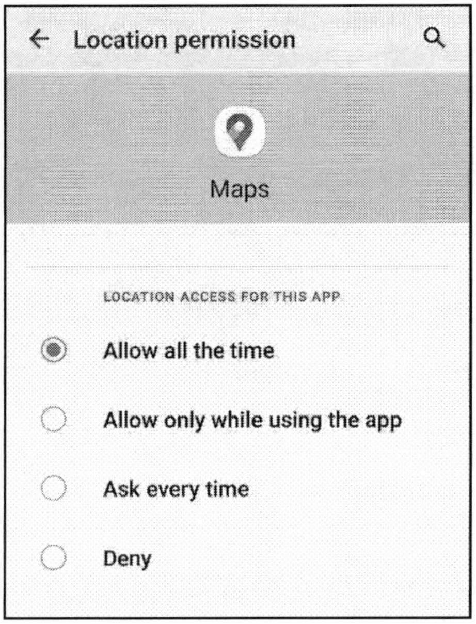

Allow background location permission

Build and run. Everything works as before. Declaring the permission in the manifest doesn't make the app ask the user for permission. You'll learn how to do that next.

Asking for permission

Here's the recommended code block for checking for permissions and requesting them if necessary:

```
when {
    checkSelfPermission(...) == GRANTED -> {
        // Perform action.
    }
    shouldShowRequestPermissionRationale(...) -> {
        // Show in-context rationale.
    }
    else -> {
        requestPermissions(...)
    }
}
```

This is the recommended flow to handle runtime permissions:

1. Check whether the app holds a given permission **before** performing any action that requires it. Unlike iOS, in Android, the developer can always perform this check successfully regardless of the permission type.This check shouldn't be cached or stored since it can get out of sync with the system state. A user can always go into the device settings and deny a permission they previously granted. Furthermore, in Android 11 and later, the system will **automatically revoke all runtime permissions** for apps the user hasn't used for some time.
2. Fail gracefully in cases where the user declines a permission.

Permissions best practices

Here are the best practices regarding permissions:

1. Request minimum permissions.
2. Only ask for access in context when the user starts to interact with the feature that requires it.
3. Don't block the user. Always provide the option to cancel an educational UI flow related to permissions.
4. Plan for users to select deny.
5. Don't access data when the user doesn't expect it.
6. Pay attention to libraries.

Lets take a look at each of these best practices in a bit more detail.

Requesting minimum permissions

Only use the permissions necessary for your app to work. Every time you ask users for permission, you require them to make a decision, increasing the burden on the user.

Look for alternatives to common use cases that may help you limit the number of permissions you ask. For example, you might consider system intents, identifiers and background for phone calls.

Be mindful of your deny rate. If you're distributing your app through Google Play, the **Android Vitals** section reports the percentage of users who deny permissions in your app. Use that to assess whether or not you should rethink your permissions strategy.

Asking for access in context

Ask for permissions only when your app needs to access it for the first time. Be transparent with your users about why you need the permission.

You want to design the UX of your app to feel natural and logical for your users to grant the requested permission, rather than abrupt, forced or accidental. If the user understands why they need to give a certain permission to carry out some task with your app, they're much more likely to grant the permission.

Once the user clicks the feature that needs the permission, first check if they granted permission by passing the permission into the `checkSelfPermissions` as you saw earlier:

```
when {
    checkSelfPermission(...) == GRANTED -> {
        // Perform action.
    }...
```

This method will return permission granted, or permission denied.If the permission returned is denied, you call `shouldShowRequestPermissionRationale` to decide whethet to show the user a UI requesting the permission.

In this UI, you need to explain clearly why the app needs the permission. You also need to give the user the option to deny the permission request before seeing a runtime prompt. Never use the runtime prompt to capture the user's decision to grant the permission. Instead, the runtime prompt is meant as a system confirmation that the user wants to use a specific feature in your app and therefore is willing to give you app access to their private data.

Planning for denied requests

There's no guarantee the user will grant the permission you request. You should always write the logic of your permission request in a way that *assumes* the user may deny the request and act accordingly. If the user denies or revokes a permission that a feature needs, gracefully degrade your app so the user can continue using your app, possibly by disabling the feature that requires the permission.

Keep these best practices in mind:

1. Expect that the user will deny the permission and gracefully degrade when that happens. Don't block users from using the app unless the permission is critical to its functionality.
2. Expect that the user might permanently deny the permission. To prevent this, make sure to ask for the permission in context and let the user deny the feature within your app's UI.
3. Use `shouldShowRequestPermissionRationale` properly, in case the user has selected "Only this time" or in case the system has automatically revoked the permission.

If the user denies a permission request, your app should help them understand the implications of denying the permission. In particular, your app should make the user aware of the features that won't work because of the missing permission. When you do, keep the following best practices in mind:

- **Guide the user's attention.** Highlight a specific part of your app's UI where there's limited functionality because your app doesn't have the necessary permission. For example, you could show a message where the feature's results or data would have appeared. Or you could display a different button containing an error icon and color.
- **Be specific.** Don't display a generic message. Instead, mention which features are unavailable because your app doesn't have the necessary permission.
- **Don't block the user interface.** In other words, don't display a full-screen warning message that prevents users from continuing to use your app at all.

At the same time, your app should respect the user's decision to deny a permission. Starting in Android 11, API level 30, if the user taps **Deny** for a specific permission more than once during your app's lifetime of installation on a device, the user won't see the system permissions dialog when your app requests that permission again. The user's action implies "don't ask again." On previous versions, users would see the system permissions dialog each time your app requested a permission unless the user had previously selected a "don't ask again" checkbox or option.

In certain situations, the permission might be denied automatically, without the user taking any action. Similarly, a permission might be *granted* automatically as well. It's important not to assume anything about automatic behavior. Each time your app needs to access functionality that requires a permission, you should check that your app is still granted that permission.

One-time permissions

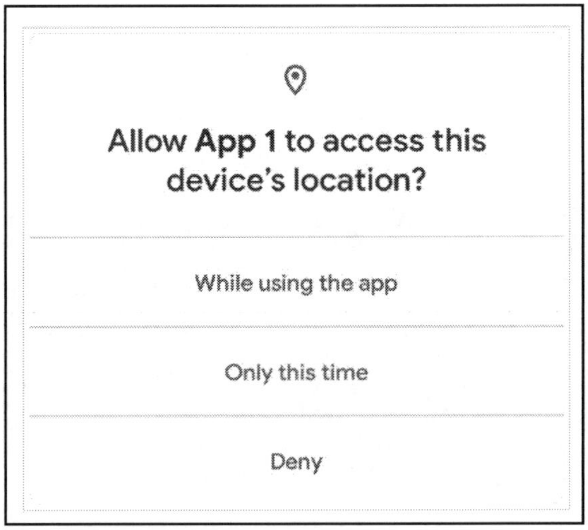

System dialog that appears when an app requests a one-time permission.

Starting in Android 11, API level 30, whenever your app requests a permission related to location, microphone or camera, the user-facing permissions dialog contains an option called **Only this time**, as shown above. If the user selects this option, they grant your app a temporary *one-time permission*.Your app can then access the related data for a period of time that depends on your app's behavior and the user's actions:

- While its activity is visible, your app can access the data.
- If the user sends your app to the background, it can continue to access the data for a short time.
- If you launch a foreground service while the activity is visible, and the user moves your app to the background, your app can continue to access the data until that foreground service stops. You must note this condition. Later, you'll see how to leverage this to get rid of background location services.
- If the user revokes the one-time permission, such as in system settings, your app cannot access the data, regardless of whether you launched a foreground service. As with any permission, if the user revokes your app's one-time permission, your app's process terminates. When the user next opens your app, and it requests access to location, microphone or camera, the user is prompted for the permission again.

Don't access private data unexpectedly

Pay attention to the time and frequency you're accessing user data to ensure it aligns with what users expect. You must provide continuous indication for mic and camera whenever you access these sensitive capabilities.

Updating Podplay to search by location

Now that you understand the best practices and UX of requesting permissions, you're ready to update Podplay to search for podcasts based on the user's location.

iTunes Search API

Podplay uses the iTunes Search API to search for podcasts.

According to Apple's developer documentation for this API, the fully-qualified URL for the API has the following format:

`https://itunes.apple.com/search?parameterkeyvalue.`

Here, `parameterkeyvalue` can be one or more parameter key and value pairs indicating your query's details.

Under **service**, open **ItunesService.kt**. You can see a companion object, `ItunesService`, that defines the base URL for this API. There's also a definition for `searchPodcastByTerm`, which takes the search term, typed in by the user, and appends it to the base URL:

```
@GET("/search?media=podcast")
fun searchPodcastByTerm(@Query("term") term: String):
Call<PodcastResponse>
```

Podplay already sends parameter `term`. Also, note `@GET` above the function signature, which defines the `media` parameter key. Now, you need to add an additional parameter key, `country`, for the user's country.

The value for this key is the country code, which you can derive directly from the location service you'll implement. To keep with coding best practices, rename the function to keep it descriptive of what it does. Change the `searchPodcastByTerm()` function to:

```
@GET(value = "/search?media=podcast")
  fun searchPodcastByTermAndCountry(@Query("term") term: String,
```

```
@Query("country") country: String): Call<PodcastResponse>
```

Alternatively, you could use `@QueryMap` instead of `@Query`. To keep things simple, adding another `@Query` is fine here.

Next, under **repository**, open **ItunesRepo.kt**. Again, you need to add the country parameter and change the function's name to reflect this change in parameters. Change the function signature of `searchByTerm` and `podcastCall` to:

```
fun searchByTermAndCountry(term: String, country: String,
callBack: (List<ItunesPodcast>?) -> Unit) {

    val podcastCall =
itunesService.searchPodcastByTermAndCountry(term, country)
```

Finally, under **viewmodel**, open **SearchViewModel.kt** and update `searchPodcasts()` like this:

```
fun searchPodcasts(term: String, country: String, callback:
(List<PodcastSummaryViewData>) -> Unit) {
    iTunesRepo?.searchByTermAndCountry(term, country) { results
->
```

You added the country code to the search functionality. Now, you need to determine which country the user is in to provide the right country code.

Implementing location service requests

As you know, you don't want to access your user's location until necessary. Hence, you don't ask for location permissions as soon as the app starts. That would surprise the user and possibly lead them to deny the request outright.

When do you need to access their location? You'll need the user's country code to append your search parameter. So, wait until the user taps the search icon to search for a podcast. First, check if the user already granted permission. If they haven't, then request the permission.

The search takes place in **PodcastActivity.kt**'s `performSearch()`. First, add the following two members to `PodcastActivity`:

```
private var searchTerm = ""
private val DEFAULT_COUNTRY = "US" // search United State, by
default
```

Here, you move `searchTerm` to the class scope, so more than one function in the class can access it. `DEFAULT_COUNTRY` contains the default country code US. You provide a default value for the country code to avoid breaking the app's existing functionality if the location can't be determined or the user denies the permission.

Add the following localized string definitions to **strings.xml**:

```
<string name="permission_rationale">Select Allow Location in
order to search for podcasts local to you. 🌍🌎🌏</string>
<string name="permission_denied_explanation">Location permission
was denied, but is needed for searching in context of your
country. Searches will use default country unless you grant the
permission.</string>
<string name="ok">OK</string>
<string name="settings">Settings</string>
```

The code above defines strings you'll use in the prompt shown to the user to request the location permission.

Next, head back to **PodcastActivity.kt** and update `performSearch()` to include a parameter for the search country, as shown below:

```
private fun performSearch(searchTerm: String, searchCountry:
String) {
  showProgressBar()
  searchViewModel.searchPodcasts(searchTerm, country =
searchCountry) { results ->
    hideProgressBar()
    toolbar.title = searchTerm
    podcastListAdapter.setSearchData(results)
  }
}
```

In the code above, you also update the method invocation of `searchViewModel.searchPodcasts()` to include the `searchCountry` parameter.

Next, add the following method to the same Activity:

```
private fun checkLocationPermissionAndSearch(term: String) {
  searchTerm = term
  when {
    // 1

checkSelfPermission(Manifest.permission.ACCESS_COARSE_LOCATION)
== PackageManager.PERMISSION_GRANTED -> {
      // Permission granted. Proceed to use the location.
      performSearch(term, DEFAULT_COUNTRY)
    }
```

```
    // 2
    // If the user denied a previous request, but didn't check
"Don't ask again", provide
    // additional rationale.

shouldShowRequestPermissionRationale(Manifest.permission.ACCESS_
COARSE_LOCATION) -> {
      // In an educational UI, explain to the user why your app
requires this
      // permission for a specific feature to behave as
expected. In this UI,
      // if possible, include a "cancel" or "no thanks" button
that allows the user to
      // continue using your app without granting the
permission.
      Snackbar.make(
              podcastDetailsContainer,
              R.string.permission_rationale,
              Snackbar.LENGTH_LONG
      )
              .setAction(R.string.ok) {
                // Request permission
                ActivityCompat.requestPermissions(
                        this,

arrayOf(Manifest.permission.ACCESS_COARSE_LOCATION),
                        LOCATION_PERMISSION_REQUEST_CODE
                )
              }
              .show()
    }
    else -> {
      // 3
      // Display the system permissions dialog when necessary
      Log.d("PodcastActivity", "Request location permission")
      ActivityCompat.requestPermissions(
              this,

arrayOf(Manifest.permission.ACCESS_COARSE_LOCATION),
              LOCATION_PERMISSION_REQUEST_CODE
      )
    }
  }
}
```

Also, the following import for `Manifest`:

```
import android.Manifest
```

The code above does the following:

1. First, if the user previously granted the permission, the search will execute as before. However, if they haven't granted permission, for example, if this is the user's first search, it won't be performed yet.
2. Next, you make the call to `shouldShowRequestPermissionRationale`, which returns a Boolean. If it returns true, you show the user an educational UI to explaining why you need the location permission. Note that typically, if this condition returns true, it's because the user previously denied this permission request from this app. If you keep trying to request the permission, your permission request won't be shown after the second time. Therefore, it's better to explain to the user *why* you need this permission. Also, note that for simplicity's sake, in these examples you'll use snackbar notifications. However, if you need to provide a detailed explanation or additional buttons for a more graceful user experience, you should show a modal popup instead.
3. If the user hasn't already granted permission, and the system isn't reporting that you need to display a rationale, then you make the permission request.

The IDE will warn you that `LOCATION_PERMISSION_REQUEST_CODE` hasn't been defined. Create a new file named **Constants.kt** inside **model**. Add the following code to it:

```
const val LOCATION_PERMISSION_REQUEST_CODE = 100
```

Go back to **PodcastActivity.kt** and add the following import for LOCATION_PERMISSION_REQUEST_CODE :

```
import
com.raywenderlich.podplay.model.LOCATION_PERMISSION_REQUEST_CODE
```

Since you added code to request permission, you also need to handle the premission request's outcome.

Add the following method to the same Activity:

```
override fun onRequestPermissionsResult(
          requestCode: Int,
          permissions: Array<String>,
          grantResults: IntArray
  ) {
    super.onRequestPermissionsResult(requestCode, permissions,
grantResults)
    when (requestCode) {
      LOCATION_PERMISSION_REQUEST_CODE -> when {
```

```
        grantResults.isEmpty() ->
          // If user interaction was interrupted, the permission
request
          // is cancelled and you receive empty arrays.
          Log.d("PodcastActivity", "User interaction was
cancelled.")

        grantResults[0] == PackageManager.PERMISSION_GRANTED ->
          // Permission was granted.
          performSearch(searchTerm, DEFAULT_COUNTRY)

        else -> {
          // Permission denied.
          Snackbar.make(
                  podcastDetailsContainer,
                  R.string.permission_denied_explanation,
                  Snackbar.LENGTH_LONG
          )
                  .setAction(R.string.settings) {
                    // Build intent that displays the App
settings screen.
                    val intent = Intent()
                    intent.action =
Settings.ACTION_APPLICATION_DETAILS_SETTINGS
                    val uri = Uri.fromParts(
                            "package",
                            BuildConfig.APPLICATION_ID,
                            null
                    )
                    intent.data = uri
                    intent.flags = Intent.FLAG_ACTIVITY_NEW_TASK
                    startActivity(intent)
                  }
                  .show()
          performSearch(searchTerm, DEFAULT_COUNTRY)
        }
      }
    }
  }
```

Also, add the following import for `Settings`:

```
import android.provider.Settings
```

Note: If you are unable to find an import for `BuildConfig`, build the app once. It will generate the required **BuildConfig.java** and you'll be able to import it.

In the code above:

1. You check whether the user granted the location permission. If they did, you continue with the search. For now, you use the default country. You'll change that shortly.
2. If the user denied the permission, you show a SnackBar with an explanation and continue the search using the default country. This lets the user continue using the app even without granting the permission.

Finally, replace the invocation of `performSearch` inside `handleIntent()` with `checkLocationPermissionAndSearch` as shown in the code below:

```
private fun handleIntent(intent: Intent) {
  if (Intent.ACTION_SEARCH == intent.action) {
    val query = intent.getStringExtra(SearchManager.QUERY) ?:
return
    checkLocationPermissionAndSearch(query)
  }
  //..
}
```

Build and run. Even though you aren't fetching the user's location yet, you ask for location permissions. Note: if you don't see the prompt asking for permissions un-install and re-install the app on your device. Search for some podcasts. Experiment with allowing and denying the location permissions.

You can go into the device's Settings to change the permissions for the app if you denied permission enough times that you no longer receive a permissions prompt. Additionally, you can set breakpoints in the code in the different permission scenarios to see how and when they're called. Tap the links in the toast messages to test the functionality of opening Settings to the permissions settings for Podplay.

Rationale toast message with link to settings app.

Fetching location

There's only one piece left to this puzzle: determine the user's country. First you'll ask the system for the user's last known location. You'll then use that location to perform a technique known as *reverse geocoding*.

Reverse geocoding is transforming a latitude, longitude coordinate into a partial address. The amount of detail in a reverse geocoded location description varies. For example, one might contain the closest building's full street address, while another might contain only a city name and postal code.

You've already updated the manifest file for the coarse location permission. Now you also need to update the app Gradle file to use Google Play location services. Add the following to the dependencies block in the app **buildgradle** and sync the Gradle file:

```
// Location Services
implementation "com.google.android.gms:play-services-
location:18.0.0"
```

Almost done! Add the following class level variabl to **PodcastActivity.kt**:

```
private lateinit var fusedLocationClient:
FusedLocationProviderClient // Location Services Client
```

Then add the following method in **PodcastActivity.kt**:

```
private fun searchUsingLocation(searchTerm: String) {
  //Create Location Services Client
  fusedLocationClient =
LocationServices.getFusedLocationProviderClient(this)

  // 1
  if (ActivityCompat.checkSelfPermission(this,
Manifest.permission.ACCESS_COARSE_LOCATION) !=
PackageManager.PERMISSION_GRANTED &&
ActivityCompat.checkSelfPermission(this,
Manifest.permission.ACCESS_COARSE_LOCATION) !=
PackageManager.PERMISSION_GRANTED) {
    return
  }
  // 2
  fusedLocationClient.lastLocation
          .addOnSuccessListener { location : Location? ->
            // Got last known location. In some rare situations
this can be null.
            location?.let {
              // 3
              val geoCoder = Geocoder(this)
              val addresses =
geoCoder.getFromLocation(location.latitude,location.longitude,
1)
              val searchCountry = addresses[0].countryCode
              performSearch(searchTerm, searchCountry)
            } ?: run {
              performSearch(searchTerm, DEFAULT_COUNTRY)
            }
          }.addOnFailureListener {
              performSearch(searchTerm, DEFAULT_COUNTRY)
          }
}
```

The code above does a few things:

1. It might seem redundant to check for location permissions again. After all, you never get to this function without first doing a permissions check. However, if you don't make the check here, you'll get a rather annoying compiler warning from Android Studio. You could also argue that always checking permissions before trying to use a dangerous permission is a best practice.

2. Both in the Android and iOS ecosystems, hardware devices are extremely well engineered when it comes to location services. Hence, location services on both platforms provide an API that relies on the combined smarts of the OS, processor and *all* the various sensors including magnetometer, GPS, accelerometer, WiFi, and cell phone antennae to provide what is known as "fused sensors". Fused sensors are a virtual construct that's more dynamic and versatile than any of the sensors on their own. It's more reliable for the programmer to simply use the fused sensors rather than try to access raw data from individual sensors.

   Furthermore, with "dangerous" location permissions on Android, if you don't require the user's exact location, you're only supposed to access "coarse location", which is the permission you implemented previously. Where and how the location is determined will vary depending on the device's sensors, what data is available from each and so on. As a programmer, you don't need to care about those details. The `FusedLocationProviderClient` provides a convenient callback that will return a `Location` object when it's available. This, in turn, provides an array of addresses.

3. You then rely on yet another convenient built-in class on Android, `Geocoder`, which provides geocoding and reverse geocoding for you. You provide it with a latitude and longitude from the `Location` object, and it provides the country code.

Next, change the first invocation of `performSearch` in `checkLocationPermissionAndSearch` to `searchUsingLocation` as shown below:

```
private fun checkLocationPermissionAndSearch(term: String) {
    when {

checkSelfPermission(Manifest.permission.ACCESS_COARSE_LOCATION)
== PackageManager.PERMISSION_GRANTED -> {
            searchUsingLocation(term)
        }
        //..
}
```

Finally, change the invocation of `performSearch` in `onRequestPermissionsResult()` in the condition where permission is granted, as follows:

```
override fun onRequestPermissionsResult(
    requestCode: Int,
    permissions: Array<String>,
    grantResults: IntArray
) {
  //..
  grantResults[0] == PackageManager.PERMISSION_GRANTED ->
    // Permission was granted.
    searchUsingLocation(searchTerm)
  //..
}
```

Voila! Your app now provides the search query with the proper country code. Build and run. Search for some podcasts!

Finding background location use

Android 10 and 11 give users better privacy controls for fine-grain location permissions. One of the biggest changes is the separation of **foreground location access**, or **while-in-use access**, from **background location access**, or **all-the-time access**.

In Android 11, you can't request both permissions at the same time. Whenever possible, Google recommends you only rely on foreground access for your location data.

If your app or the libraries it uses require background location, determine if you can switch to foreground location instead.

Updating your own code is straightforward, but you need to be mindful of permissions required by third-party libraries you're using.

Updating your code

Find any location APIs in your code to determine if they're used in the background.

1. Search through your code and look at your use of location services. This part is pretty straight forward. You're just reviewing your own code and figuring things out.

2. Next, examine how your app uses location. Specifically, do you really need background location? You should evaluate whether background location access is critical to your app's core functionality. You can realize many use cases with only foreground location. If you don't need location access in the background, either migrate to foreground location access or remove it altogether. In both cases, it'll simplify your app and codebase. Keep in mind, for Android 10 and later, you need to remove the `ACCESS_BACKGROUND_LOCATION` permission from the manifest.

3. If you determine background location is critical, make sure to follow the best practices and review Google's current policies on location services.

Suppose you want to migrate some background location service code to foreground location instead. What are your options?

1. You could only retrieve location while your activity is viewable. This is the most common approach. So, don't request location data, like "get last location" when your app isn't visible. Update your code so it stops listening to location updates whenever the UI goes out of view.

2. There's another option for foreground location. Your app can retrieve location via a foreground service without the background location permission. This is a little more difficult to implement and debug. For example, you can have a navigation app that only gets updates using the foreground location service. Here, the trick is to transition the service to a foreground service and tie it to a notification. That way, your app is still in use, and you can continue to get location updates without background location access. However, it's important to note that you shouldn't replace all code retrieving location in the background with this approach.

When your app is paused, the trick is to transition the location service being used in the app as a foreground service to a foreground service that's instead tied to a notification. That way, your app is still "in use" and you can continue to get location updates without background location access.

1. First, determine if you should retrieve location data in that instance. In most cases, you should only request location data in the foreground if the user-initiated an action that requires location, like navigating to another place.

2. If you take the time to architect things with proper separation of concerns, all your location code should be separated. That way, you'll know that when the subscriber unbinds from the class using location services, that the activity is going away since it's no longer visible. So if they actively subscribe to location changes and you get an unbind request, you know you need to transition the service to a foreground service. In that case, you create a notification and then transition it to a foreground service. Then, if the activity comes back and re-binds to this class, you transition it back to a foreground service.

You're using a service to retrieve the activity's location via binding. Then you promote that service to a foreground service for the notification when the activity is no longer visible. That way, you still get location changes, even when the app isn't technically visible. It's within the notification, but you don't have an activity visible, and you don't need background permissions.

For an example of how to implement this type of switching between a foreground location service and notifications, see this Google Codelab: https://codelabs.developers.google.com/codelabs/while-in-use-location/?hl=ko#2

Finding permissions required by third-party libraries

You inherit permissions every time you include a third-party library in your code. Users will generally attribute those permissions to your app, not to the library.

If you need to figure out which library requires a specific permission, you can use two APIs Google introduced in Android 11.

The first API is a **callback on data access**. This API tells the system to backtrace an app's specified callback each time the app accesses sensitive data. The callback provides various information, including the type of data being accessed, a stack trace, the frequency and time of data access. For more information on this API, see the official documentation https://developer.android.com/guide/topics/data/audit-access.

The second API is **feature tagging**. It lets developers attribute access to logical features within their app by tagging certain parts of the app. You can learn more about this API at https://developer.android.com/guide/topics/data/audit-access#audit-by-attribution-tag .

Simplifying multiple permission requests with Android Jetpack

The code and techniques you used so far are fine when you only need to request one or two permissions. But some apps need access to multiple permission types. Using `requestPermissions()` and then checking the request code in `onRequestPermissionsResult()` for many different types of permissions can start to make your code complex.

Alternatively, with Jetpack and AndroidX, you can request permission using an activity result registry with the request permission result contract. This removes the need for request codes and overwriting activity APIs. However, it does introduce a bit of its own complexity, and requires you to add yet another Gradle dependency to your app. But, if your app requires many permissions, or if you're using `ActivityResult` API for some of the many other features it offers, it might be something to look into.

Key points

You covered quite a lot in this chapter! Here's a quick recap of some of the salient points:

- Never ask your users for permissions out of context. Wait until you need to access the feature which requires the permission, and then clearly explain why you need it.
- Try to fail gracefully or work around lack of permissions, if you can.
- Architect your apps in a way that plans for the user to deny you permissions.
- Third-party APIs can introduce their own permissions dependencies, but your users will assume this is coming from your app. They don't know or care about third-party libraries. It's good to debug both your app and your library dependencies to see where your user's data is being accessed.

Where to go from here?

In this chapter, you got hands-on experience with some location services and the permissions around them. However, your app many need access to many other kinds. See *Saving Data on Android* for all the many ways you can access data on a device, including disk and database access, network access and `SharedPreferences`, which you'll touch on from the security standpoint in the next chapter. You can find the book here: https://www.raywenderlich.com/books/saving-data-on-android/.

Chapter 6: Security Best Practices

by Fuad Kamal

Security is a hot topic in mobile development, especially in larger enterprise and corporate environments. Many companies pay top dollar for security experts to run penetration tests and other security tests on their apps. Some companies license scanning tools, such as Veracode. There's even a relatively new career path for people who have cross-domain knowledge in mobile development and security.

However, security starts with the architecture and code you write to develop your app. Following security best practices ensures your users' safety, which is the ultimate goal. In this chapter, you'll examine some of the techniques and best practices for securing and hardening your app.

Data storage domains

Securing user data is of paramount importance in mobile apps, both on-device and in transit on networks. Protecting access to source code, API endpoints and keys is a top security concern for corporations.

But for your users, the most critical security concern is protecting their data. You need to protect their data when transmitted to or from the app, which falls under networking. HTTPS (SSL) handles Network traffic.

You also need to protect data stored locally on mobile devices, which falls under data storage. On-device, encryption is the primary way to secure data. Since Android 5.0, the OS encrypts the contents of the user's data partition by default.

But sometimes, you want to provide an extra layer of protection for sensitive data. For example, you may want extra protection when using shared storage and handling sensitive information, such as personally identifiable information (PII), financial records or any especially sensitive data. Also, starting with Android 10, full disk encryption is no longer an option, and your app must do some form of file encryption to secure sensitive data written to files.

In Android, there are three domains concerning data storage:

1. **Internal storage** is the default storage mechanism and has built-in encryption provided by the system.

2. You can also store files on **external storage**, such as SD Cards or even internal disk space your app considers external. If you need to support this type of storage and the data is sensitive, use the **Jetpack Security Library**. You'll read about it in more detail later in this chapter.

3. Finally, **content providers** are an encapsulation method for data storage that provides mechanisms for apps to manage private, self-only access or access to data provided by other apps, such as getting information from Contacts or Gmail, and for sharing data with other apps. Even if your app doesn't share data with other apps, you might use content providers to benefit from the abstraction layer. However, if you do, make sure you disallow access to your app's content providers by setting `android:exported=false` in your app manifest file for the content provider.

Securely storing data

In the past, learning how to encrypt data on Android often meant long hours spent searching the web, and much of what you found was outdated or incorrect. Fortunately, now you can leverage Jetpack Security to easily add an extra layer of security and data protection to your apps.

The Android Keystore stores cryptographic keys in a container to make them more challenging to extract from the device. Once keys are in the keystore, you can use them for cryptographic operations in the trusted execution environment, and the key material isn't exportable. The Android Keystore also provides options such as **Strongbox** to store and operate on keys in a secure hardware chip.

StrongBox Keymaster is a **Hardware Abstraction Layer**, or **HAL**, that resides in a hardware security module with its own CPU, secure storage and a true random number generator. Keep in mind, since this is a hardware feature, it's limited to devices that support it, such as the Google Pixel series.

Jetpack Security, or **JetSec**, uses the Android Keystore to keep encryption keys in hardware, making unauthorized access to the key material difficult. It also provides high-level abstractions for encrypting files and shared preferences to let developers encrypt their data safely without understanding algorithms, block modes and other security field specializations.

Jetpack Security is built on top of **Tink**, a cross-platform Open Source library from Google that provides cryptographic APIs. Jetpack Security focuses on two primary means of securing data persisted to the device: `EncryptedSharedPreferences` and `EncryptedFiles`.

Jetpack Security uses a master key that's hardware-backed and optionally locked by biometrics like fingerprint or face identification. This master key, in turn, secures key-sets treated per cryptographic algorithm using Tink. Biometric security, such as fingerprint authentication, isn't part of the Jetpack Security library but rather part of the AndroidX library. They work well together to offer advanced encryption options.

Securing the Organized Simple Note app

Open the starter project for this chapter and build and run. Running the project for this chapter is best done on an Android device and not on an Android emulator due to the use of device hardware for encryption.

The **Organized Simple Note** app lets you create, edit and delete notes saved in the internal file system. In the **options menu** items, there's an option to change the background color. You can also filter the notes by priority or sort them by specific sort order.

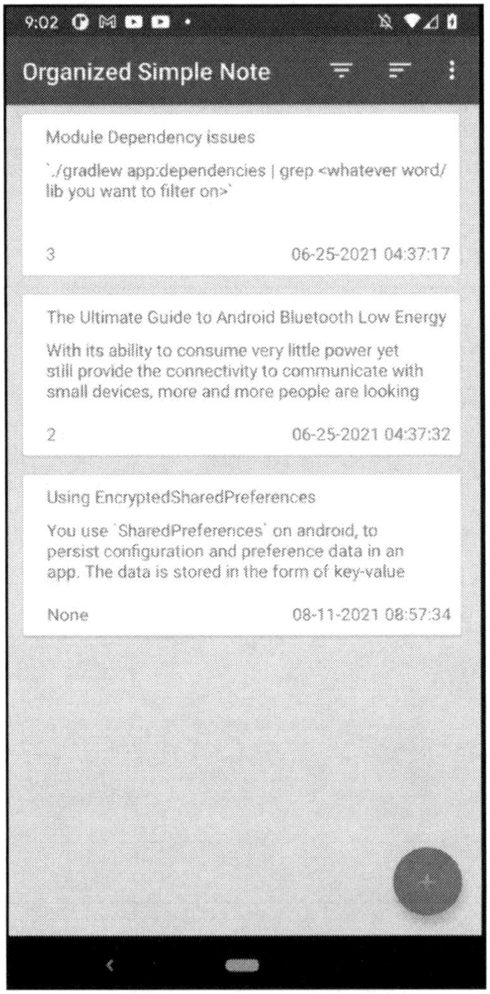

The SimpleNote App Interface

Select a new background color, set a sort order and one or more priority filters. Now, quit the app and rerun it.

When the app reloads, the background color you selected persists. That's because the background color you selected saved to prefs and applied when the app reran. The sort order and priority filters reset to defaults. They weren't stored in prefs. You'll enable these features using encrypted shared preferences.

You may have noticed another menu item, **Set Encryption Key**, below the menu item for changing the background color in the overflow menu. If you tap it now, it'll open a dialog to enter a numeric key, but currently, saving it does nothing.

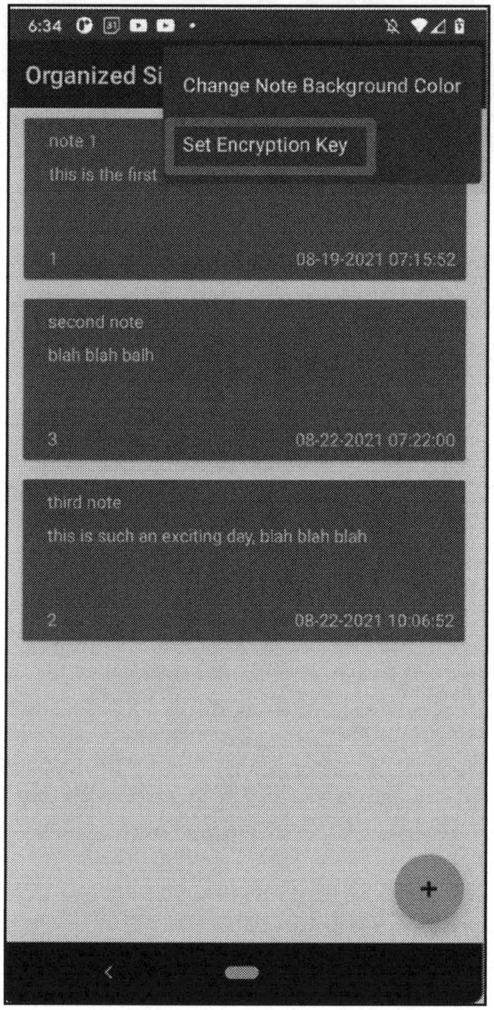

The SimpleNote App Interface

The notes themselves write to disk, not to shared preferences. They're currently not encrypted: You'll use JetSec to encrypt the files as well.

Data encryption: Encrypting files and shared preferences

To protect your users' sensitive data, you should encrypt shared preferences as well as files that may contain such data. Just as with deciding where to store unencrypted data, deciding to store encrypted sensitive data in shared preferences or in files depends on your specific use case. If you need to store some small amount of data in key value pairs, then `EncryptedSharedPreferences` is certainly the easier path to take. If you have a lot of data or complex data, go with encrypted files.

Using EncryptedSharedPreferences

You use `SharedPreferences` on Android to persist configuration and preference data in an app. The data stores in the form of key-value pairs. JetSec provides an encrypted version of `SharedPreferences`, named `EncryptedSharedPreferences`, that provides strong security while maintaining performance for reading the key-value data. Keys and values can both be encrypted.

To create and use `EncryptedSharedPreferences`, you need to provide three things:

1. A **master key** stored in the Android keystone on your device. The master key encrypts all sub keys used for each cryptographic operation.

2. A **value encryption scheme** such as the fast AES-256 GCM algorithm. This algorithm is also used for the master key.

3. If you also want to encrypt the keys, provide a **key encryption scheme**. Encrypting keys is usually optional, but it's necessary if the keys themselves hold sensitive data.

For Organized Simple Note, you'll let the user create a key they'll later use to encrypt the notes themselves. You'll store the key the user creates in `EncryptedSharedPreferences`.

Note that the key acts like a password. In this case, it's OK to store the encrypted key as secret data for the app. However, don't take this approach to store user account passwords for backend systems. In that case, store a salted and hashed password on your backend and not the password itself.

Salting is the process of using random data as input to a function that hashes the password. That way, if your backend server ever has a data breach, an attacker can only get access to salted password hashes and not your users' passwords themselves. You can learn more about salting and hashing in the first section of the *Saving Data on Android* book from raywenderlich.com.

Key management: Creating and securing encryption keys

To use Jetpack Security, first, you need to add it to the app build dependencies.

Open the Simple Note **starter project** for this chapter. Then open the project **build.gradle** and add the following definition to the `ext{}` block:

```
security_version = "1.0.0"
```

Then open the app **build.gradle** and add the jetpack security dependency to the `dependencies` block:

```
implementation("androidx.security:security-crypto:
$security_version")
```

Sync the gradle dependencies.

Next, open **MainActivityViewModel.kt**. Create a `sharedPreferences` in the ViewModel that you'll lazily instantiate by adding the code below:

```
private val sharedPreferences by lazy {
  // 1
    val masterKeyAlias =
MasterKeys.getOrCreate(MasterKeys.AES256_GCM_SPEC)
  // 2
  val keyEncryptionScheme =
EncryptedSharedPreferences.PrefKeyEncryptionScheme.AES256_SIV
  // 3
  val valueEncryptionScheme =
EncryptedSharedPreferences.PrefValueEncryptionScheme.AES256_GCM
    // 4
  EncryptedSharedPreferences.create(
        ENCRYPTED_PREFS,
    masterKeyAlias,
    context,
    keyEncryptionScheme,
    valueEncryptionScheme
    )
}
```

Hit **option-return** on Mac or **Alt-Enter** on PC to pull in the necessary import statements as needed.

In the code above, you:

1. Create a master key alias that gets the master key from the Android keystore. JetSec lets you create a master key with just one line of code. By default, it uses the AES256 bit key, which is sufficient for most use cases.Google recommends tying hardware-backed keys to user presence via a biometric credential. The Android Keystore enforces biometrics at a hardware level so that keys aren't available for use without authorizing the device. Furthermore, for time-bound master keys, the Jetpack biometric prompt is a quick and easy way to show a backward-compatible biometric check on the device.
2. Set up an encryption scheme for the preference keys. You use the AES256_SIV scheme for the keys. Encrypting keys is optional but necessary if the keys themselves hold sensitive data.
3. Add a value encryption scheme. You use AES256_GCM for the encryption values, the same algorithm used by default for the master key.
4. Finally, call `create` on the encrypted shared preferences class to create the shared preferences instance. You pass in the values you created, along with a constant name for the preferences in the starter project and a context object from the view model.

MainActivity uses `getEncryptionKey()` and `setEncryptionKey()` in the ViewModel when the user interacts with the **Set Encryption Key** menu item you examined earlier.

The starter project's ViewModel class has stubs for those methods.

You can interact with the encrypted shared preferences in the same way you do with normal shared preferences, calling `get` methods to get values and `put` methods to save values. Replace the contents of `getEncryptionKey()` with the code below:

```
fun getEncryptionKey(): String? {
    return sharedPreferences.getString(
    ENCRYPTED_PREFS_ENCRYPTION_KEY,
    null
  )
}
```

In the code above, you make a call to `getString` on `sharedPreferences`, passing in a key string named `ENCRYPTED_PREFS_ENCRYPTION_KEY`, the key for the log key value. You also set the default value on the `getString` call to null, so if there's no log key saved in encrypted shared preferences, this method will return null.

Replace the contents of `setEncryptionKey()` with:

```
if (current != getEncryptionKey()) {
  _snackbar.value =
context.getString(R.string.error_current_encryption_key_incorrec
t)
  return
}
//1
if (new.isNullOrBlank()) {
  //2
  sharedPreferences.edit().putString(
    ENCRYPTED_PREFS_ENCRYPTION_KEY,
    null
  ).apply()
  _snackbar.value = context.getString(
    R.string.message_encryption_key_cleared
  )
} else {
  //3
  sharedPreferences.edit().putString(
    ENCRYPTED_PREFS_ENCRYPTION_KEY,
    new
  ).apply()
  _snackbar.value = context.getString(
    R.string.message_encryption_key_set
  )
}
```

In the code above, you:

1. Add a conditional to first check whether a new log key being set is null or blank. If it is, clear the log key by sending null to put the string and then update the `_snackbar` LiveData value in the view model.
2. Just as you would with typical shared preferences, you use `edit` and `apply` calls on the encrypted shared preferences.
3. If the new log key isn't null or blank, set the new value using `putString`. Apply the change and update the SnackBar.

Now build and run. From the overflow menu, tap **Set Encryption Key**. Set an encryption key in the dialogue. Then, tap **Set Encryption Key** again, enter your original key and enter a new key.

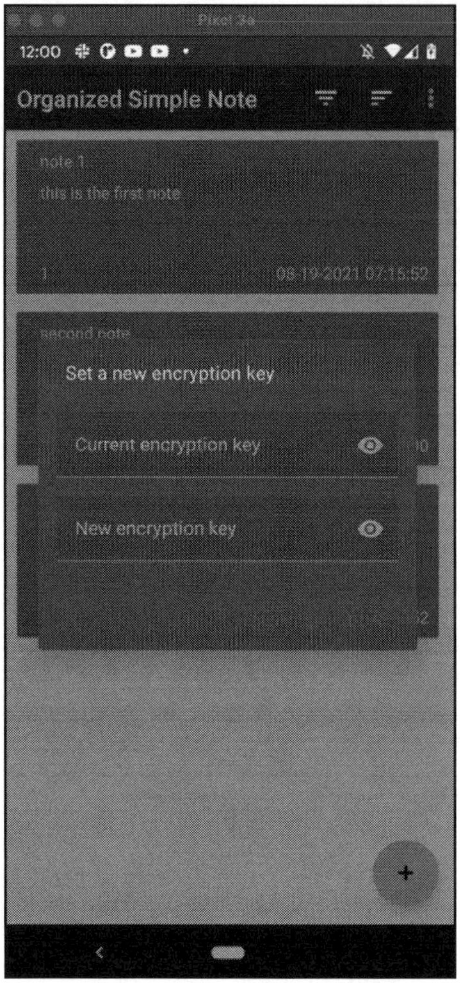

The SimpleNote App Interface

Encrypted files

For persisting and securing the primary app data with Jetpack Security, use encrypted files. Both files and shared preferences are abstractions that provide **authenticated encryption with associated data**, or **AEAD**. AEAD ensures both the confidentiality and integrity of data.

In the past, encrypting files was challenging because of size limitations. You had to load the entire file into memory. `EncryptedFile`, the Android class used to create and read encrypted files, uses streaming AES encryption to handle files of all sizes. The only limiting factor is the remaining disk space.

You can treat `EncryptedFile` similar to a standard file in Android. Once you create the encrypted file object, you can operate on the file with the provided file input/output stream APIs.

The API for getting an encrypted file is similar to getting shared preferences: You need a master key and an encryption scheme. You also need to specify a filename that acts similarly to a key in a key-value pair, uniquely identifying the file in the file system.

Reading an encrypted file

Open **InternalFileRepository.kt** and add the following function:

```
private fun getEncryptedEntry(name: String): EncryptedFile {
  // 1
  val keyGenParameterSpec = MasterKeys.AES256_GCM_SPEC
  val masterKeyAlias =
MasterKeys.getOrCreate(keyGenParameterSpec)
  // 2
  val fileEncryptionScheme =
EncryptedFile.FileEncryptionScheme.AES256_GCM_HKDF_4KB
    // 3
  return EncryptedFile.Builder(
    // 4
    File(context.filesDir, name.urlEncode()),
    // 5
    context,
    masterKeyAlias,
    fileEncryptionScheme
    // 6
  ).build()
}
```

Here's a code breakdown:

1. As with encrypted preferences, you need a master key to access encrypted files. `keyGenParameterSpec` is the same value you used for the master key earlier.
2. Next, like you did for keys and values for encrypted shared preferences, you add a file encryption scheme. You use the **AES256_GCM_HKDF_4KB** algorithm to encrypt files.
3. Then, you use the builder pattern to return an encrypted file.

4. In the builder, you first pass in a file object using the context files directory and the file's name. You use a helper method from the starter project to URL encode the filename, so you don't run into problems with any input data the user chooses to use for the filename.

5. Next, you pass the builder the context, the master key alias and the file encryption scheme.

6. Finally, call build on the builder to finish retrieving the encrypted file.

Next, you need to write data to the encrypted file and then read the encrypted data back in. In `addNote()` replace this line:

```
context.openFileOutput(note.fileName, Context.MODE_PRIVATE).use{
output ->
    output.write(text.toByteArray())
}
```

With the following `try/catch` block:

```
try {
  // 1
    val encryptedFile = getEncryptedEntry(note.fileName)
  encryptedFile.openFileOutput().use { output ->
    output.write(text.toByteArray())
  }
} catch (e: Exception) {
  // 2
    e.printStackTrace()
  _snackbar.value =
context.getString(R.string.error_unable_to_save_file)
}
```

Here's a quick breakdown:

1. In the try block, you attempt to write to the file. You obtain a handle to access the file. `openFileOutput()` grants output access to the file, and then you pass in a Lambda to actually write to the file.

2. You handle any exceptions that occur while trying to write to the file. This example uses a general exception, but you might want to use an IO exception instead.

The method to read from an encrypted file is similar to the operation for writing to the file. Update `getNote()` as follows:

```
override fun getNote(fileName: String): Note {
    val note = Note(fileName, "", 0)
    try {
        context.openFileInput(fileName).use { stream ->
        val text = stream.bufferedReader().use {
        it.readText()
      }
        note.dateModified =
Date(noteFile(fileName).lastModified())
        note.priority = text.takeLast(1).toInt()
        note.noteText = text.dropLast(1)
        return note
        }
    } catch (e:Exception) {
        e.printStackTrace()
    _snackbar.value =
context.getString(R.string.error_unable_to_decrypt)
    return note
    }
}
```

In the code above, the main difference is that you wrap the file reading operation in a try-catch block.

Build and run. Try creating a new note, and then try to read it back. Congratulations, now you know how to securely encrypt your users' data!

Challenge

The sort order and priority filters still reset to their default values when you reload the app. They didn't store in `EncryptedSharedPreferences` yet. As a challenge, update the app so that these values persist in `EncryptedSharedPreferences`.

Key points

- Adding Jetpack Security to your project is quick and easy. The defaults work great out of the box.
- Encrypted files use AES encryption to handle files of all sizes.
- You use an encrypted file like a standard file with minor exceptions.
- Keys for `EncryptedSharedPreferences` are encrypted deterministically.
- `EncryptedSharedPreferences` implement `SharedPreferences` for interoperability.

Where to go from here?

The book *Saving Data on Android* is an in-depth exploration of the various ways to store data on a device. You can find more information about shared preferences, as well as the various storage scopes and domains on Android, here: https://www.raywenderlich.com/books/saving-data-on-android/

You may also want to review:

- raywenderlich.com course on Jetpack Security: https://www.raywenderlich.com/10135609-jetpack-security
- Data Privacy for Android tutorial on Ray Wenderlich: https://www.raywenderlich.com/6901838-data-privacy-for-android
- The book *Real-World Android by Tutorials* has an entire section on "Securing your App": https://www.raywenderlich.com/books/real-world-android-by-tutorials/v1.0/
- Securing your app for work - Enterprise Dev Training: https://www.youtube.com/watch?v=2y9Ol2N1I4k
- Android Keystore Documentation: https://developer.android.com/training/articles/keystore
- EncryptedFile documentation: https://developer.android.com/reference/androidx/security/crypto/EncryptedFile

Chapter 7: Optimizing App Size & Obfusticating the APK

By Evana Margain Puig

You have two options when releasing an app to your users:

1. You can launch it exactly as it was when you, or one of the developers in your team, typed the last line of code.
2. You can implement optimizations on your code and app to make it run better and occupy less space in your users' smartphones.

At this point, you may be thinking the obvious best option is the second one. But it would surprise you how many companies release apps with the default settings because of the time contraints most teams are under.

In the first section of this book, you learned how to release an app with the basics. If you've gotten this far, I assume you care for your users. The last chapter was the first step in making a more robust app.

In this chapter, you'll learn and implement techniques to optimize your app in several ways that will make your app smaller, give it better performance, and overall, provide a better experience for your users.

Why is optimization important?

The answer to this question may come from the word *optimization* itself. In today's world, we often talk about optimized things as better or enhanced, but why is it important for your app?

To understand this, take a step back. You probably own a smartphone, and with it, you use several apps. Think about what qualities make you like or dislike an app. Do you dislike apps with a lot of bugs?

When users judge apps and choose which to uninstall, they look for several things. For example, they might look at:

1. App size if they are looking to free space on their device.
2. Loading times from screens and actions in the app.
3. How much battery the app consumes.

These examples pertain to optimization. If you want a happy userbase and want your app to perform well, you'll want to optimize it.

Terminology

Throughout this chapter, you'll learn terms that may be confusing or unknown to you. Take a look at some of those terms to establish the base for what you'll learn.

App size

The term refers to the amount of disk space your app takes up on the user's phone and the amount of data they'll require to download it.

It's important to consider that users connect to 2G or 3G networks in many countries where network providers charge based on the size of the things they download. So, you want to make your app and assets as small as possible.

Shrinking

Shrinking, as the word implies, refers to making your app smaller. There are two types of shrinking, one for code and another for resources. Take a look at each of them.

Code shrinking

Code shrinking is when you use tools to run through your app code and find what you don't use. This kind of tool removes unused things in your code, like classes and variables. This process generates a thinner version of your app with only the necessary code. It may sound like magic, but you'll learn how useful this can be.

Resource shrinking

Based on the definitions above, you may have an idea of the meaning of resource shrinking. As with code shrinking, these tools scan your project's resources, which have a wide range including images, strings and XML files. Then, they remove the unused ones.

Obfuscation

Obfuscation is a process performed by a program that reduces the names of classes, methods and variables, from your human standard syntax to something like a group of letters and identifiers to make the code smaller. After obfuscation, the process of debugging changes since you won't know exactly what the class refers to.

Optimization

This step is like code shrinking but involves some more advanced techniques. The tools analyze your code and rewrite some things, so your code works faster.

Best practices for reducing your app size

There are many things you can do to make your app smaller. Options range from reducing image quality to letting the Google Play console build your APK. In this part, you'll take a look at the recommended options for reducing app size.

Android App Bundles

One of the best things you can do to reduce your app size is to create an **Android App Bundle**, or **AAB**. You already did this in Chapter Two.

An AAB reduces your app size because once you upload your app in this format, Google Play takes charge of creating an APK for the user's device. This APK includes only the necessary things for their device and the Android version it has.

For example, if you're bundling your apps with images of different sizes for specific DPIs, it'll only bundle the ones that correspond to the user's device's size.

If the Google Play Console detects your app may have a download size above 150Mb in any of the versions, it'll warn you. You won't be able to release until you get below this hard limit.

Note: If for any reason you decide to upload an APK instead of an AAB this limit will go down to 100Mb.

APK Analyzer

APK Analyzer, a tool included in Android Studio by default, will help you notice the resources that increase your app's size the most.

Performing an APK analysis

Before running the analysis you need to ensure that the APK you're using doesn't have instant run, as this may give you false information. To ensure this, go to **Build ▸ Build Bundle(s) / APK(s) ▸ Build APK(s)** as shown in the image below.

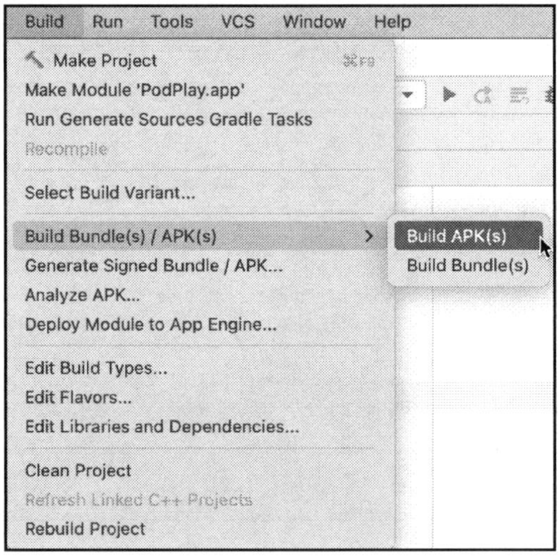

You'll get a Gradle Build indicator at the bottom. When it's finished, you can run the analysis by going to **Build ▸ Analyze APK...**. Once the analysis finishes, the analysis window will appear on the main screen as in the following image:

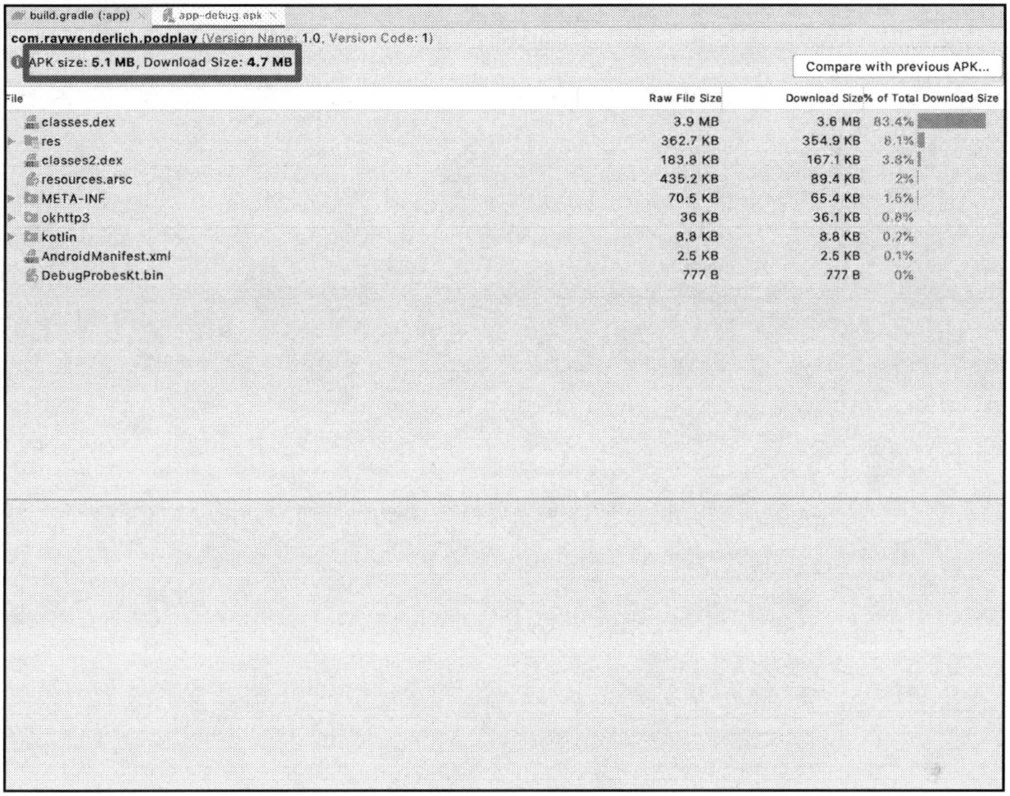

First, notice how the analyzer gives you basic data about your app:

- APK size
- Download size
- Version name
- Version code
- List of files inside the APK

Then, notice in the image above that you have **classes.dex** and **classes2.dex**. This might be different for you, but it's important to observe. The term for this is **MultiDex**, which means you have more than one **classes.dex**, and each has a number.

Android has a rule where you can't exceed 65,536 method references. To see how many references your project has, click the first classes.dex and take a look at the info message that appears.

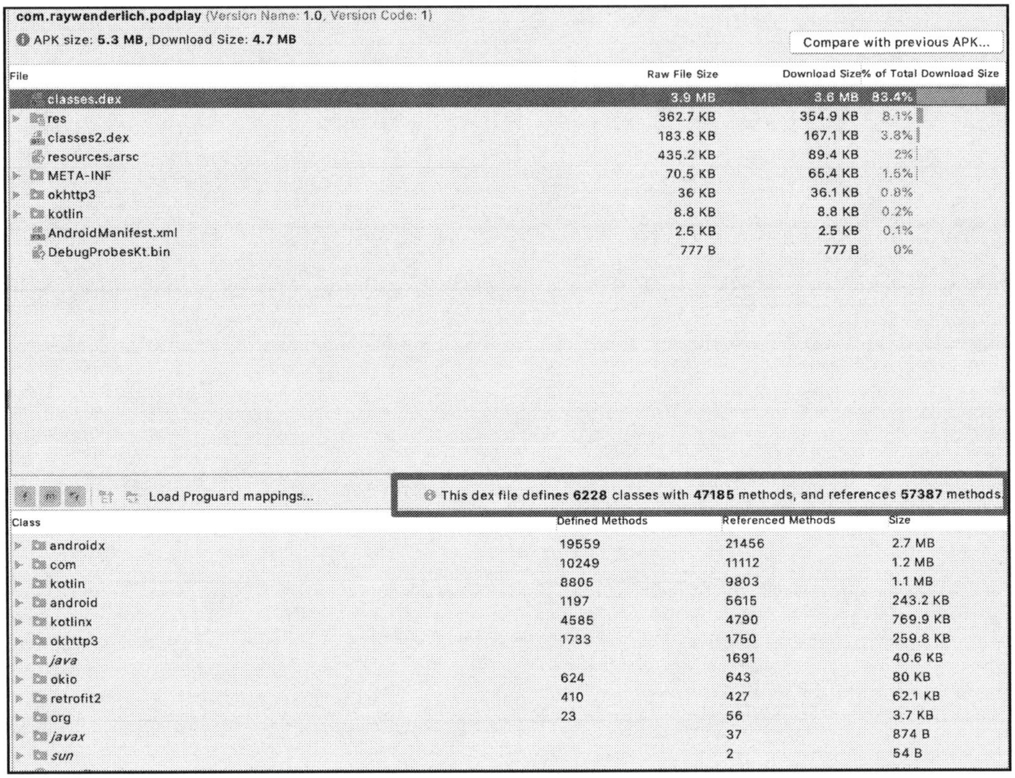

In the image above it says there are 57,387 references. If you do the same with classes2.dex, it mentions 1,503 references. Interestingly, this app doesn't exceed the number of references, but Android Studio decided to automatically separate them since it's close to the limit.

Since Android 5.0, the build process can decide whether or not to create multiple dex files. Ideally, you would only want to have one. But in today's world, with apps being more powerful and large every day, this can become difficult.

Understanding APK Analyzer results

What you do with the analysis results will vary greatly depending on your app. Despite that, there's a couple of important things to observe here:

1. By clicking on **classes.dex** you can see how much space each of the libraries you included uses. In this case, notice the AndroidX libraries are the ones with more references.
2. You can explore your resources and see particular ways to optimize your app that Android Studio may not have identified.

The rest will depend on the app itself.

Finally, notice there's a button at the top that says **Compare with previous APK**. Once you finish with your optimizations, you can compare the new APK and see what improvements you got.

Other improvements you can do with the analysis

Besides the app specific things that you may get from the analysis, here are some best practices to improve your app size.

Optimizing images

As you may already know, images play a significant role in determining an app's size. Experienced designers have a variety of non-coding techniques they will do to reduce these sizes. But, as this book is about coding, we are going to take a look at what you can do code-wise to reduce the size of images.

Focus only on certain densities: Generating the resources from the largest DPI

One of the easiest but most ignored things you can do is create your resources for only one density, in particular the biggest one you'll support.

When Android gives you the option of providing resources for every Screen Density, you may think the best thing to do is to provide them all to make a complete app. Although that is a solution that will work, it's important to know that Android itself can downsize resources to lower densities whenever needed. So the only reason you would need to provide a resource for another density is when the smaller one changes in dimensions or is a different resource. But if all you're doing is downsizing them, let Android do it for you.

Bitmap images

Whenever you reference a bitmap, the first thing that may come to mind is one of those old school video games where you have a pixelated image. The reality is most of the images you use on your computer are bitmap formats, such as JPG, PNG and GIF.

> **Note**: For handling bitmaps, Google recommends using Glide (https://github.com/bumptech/glide), which is a library that works together with your app to optimize these images at runtime. Glide won't help reduce your app size, but it will help your app perform better at runtime and make your users happy.

PNGs: Portable Network Graphics

If you've done development in the past couple of years, it is likely that you have used several PNG resources in your apps. That said, this is a heavy format that contains more detail than you need for an Android application. If you include it in your Android project, make sure it's gone through Photoshop's 'export to web' tool or use a similar technique to reduce its size.

JPG or PNG

JPG is a bit older than PNG. Generally, there's no noticeable difference from other formats if your app is not exploring images in detail.

Often, for web and mobile, many developers prefer using PNG over JPG becuase PNG uses lossless compression.

Beyond the image quality improvement, another significant advantage PNGs have over JPGs is that PNGs support transparency. If you've downloaded an image from the internet in JPG format and ended up having a white square surrounding the image you understand why this is important. From a size perspective though, it is still larger than we would like it to be.

Now that we've criticized the two most common image formats, you are probably wondering if there is a better option.

WebP

In 2013, Google introduced this new image type. Don't worry if you haven't heard of it. It's relatively new and not as widespread as it should be. In short, WebP allows you to use lossless compression like you do for PNG, but with savings of 24% to 35% in size. There is also an option to apply lossy compression to a WebP image to make it even smaller.

While this may sound like a small amount of savings, think a little deeper. Imagine you uploaded an app within the 150Mb size limit, of which 100Mb are JPEG images. When you transform them to WebP, your app is at least 24Mb smaller. You turn a 150Mb app into a 126Mb app. That's significant for someone with a limited data plan.

AAPT: Android Asset Packaging tool

Android Studio has a tool called **Android Asset Packaging tool**, which runs by default on any project with Android Gradle Plugin 3.0.0 and above.

This tool runs tests on your images and optimizes them accordingly through algorithms. It's important to remember AAPT only optimizes resources under **res/drawable**, and nothing in the **asset/** folder.

Vector graphics

You may have noticed that Android offers a wide range of possibilities when using images. **Vector graphics**, also known as **SVGs**, are another trending image format often used in Android apps. Android has its specific sub-version of SVGs called **Vector Drawables**.

Vectors are fantastic because you can resize them to any dimension needed. Designers have used them for a long time.

However, they have a particular disadvantage in Android: They are slow to draw on the screen. That said, it's not unusual to see them used, and abused, in many Android apps. Even though they're a great tool, users dislike slow apps as much as they dislike large apps, so be mindful when using Vector Graphics.

Making variations of the same image

This last image optimization tip is as underestimated as it is useful. The simplest example of this is an arrow. Say your app needs a set of arrows as assets, each pointing in a different direction. The most common thing to do is export each of the arrows and upload them as assets. But what if you upload one arrow and reuse the asset by using code to rotate it?

This is a simple memory-saving technique you can use while coding. Your users will thank you for being mindful of such details.

The same thing goes on altering the color of an asset through code. If you need a red and a blue version of the same assest, leave the color change to code instead of uploading several assets.

Making changes in your images

Now that you reviewed the best practices for images in Android, you can optimize them for reducing **PodPlay**'s size.

Converting images to WebP

Navigating through the structure of the analyzer results, go to **res ▸ drawable-xxhdpi-v4 ▸ ic_play_arrow_white.png**. You will get a preview of the image at the bottom of the APK analyzer.

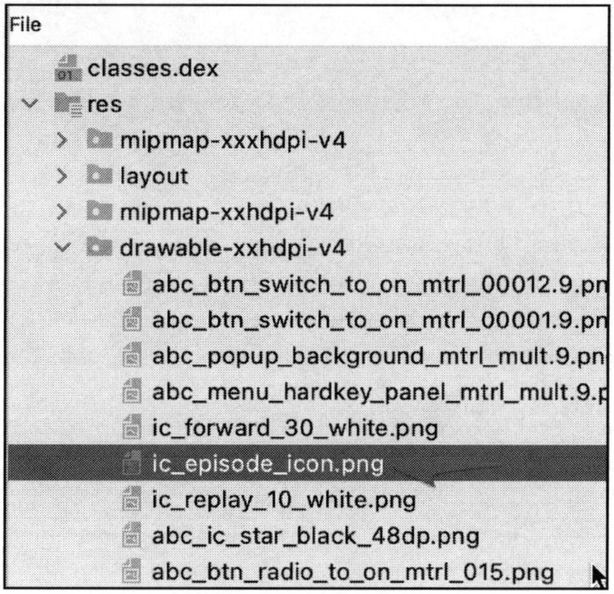

Of course this image doesn't have a very large size, but this is just for you to learn how to do it. Right click on the image preview and you will get a list of options.

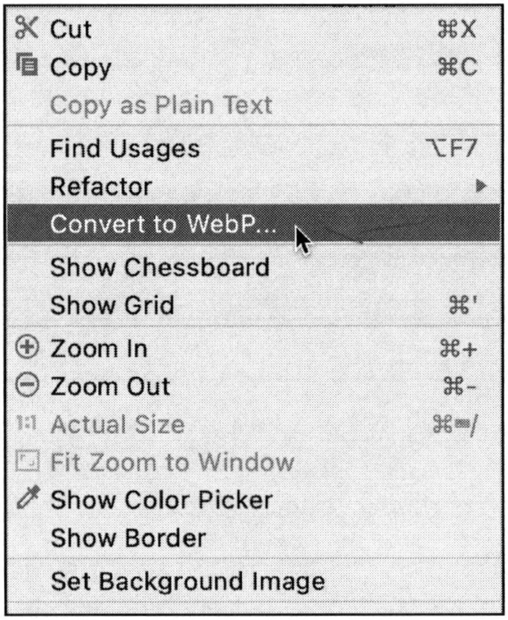

Click on **Convert to WebP** and you will see a dialog open like in the image below.

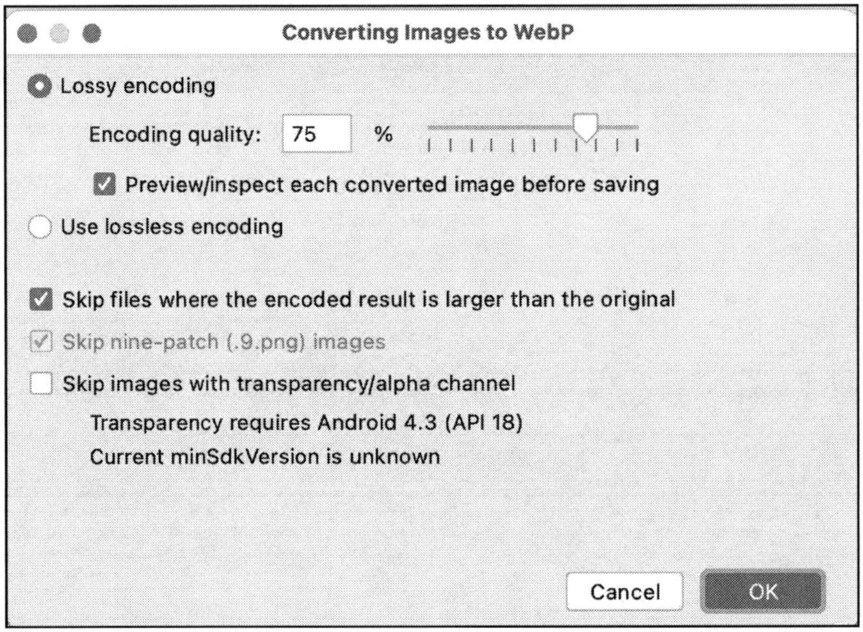

As a general recommendation, the default options are a good start, but you may need to play a little with the options depending on the desired image quality. This is mainly an exercise of balancing the reduction of the image size with the level of quality to come up with a combination that works for you.

Click on the *OK* button and you will get a comparison of both images and a slider that you can adjust to preview the change. Play with the slider and see if you notice any difference. In this kind of basic images you will rarely see a change, which is good news! You can have a smaller file without any visible changes.

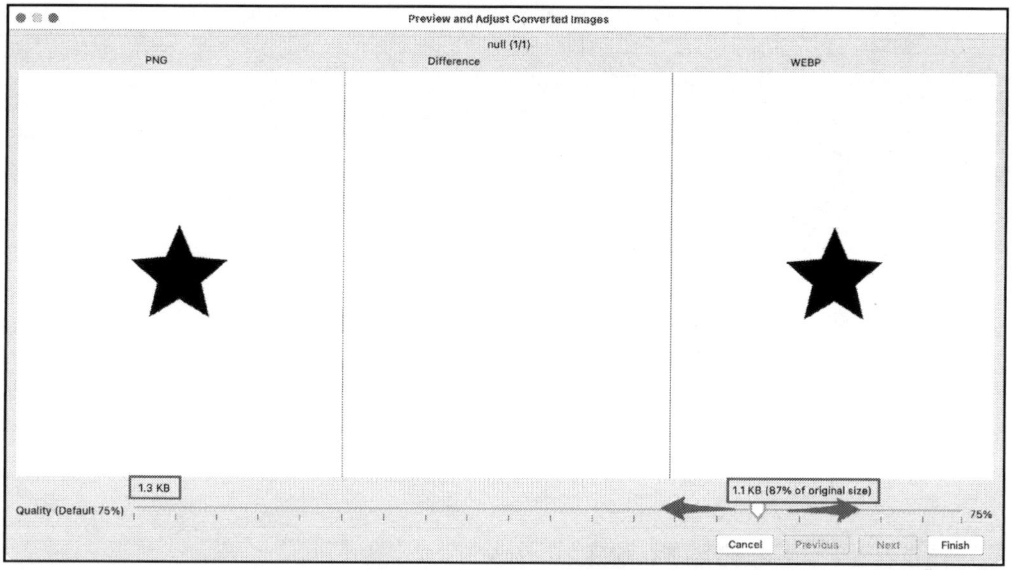

Note: In the current version of Android Studio at the time of writing, Android Studio 4.2, there is a bug where the image doesn't change to webP. Another option is to do the same process but through *Android Resource Manager*, in the exact same way, right-click the image and select convert to WebP, you will get the same dialogs as above. The image below shows you where to locate *Android Resource Manager*

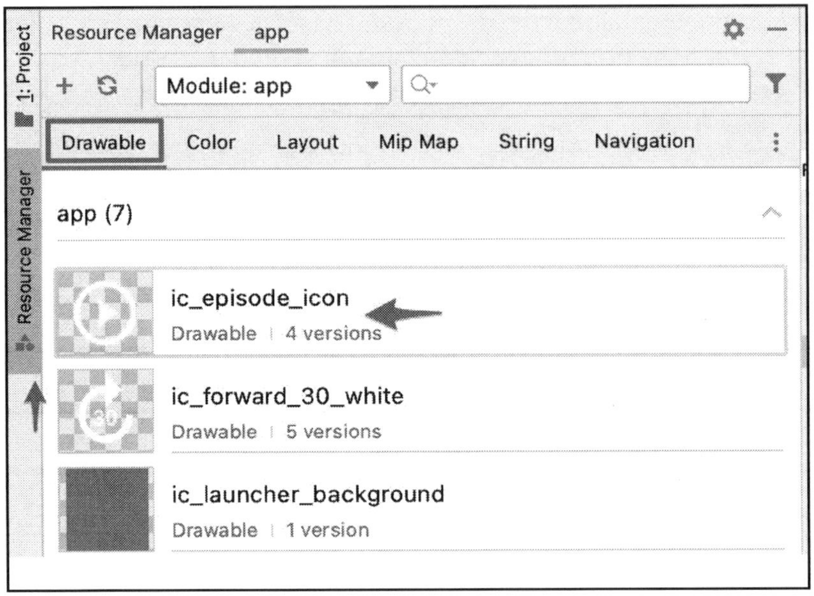

Large files

The next suggestion is to review large files. A common recommendation is to add the images through a **dynamic-feature**. You'll learn how to do this in the next chapter.

Unused resources

Another thing you can do is remove unused resources, but this is not easy to spot through APK Analyzer.

The PodPlay app, has no unused resources because it was created for another book, so add one empty method by going to **app ▸ java ▸ ui ▸ PodcastActivity.kt** and at any point in the file add the following code:

```
fun myUnusedMethod() {
    // this is a useless method
}
```

> **Note**: In a production app, ensure the code isn't used before deleting it. The technique you will see below may not catch all references to files, particularly if any library uses them through code generation.

Once you have that method added, in the top bar of Android Studio select: **Analyze ▸ Inspect Code**.

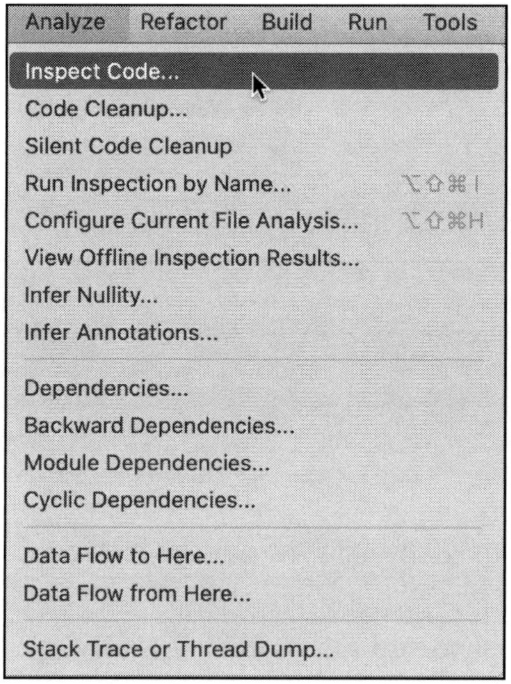

The process will take a couple of minutes and eventually an *Inspection Results* screen will appear in the bottom part of your screen.

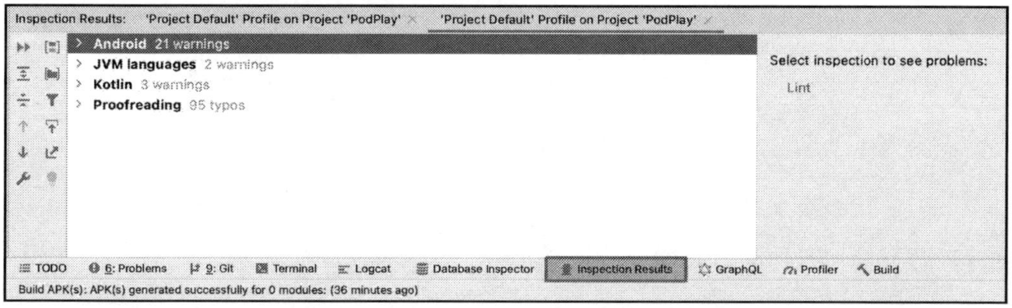

You will see a lot more suggestions that you may want to address and will be unique to each project, but for now focus on identifying the unused method. Navigate in the results to **Kotlin ▸ Redundant Constructs ▸ Unused symbol**. There you will find a message showing you that the method you just created isn't being used.

If you click on the message, you will get the function in the code editor to the right. There is also a *Safe delete* option there.

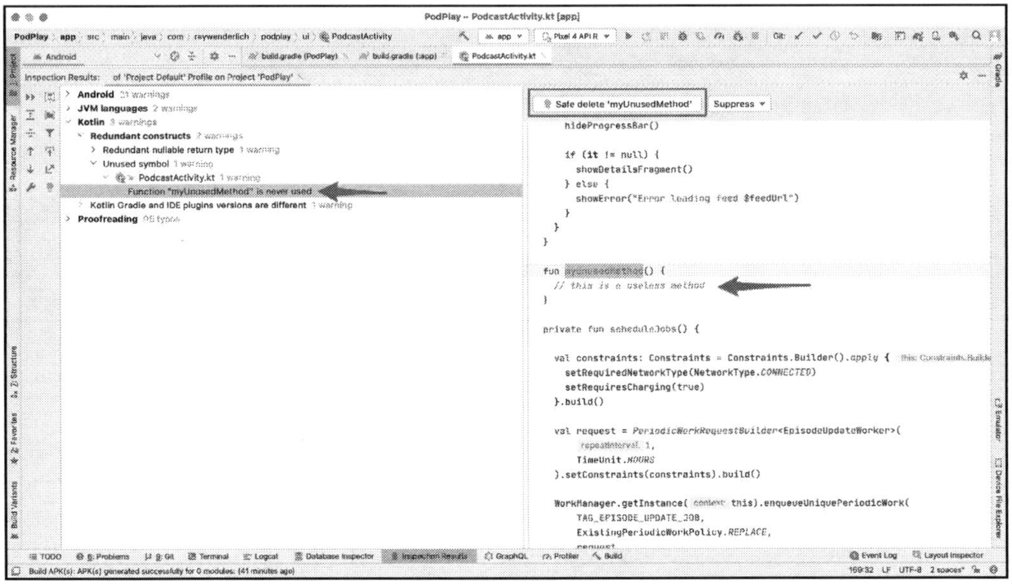

Click on *Safe delete*. You will get a message which will show you two checkboxes that can run the checks again to ensure there wasn't a mistake.

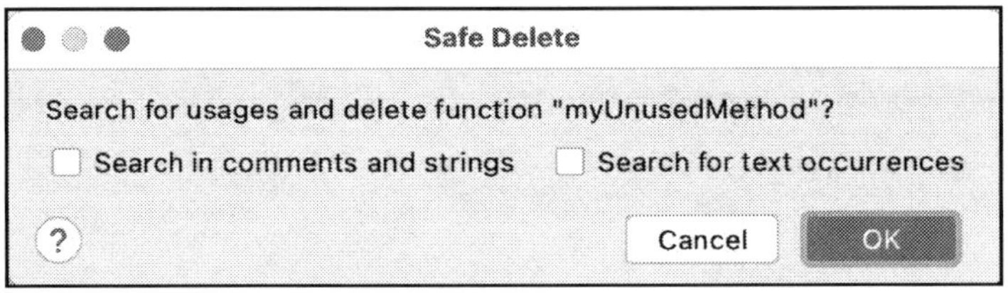

In this case you are sure this method isn't used so click on *OK*.

Enabling Proguard / R8

The last recommendation is enabling Proguard or R8. You'll learn how to do this later in this chapter, so don't worry about it for now.

That's it for automatic recommendations. As you may have noticed, most are pretty straightforward, and Android Studio will help you reduce your app's size.

Size reductions to make directly in your code

Besides the changes mentioned above, developers can do some recommended optimizations to reduce the size of the APK:

1. Look for code generated by libraries that may not be necessary.
2. Some libraries include code intended for web or other platforms. Make sure this isn't part of your APK.
3. Enums require a lot of space, so beware of abusing them.

Going one step further in optimization

You now understand the basics of optimizing your apps. At the beginning of the chapter, there was a mention of a so-called **ProGuard** or **R8**. In this section, you'll learn about ProGuard, and its successor R8, which will let you configure your optimization even further.

ProGuard

For a long time in Android, ProGuard was the standard for code obfuscation. If you're using Android Gradle plugin 3.4.0 or higher, you're probably not using ProGuard anymore. Even when the loaded file is from ProGuard, you're using R8.

What is ProGuard?

In short, it's a code optimizer for Java Bytecode. Even when you're using Kotlin, the compiler will transform your code into Java, and Google recommends using a code optimizer. ProGuard and R8 are similar, but ProGuard is a bit more complicated.

> **Note**: It's important to note that you can still use ProGuard in your projects by adding the following code to **gradle.properties:**
>
> ```
> android.enableR8=false
>
> android.enableR8.libraries=false
> ```

Using R8: Shrinking, obfuscation and optimization

Shrinking, obfuscation and optimization aren't enabled by default in newer versions of Android Studio for two main reasons:

1. The compilation time is longer, which may be inconvenient for developers.
2. They may cause some bugs, particularly when dealing with third-party libraries.

Enable the features by adding the following code to the `buildTypes` block inside your *project-level* **build.gradle**:

```
android {
  buildTypes {

    // 1
    debug {

      //2
      minifyEnabled true

      //3
      shrinkResources true

      //4
      proguardFiles getDefaultProguardFile('proguard-
android.txt'), 'proguard-rules.pro'
    }
  }
  ...
}
```

Here's a code breakdown:

1. Enables the features for your project's **debug** build type.
2. This line enables code shrinking, obfuscation and optimization.
3. As the name implies, it enables resource shrinking.
4. Enables the default ProGuard rules, which have the most commonly used rules for optimizing your code.

Once you have this in your code, make sure you're building the debug version by clicking on the left panel. Then click the dropdown to select **debug** as in the image below:

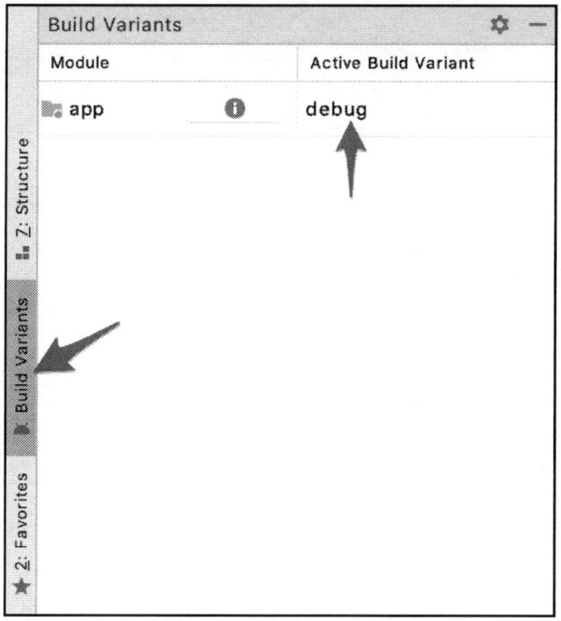

Now repeat the steps you did with the APK analyzer to create an APK.

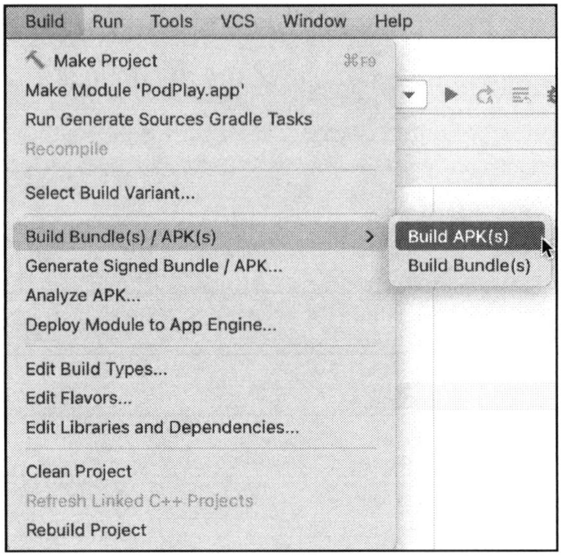

Next, trigger the APK Analyzer again to see how much of a difference enabling these three features made.

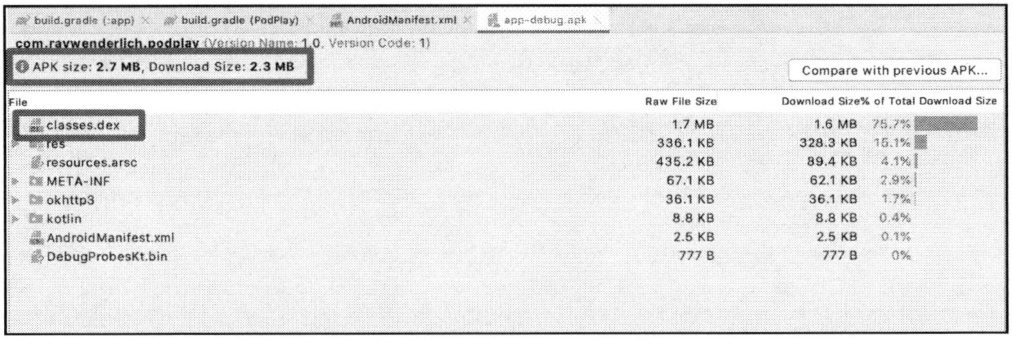

In the case of **PodPlay** you can see the changes in the screenshots above:

1. The app size reduced from **5.1MB** to **2.7MB**, which is a reduction of almost half the app's size.
2. The download size has also reduced from **4.7MB** to **2.3MB**, in this case, more than half.
3. In this case, the classes.dex is only one file and not multiple.

Now, look at obfuscation. Click **classes.dex**. You'll get a list of the files and folders inside the APK. You will see packages and files named with the letters a, b, c and so on.

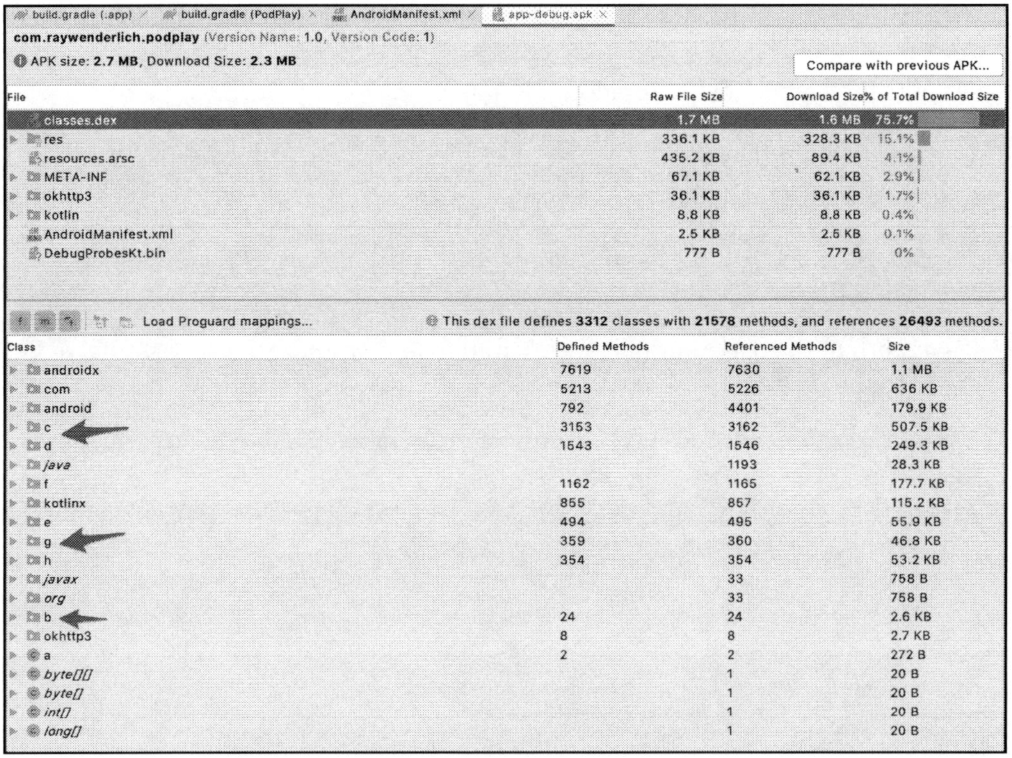

These folders have those names because of the obfuscation process discussed earlier. Names of classes, variables and other things in your projects will change to letters that the compiler can understand, but are difficult for a human to trace.

Key points

- App size is one of the most important features for your users.
- It's better to bundle your app as an AAB rather than using an APK.
- Google Play won't allow Android App Bundles larger than 150MB in size.
- PNG is a great format, but you should take care of the size of your images.
- WebP is the recommended image format by Android.
- You can use APK Analyzer to understand the format of your APK and find ways to optimize it further.
- It's important to enable shrinking, obfuscation and optimization in the final builds of your app.
- R8 is the recommended tool for cleaning up your project and reducing your app's final size.

Chapter 8: Adding Features Dynamically

By Evana Margain Puig

With AABs, or Android App Bundles, Android lets you deliver features dynamically. In this context, dynamically means several possibilities. For instance, users can download only the parts of the app they need, or you can prompt them to download specific information if they access a specific part of your app.

Besides delivering features dynamically through your AAB, you can use another technique, called **Feature Flagging**. This term refers to conditional statements, controlled either by the server or the code itself, which tell the app whether to show or hide specific features.

What are dynamic features?

You'll start this chapter by learning how to deliver features through a tool called **Play Feature Delivery**. This term refers to the features you can deliver after the user downloads the app on a per-need basis or any criteria you or your team determine.

Why are dynamic features useful?

There are many reasons why you might want to deliver features dynamically. Take a moment to explore some examples:

1. You want to reduce your app's download size, either because of **Google Play Store**'s size limitations or because you want to help users with constrained amounts of data.
2. You want to support a wide variety of devices, but you have certain features that need specific hardware. In that case, you can let devices with a particular capability to download a feature, while those without that capability keep the original functionality.
3. You have users with certain 'privileges' that may have access to sections of your app that aren't available to the rest of the user base.

Dynamic feature options

Android provides four delivery options:

1. **Install-time delivery**: The device downloads these features on the app's first launch. You often see this in mobile games: You get the game, and then on the first launch, after the splash, the app downloads several megabytes of data.
2. **On-demand delivery**: This is the most common use case. On-demand is when users download a section not included in the original download as they need it.
3. **Conditional delivery**: This option relates to the device's capabilities, either at the hardware or API level. Users with the required capabilities get some extra features, while those without those capabilities get the app as-is.
4. **Instant features**: This option lets you give users access to certain features without downloading your app. You'll learn about this topic in detail later.

Feature flagging

Feature flagging isn't an Android-specific term. It's used in various applications and is more of a software development principle. Feature flagging gives you a way to enable or disable individual modules of your app depending on certain conditions. In this chapter, you'll learn about this powerful tool.

Delivering dynamic modules

With basic definitions out of the way, it's time to start really learning! In this section, you'll add a series of dynamic modules to **Pod Play** and explore different delivery options.

First, you need to choose your base module. The base module should have this line of code in its **build.gradle**:

```
apply plugin: 'com.android.application'
```

If you created the project with Android Studio, this code is already there. To be sure, look at the gradle file on the module. Validate that the first line of **PodPlay** contains that line of code, as shown in the image below:

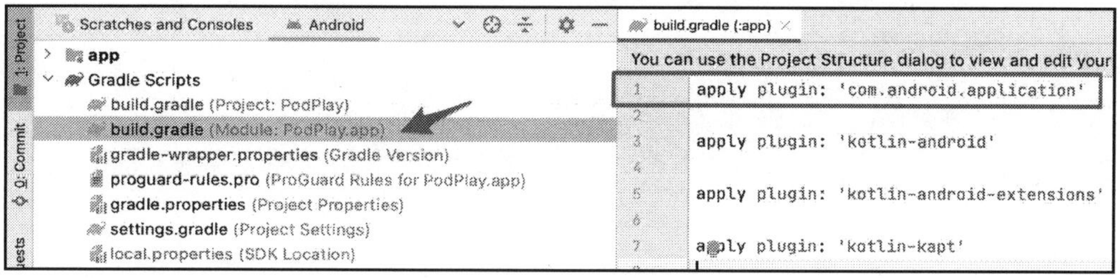

Now that you know that this is your app's base module, there are a series of things you need to check:

1. Make sure you include all the images and resources required by the base module in the initial APK. You can't move them to another module.
2. This module's manifest will be the base manifest, and the APK will take data, like version name and version code, for the full app. This manifest is also where you specify your app's entry point.
3. Even though this module has the main manifest, the build process will merge all the other modules' manifests into one file.

In a production app, you would look at the details of everything listed above to suit your needs. However, in **PodPlay**, this is mainly taken care of in the starter project.

Install-time delivery

You'll start by creating an install-time delivery feature. There are three main reasons to choose this approach:

1. Reducing the size of your initial APK.
2. Modularizing your app from the beginning of development and later converting to on-demand modules. Otherwise, your app will require a huge refactor if you decide to do this later.
3. Showing the user a one-time feature and then uninstalling it to reduce the space your app occupies. An onboarding module that the users ask not to see again is an example of a one-time feature.

Creating a new module

Open up the starter project. Then create your new module by clicking **File ▸ New... ▸ New Module**. The menu will look like this:

After clicking this, you'll get a menu with the different modules you can create. Since you're focusing on **install-time delivery** in this part of the chapter, select **"Dynamic Feature"**, as shown here:

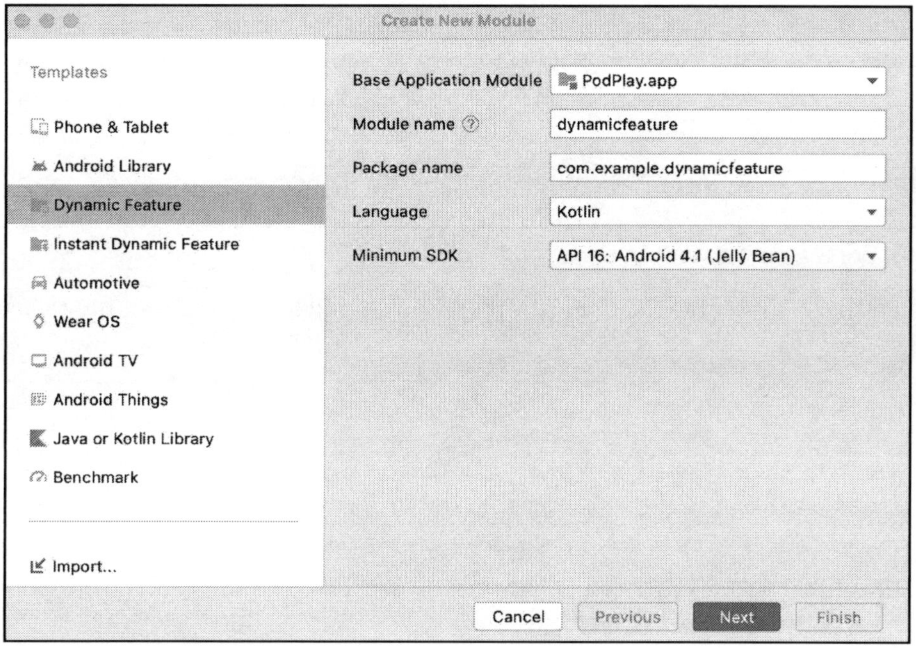

The information you need to fill in will be specific to each of your apps, but explore the current example options:

1. **Base Application Module**: In the case of **PodPlay**, you only have one base module, **PodPlay.app**. In other apps, you may have more than one. This option gives you control over which module is the parent of the new module you create.
2. **Module Name**: You want to give your module a name so you can identify it in your project and throughout the areas where you'll make configurations for it, in this case use **InstallTimeDeliveryExample**.

3. **Package Name**: This is similar to the base app's package name. It'll automatically generate for you when you input **Module Name**, but you can click the edit button and change it yourself. The recommended practice uses reversed domain names, as you do when naming apps.
4. **Language**: While it would be ideal to use the same language your project uses, it's not necessary. For example, you can have an app written in Java code with a module written in Kotlin.
5. **Minimum SDK**: Ideally, the minimum SDK would be the same as your app or a more recent version. Otherwise, there may be compatibility issues if your app supports a newer version than your module.

If you want to know how the final configuration should look, check out the image below:

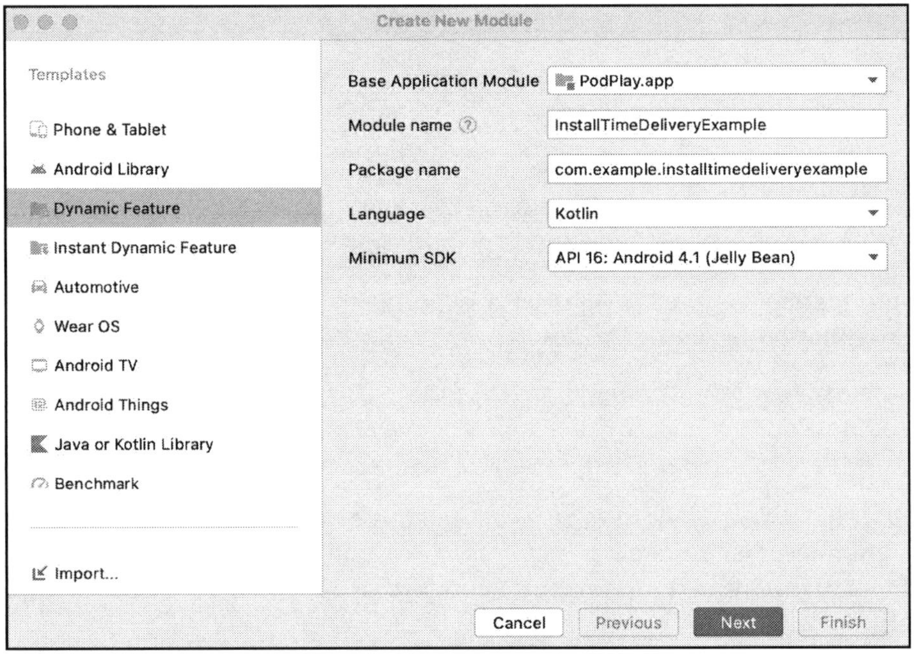

After inputting all the data, click **Next**. Another window will appear, letting you configure your module's behavior and the user-facing name. As in the previous screen, look at each of the items:

1. **Module title**: As the field description mentions, users may see the module's name. For example, they would see the name if the app requests permission to install the module. So, make this title as descriptive and straightforward as possible.
2. **Install-time inclusion**: This item determines which type of module you create. For this first example, you'll choose **Include module at Install-Time**, which means as soon as the user downloads the app, the app will download this module.

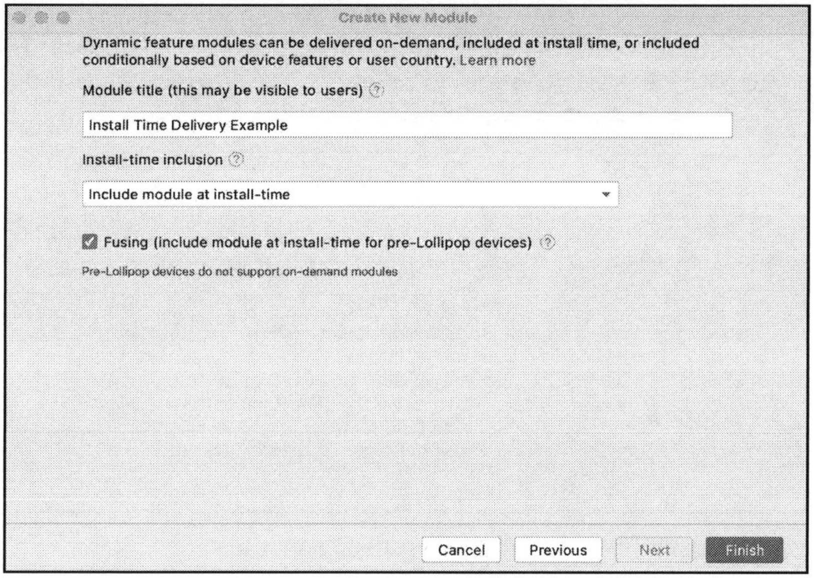

Click **Finish**, and wait for Android Studio to create your module. While it may not look like it's doing anything, the status text at the bottom of the screen will tell you it's working.

Once it creates the module, you'll find it listed to the left of Android Studio, below your main module, as in the picture below:

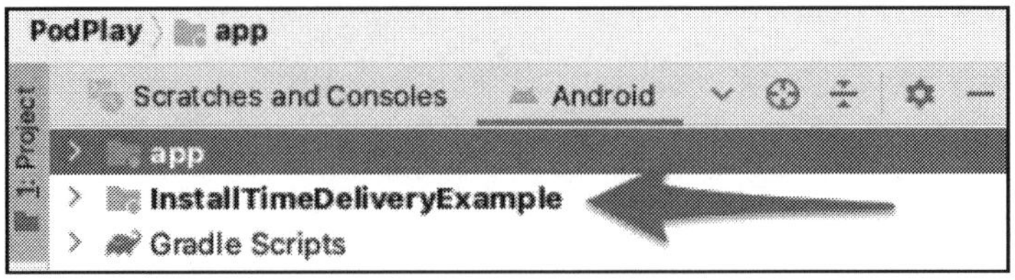

Understanding your module configuration

The information you previously selected in the dialogs will mostly be in the newly created module's Android Manifest. Open the **Android Manifest** for this new module. It is located in **nameOfYourModule ▸ manifests ▸ AndroidManifest.xml**. The three lines you need to pay attention to are:

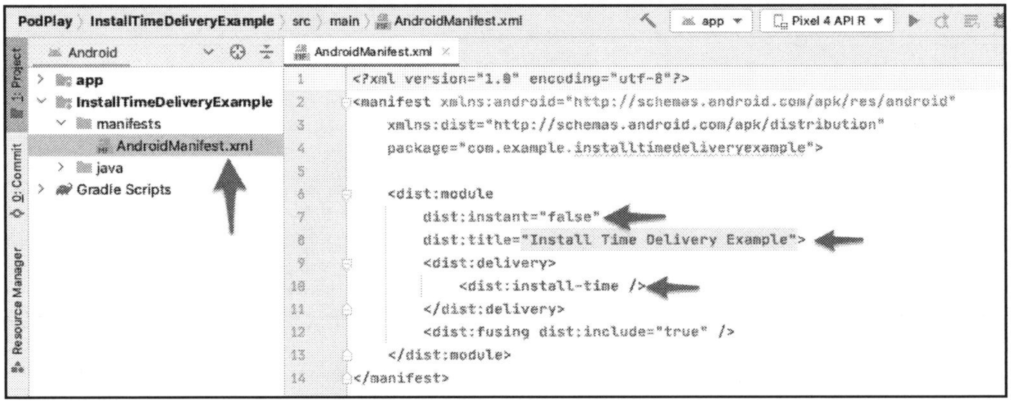

1. This isn't an instant feature but an 'installable' module.
2. Here's the user-facing title. If you don't like the title you chose in the assistant, you could change it here.
3. This indicates the feature is an **install-time** feature.

Android Studio also modified **build.gradle (:app)** when creating the module. Open this file by going to **Gradle Scripts ▸ build.gradle(Module: PodPlay.app)**. There, at the end of the curly brackets with the 'android' label, you'll see the following line:

```
dynamicFeatures = [':installTimeDeliveryExample']
```

Note that `dynamicFeatures` is an array, so if you had more than one module, it would contain a comma-separated array of modules:

```
dynamicFeatures = [":module1", ":module2"].
```

> **Note**: Android recommends having no more than ten install-time modules. Otherwise, the app install and download can take a long time and affect your users' engagement.

Finally, take a look at the created module's gradle file, **Gradle Scripts ▸ build.gradle(Module: PodPlay.installTimeDeliveryExample)**. This file also references the main app with the line of code at the top of the dependencies curly brackets:

```
implementation project(":app")
```

By adding those two lines, you, or the Android Studio assistant, create a relationship between the app and the module.

Adding a screen to your install-time delivery module

Adding files to modules is a pretty straightforward process. It's the same process that you use for your main module. You are going to add a screen to see how it works.

Right click the module and go to **com.raywenderlich.installtimedeliveryexample ▸ New ▸ Activity ▸ Settings Activity**:

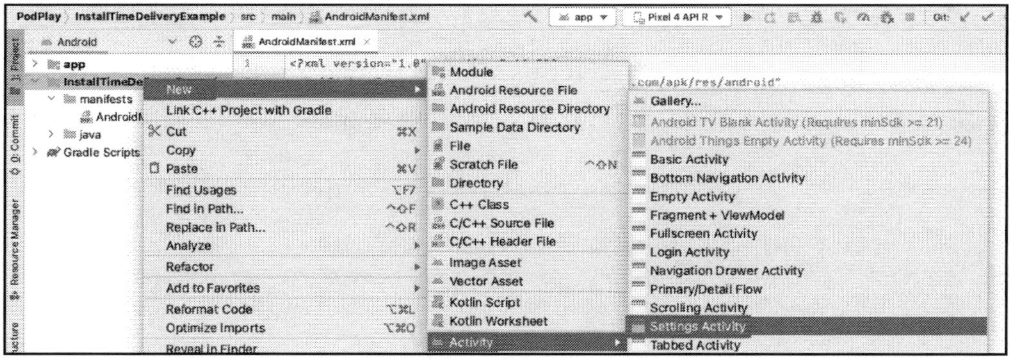

Leave all the default settings like this:

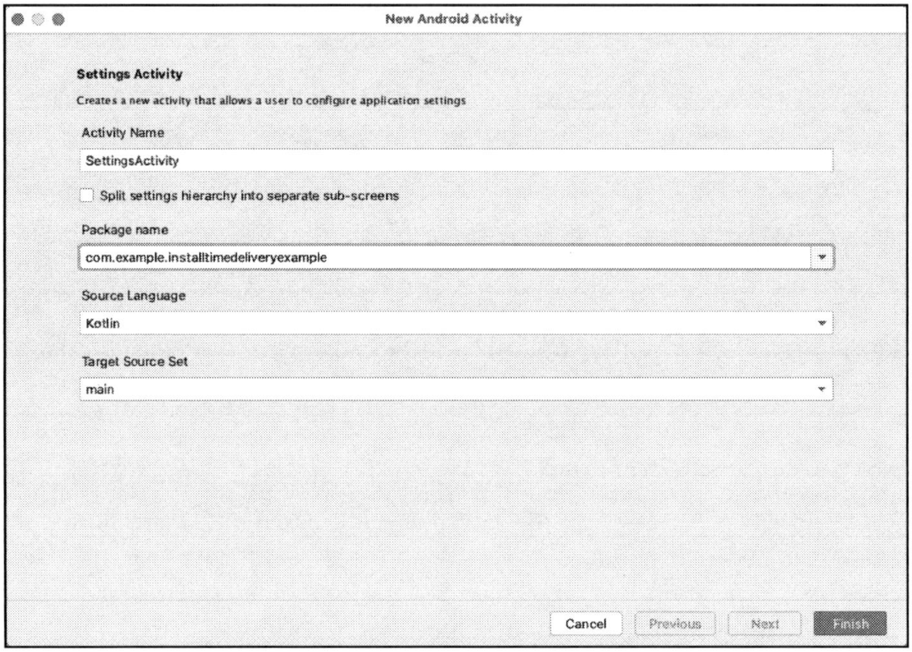

Clicking this creates a dummy settings activity to test your module.

Go back to your main module and open **res ▸ menu ▸ menu_search.xml**. Add the following item to the menu:

```
<item
    android:id="@+id/install_time_delivery_button"
    android:title="@string/install_time_delivery"
    android:icon="@android:drawable/ic_menu_preferences"
    app:showAsAction="collapseActionView|ifRoom"/>
```

Then, open **PodcastActivity.kt** and look at the top of the file. The Activity already has two variables for this item, **isInstallTimeModuleAvailable** and **settingsMenuItem**.

At the bottom of **onCreateOptionsMenu**, right before the last **return true**, add:

```
val SETTINGS_CLASS_NAME =
"com.example.installtimedeliveryexample.SettingsActivity"
val TAG_ACTIVITY = "PodcastActivity"

var settingsMenuItem =
menu.findItem(R.id.install_time_delivery_button)

try {
  Class.forName(SETTINGS_CLASS_NAME)
  isInstallTimeModuleAvailable = true
  settingsMenuItem.isVisible = true
} catch (e: Exception) {
  settingsMenuItem.isVisible = false
  isInstallTimeModuleAvailable = false
  Log.d(TAG_ACTIVITY, "Couldn't start SettingsActivity, the
class doesn't exist")
}

if (isInstallTimeModuleAvailable) {
  settingsMenuItem.setOnMenuItemClickListener {
    val intent = Intent().setClassName(this,
SETTINGS_CLASS_NAME)
    startActivity(intent)
    true
  }
}
```

Build and run. You'll see a **tool** button at the top. Click it, and it'll redirect you to the settings screen.

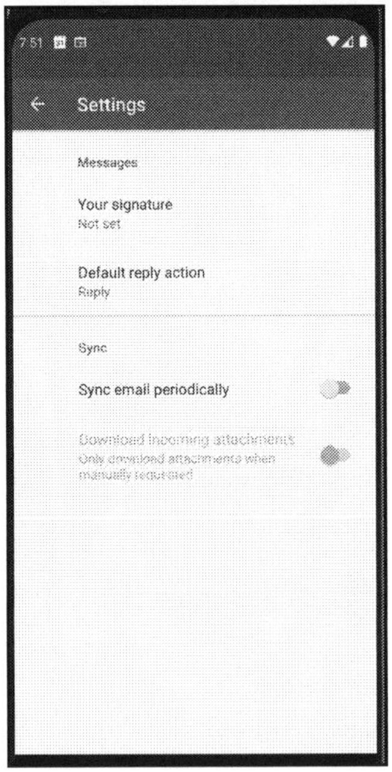

Testing your app with and without the modules

You will want to ensure your app works with or without some of your modules in certain cases. For example, maybe you want to disable a module for your users but want to be sure it doesn't break the app. To configure this, go to **Run ▸ Edit Configurations...** in the top menu:

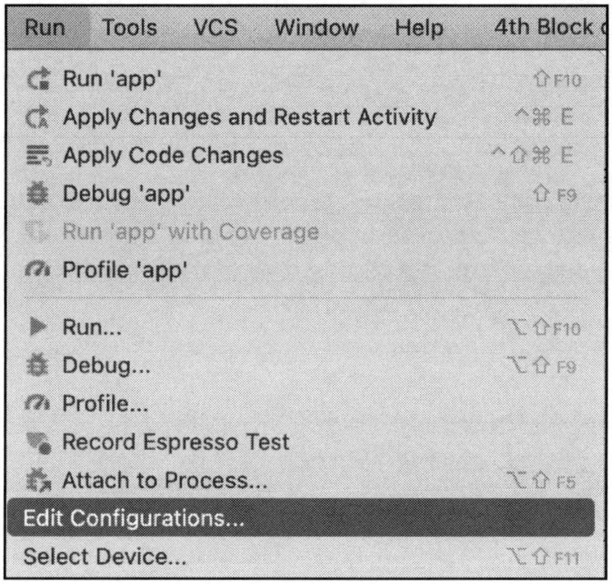

You can check or uncheck the modules you want to install in that menu when running your app. Uncheck it now and change the variable `isInstallTimeModuleAvailable` at the top of the file to false.

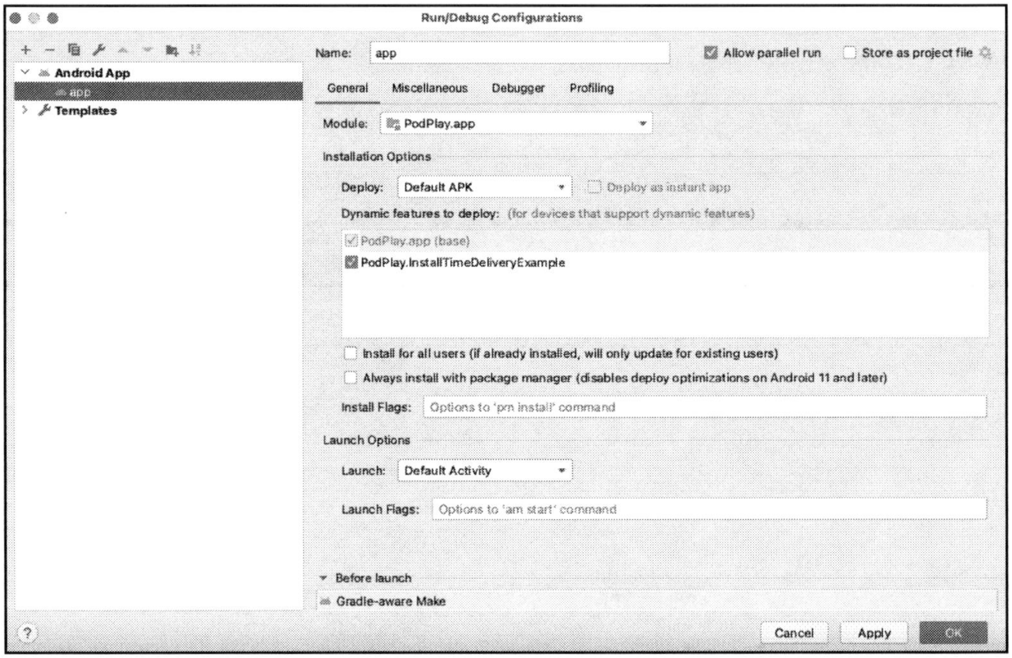

Build and run. The main app functionality will remain unchanged, but your settings will only be available if you include it in your build configuration.

> **Note**: Depending on the version of Java you have installed, you may encounter an error with the text: **Invoke-customs are only supported starting with Android O (–min-api 26).** If that's the case, go to your module's **build.gradle** and inside the android { ... } part of the gradle file add:

```
compileOptions {
  sourceCompatibility JavaVersion.VERSION_1_8
  targetCompatibility JavaVersion.VERSION_1_8
}
```

On-demand delivery

Creating an on-demand module is similar to creating an install-time module. You will go through the same steps you followed for **install-time**, but with some tweaks.

Create your new module by clicking **File ▸ New... ▸ New Module**. The menu will look like this:

After clicking this, you'll get a menu with the different modules you can create. Since you're focusing on **on-demand delivery** in this part of the chapter, select **"Dynamic Feature"**, as shown here:

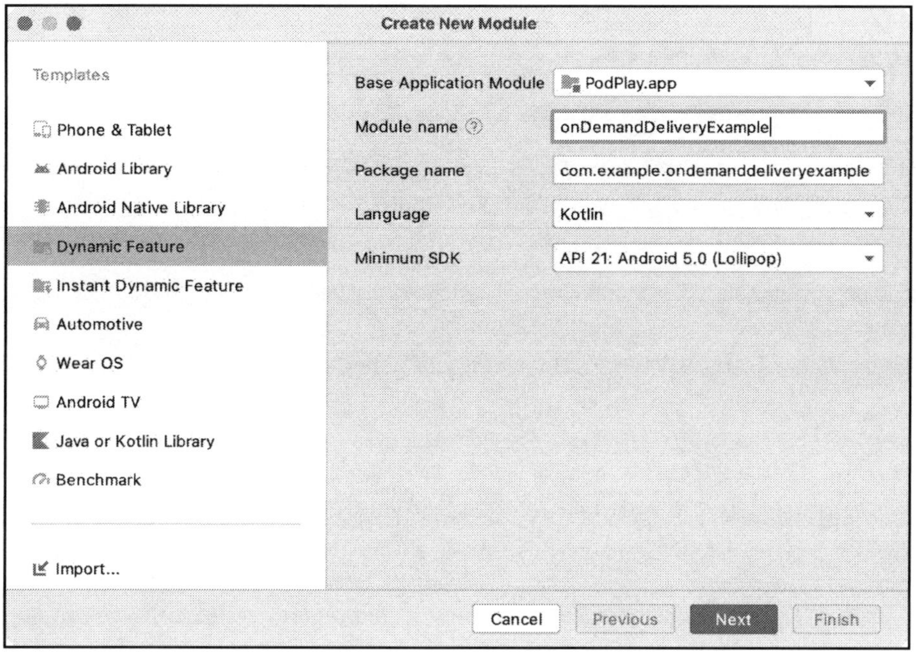

1. **Module name**: Two modules can't have the same name, so name this one **onDemandDeliveryExample**.

2. **Package name**: This needs to be unique too, so put something like **com.yourdomain.ondemanddeliveryexample**.

After inputting all the data, click **Next**. Another window will appear, letting you configure your module's behavior and the user-facing name.

1. **Module title**: Make sure this one is also unique, although it may not be required depending on your version of Android Studio, you don't want to get confused between your modules.

2. **Install-time inclusion**: Last time, when you reached this prompt, you chose **Include module at install-time**. This time, select **Do not include module at install-time (on-demand only)**.

Check out the picture below to see how the options look before clicking **Finish**.

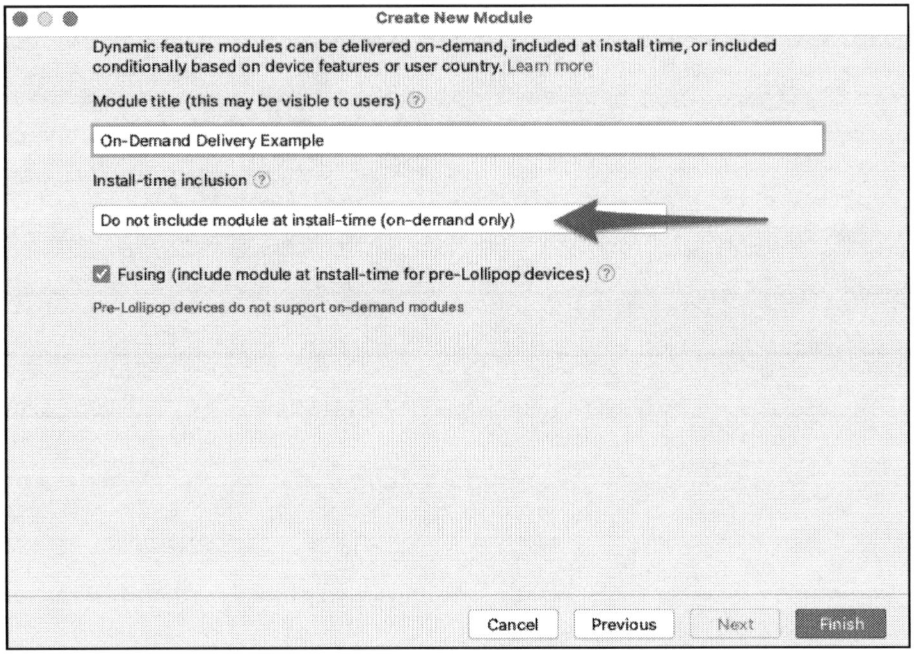

Click **Finish** and once again wait until the module appears. Now you have an app with three modules:

That's about all you need to create an **on-demand** module. But, as its name states, you need to request this module for your users to get it. You'll learn that next.

Play feature delivery

Google provides **Play Feature Delivery**, an API for getting on-demand modules. This API is available for Kotlin, Java, Android NDK and Unity. For this example, you'll focus on Kotlin.

Open your app's **build.gradle** located in **Gradle Scripts ▸ build.gradle(Module: PodPlay.app)**. Now, look at the **dependencies** section of the code, which is the last group with curly braces, and you will notice the following:

```
implementation "com.google.android.play:core:
$google_play_core_version"
implementation "com.google.android.play:core-ktx:
$google_play_core_ktx"
```

The first line is the standard library that works for Android and Kotlin. The second one adds optional functionality specific to Kotlin, like coroutines.

You are now ready to create your first dynamic feature!

Split install manager

To get the on-demand module, you need to tie it to a button, or any other part of your app, to download it. There are no limitations on where you can trigger this download.

Adding a button to trigger the on-demand download

Now, you'll add a button in the top menu bar on the home screen, next to the search icon. Navigate to **menu_search.xml**, which you can find in the main app **module ▸ res ▸ menu**. Switch to the editor's code view and add the following lines before the </menu> closing tag:

```
<item android:id="@+id/download_on_demand_module_item"
 android:title="@string/download"
 android:icon="@android:drawable/stat_sys_download"
 app:showAsAction="always"/>
```

Look at the preview in the editor. The menu will look like this:

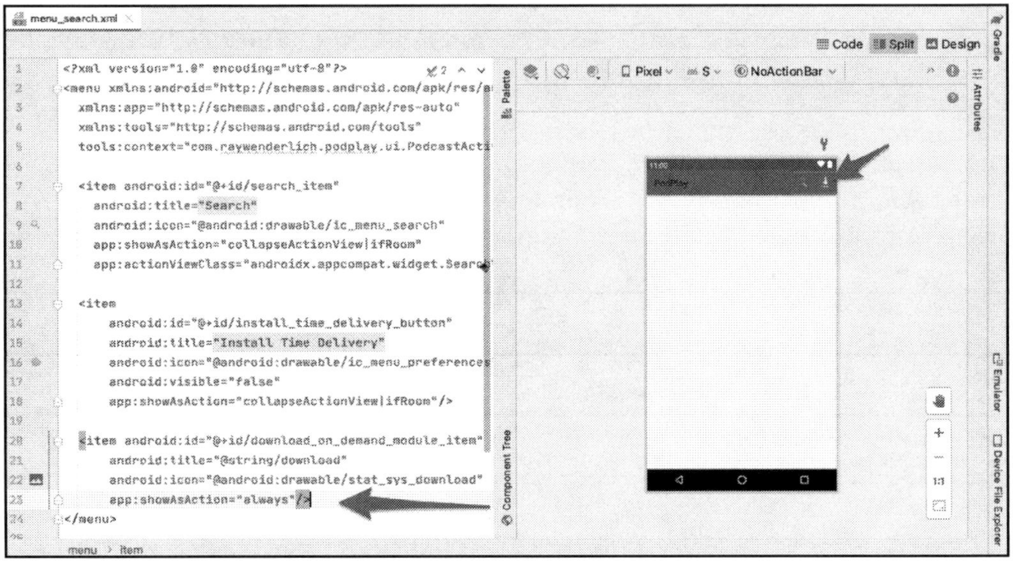

In **app ▸ java ▸ ui ▸ PodcastActivity**, open **PodcastActivity.kt**. There, you have a function called `onCreateOptionsMenu`, which is a function you can add in any activity for storing all the code related to your menu items. At the bottom of this function, before the `return true` statement located above the closing bracket, add:

```
downloadMenuItem =
menu.findItem(R.id.download_on_demand_module_item)

downloadMenuItem.setOnMenuItemClickListener {
 downloadModule()
}
```

In the code above, you get the XML item you created for the menu and set its `onClickListener` to a function call to `downloadModule()`, which you'll implement next.

In the same file, add a new function with the following code:

```
private fun downloadModule(): Boolean {
  // 1
  val splitInstallManager =
SplitInstallManagerFactory.create(applicationContext)

  //2
  val request = SplitInstallRequest
    .newBuilder()
    .addModule("onDemandDeliveryExample")
```

```
        .build()

    //3
    splitInstallManager
        .startInstall(request)
        .addOnSuccessListener { sessionId ->
          Toast.makeText(
            applicationContext,
            "Module installed successfully with sessionId
$sessionId",
            Toast.LENGTH_LONG
          ).show()
        }
        .addOnFailureListener { exception ->
          Toast.makeText(
            applicationContext,
            "Module not installed with exception $exception",
            Toast.LENGTH_LONG
          ).show()
        }

      return true
  }
```

This function is pretty long, so lets take a look at it step-by-step:

1. You use **SplitInstallManagerFactory**, a method the Play Feature Delivery API provides for making operations on modules.
2. You create a request to get the module with the name `"onDemandDeliveryExample"`. This builder is the same for all modules. The only change is the module's name.
3. You execute the install and add a listener for the success and error cases. In this case, you're adding a toast to show whether it was possible to install it or not.

You may need to import some new classes if they were not automatically included by Android Studio:

```
import android.widget.Toast
import
com.google.android.play.core.splitinstall.SplitInstallManagerFac
tory
import
com.google.android.play.core.splitinstall.SplitInstallRequest
```

Build and run. Click the download button, and you'll see the success toast:

Note: In the latest versions of Android Studio you may be getting an issue saying `Task :app:checkDebugLibraries FAILED Execution failed for task ':app:checkDebugLibraries'. [:InstallTimeDeliveryExample, :onDemandDeliveryExample] all package the same library [androidx.concurrent:concurrent-futures]`. To fix this open **build.gradle (:onDemandDeliveryExample)** and delete all the dependencies except `implementation project(":app")`. After that change the dependencies bracket should look like this.

```
dependencies {
    implementation project(":app")
}
```

Conditional delivery

Now, let's take a look at the third type of dynamic module, **conditional delivery modules**. These modules are only delivered when the device has specific capabilities.

Follow the same steps you did for the previous two modules, and stop at **Install-Time inclusion**. Select **Only include module at install-time for devices with specified features**. You'll notice a small button appears with the legend **+ device-feature**. Click it, and another dropdown will appear.

As this is a podcast app, say you only want to install this feature for devices with an audio output. Select **Name**, meaning you'll determine the condition for the name of the feature you want the users to have.

Try typing a couple of letters and notice how Android Studio suggests features. Select **android.hardware.audio.output**, which will tell the AAB to install the feature only if the device has an audio output. Otherwise, why would the user want a podcast app?

Look at the image below to see how the dialog looks before clicking finish:

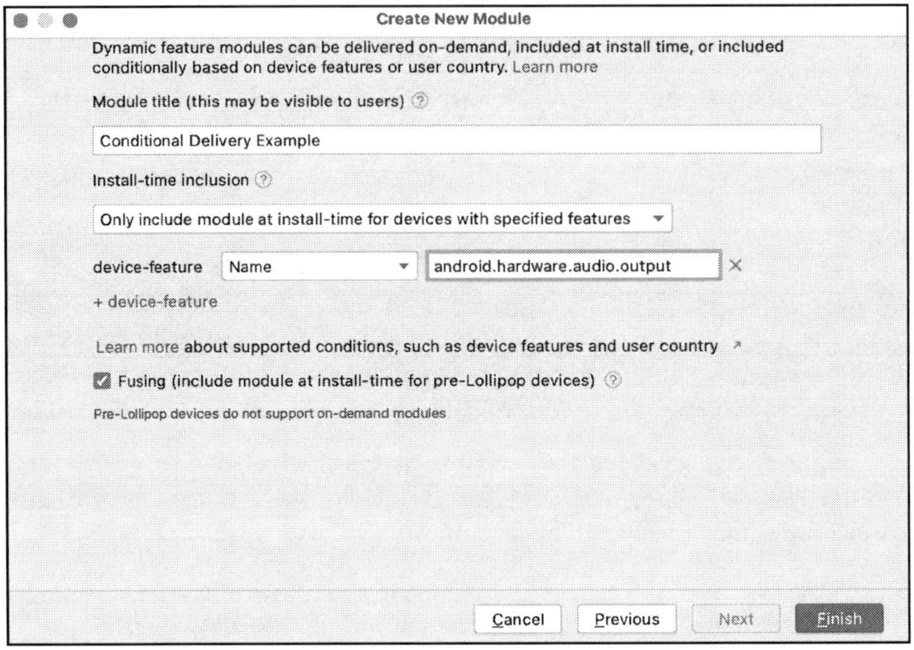

Note: You can add as many conditions as you want for your module. Maybe you have several pre-requisites for a specific module. You can add all of them.

Just as in the previous examples, after a couple of seconds, the new module will appear. Now your app has four modules, and the project looks like this:

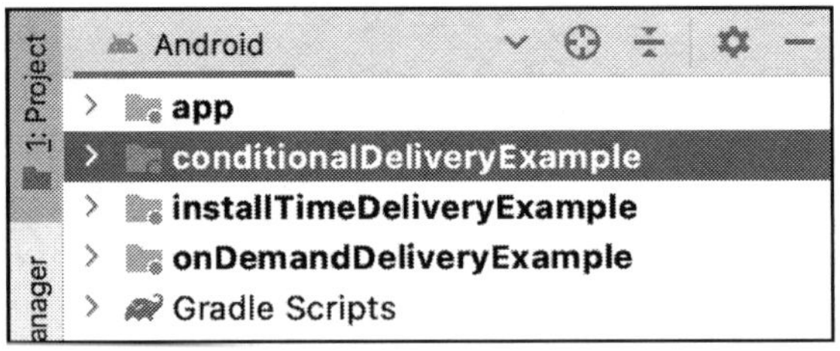

Conditional delivery by country

You can also download individual modules depending on the user's country. This is another option for conditional delivery that isn't available from the **New Module** assistant.

For example, you may want to support specific payment methods for different countries. You can create a module for each country's methods to provide users with only the necessary options.

Go into the **AndroidManifest.xml** of the sample module you created. You'll notice Android already provides a comment on how to make country-based conditionals, like in the image below.

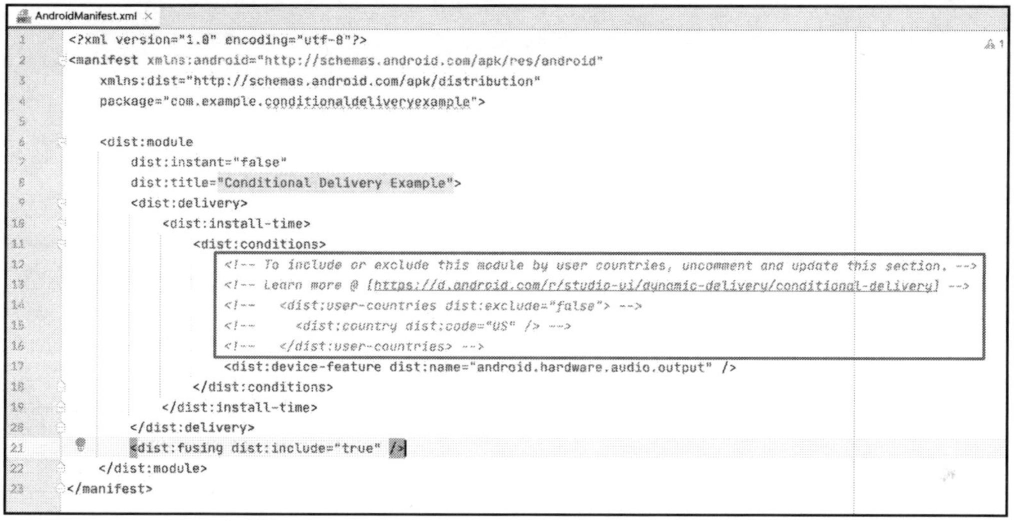

Replace that comment with:

```
<dist:user-countries dist:exclude="true">
  <dist:country dist:code="US" />
</dist:user-countries>
```

Now your file will look like this:

AndroidManifest.xml

```
<?xml version="1.0" encoding="utf-8"?>
<manifest xmlns:android="http://schemas.android.com/apk/res/android"
    xmlns:dist="http://schemas.android.com/apk/distribution"
    package="com.example.conditionaldeliveryexample">

    <dist:module
        dist:instant="false"
        dist:title="Conditional Delivery Example">
        <dist:delivery>
            <dist:install-time>
                <dist:conditions>
                    <dist:user-countries dist:exclude="false">
                        <dist:country dist:code="US" />
                    </dist:user-countries>
                    <dist:device-feature dist:name="android.hardware.audio.output" />
                </dist:conditions>
            </dist:install-time>
        </dist:delivery>
        <dist:fusing dist:include="true" />
    </dist:module>
</manifest>
```

Look at the code of this file. You'll see that this module now has two pre-conditions, inside the tag `<dist:conditions>`:

1. Located in the US.

2. Having a device with audio output.

That's it for conditional delivery. If the device fulfills the requirements, it'll install these modules at download time.

Checking whether the conditional module was downloaded

Just as you did in the previous examples, you will add a button in the navigation bar that will show a toast telling you whether the module was installed or not.

Navigate to **menu_search.xml**, which you can find in the main app **module ▸ res ▸ menu**. Switch to the editor's code view and add the following lines before the closing tag:

```
<item android:id="@+id/download_country_restricted_module"
  android:title="@string/download"
  android:icon="@android:drawable/btn_star"
  app:showAsAction="always"/>
```

The code above will show a star icon, which you will be able to see in the preview of the xml editor.

In **app ▸ java ▸ ui ▸ PodcastActivity**, open **PodcastActivity.kt**.

At the top of this class add:

```
private lateinit var downloadConditionalModule: MenuItem
```

Now, look for a function called **onCreateOptionsMenu**, where you added the code for the on-demand delivery module. At the bottom of this function, before the return true statement located above the closing bracket, add:

```
downloadConditionalModule =
menu.findItem(R.id.download_country_restricted_module)

downloadConditionalModule.setOnMenuItemClickListener {
 downloadConditionalModule()
}
```

In the same file add a function at the bottom for the execution of the code above.

```
private fun downloadConditionalModule(): Boolean {
  // 1
  val splitInstallManager =
SplitInstallManagerFactory.create(applicationContext)

  //2
  val request = SplitInstallRequest
    .newBuilder()
    .addModule("conditionalDeliveryExample")
    .build()

  //3
```

```
    splitInstallManager
      .startInstall(request)
      .addOnSuccessListener { sessionId ->
        Toast.makeText(
          applicationContext,
          "Conditional Module installed successfully with
sessionId $sessionId",
          Toast.LENGTH_LONG
        ).show()
      }
      .addOnFailureListener { exception ->
        Toast.makeText(
          applicationContext,
          "Conditional Module not installed with exception
$exception, you don't match the conditions",
          Toast.LENGTH_LONG
        ).show()
      }

    return true
  }
```

This code is very similar to the previous examples, but in case you want to look at what it means:

1. You use **SplitInstallManagerFactory**, a method the Play Feature Delivery API provides for making operations on modules.
2. You create a request to get the module with the name `"conditionalDeliveryExample"`. This builder is the same for all modules. The only change is the module's name.
3. You execute the install and add a listener for the success and error cases. In this case, you're adding a toast to show whether it was possible to install it or not.

Note: If you are using an Android emulator this may be tricky, as the set country may be different than the one you are located on, so preferably, test it in an actual device. If you keep having problems you may need to deploy the app to a beta lane in the Google Play Store.

Instant delivery

Instant delivery is the last option for dynamic features. It's interesting and has gained a lot of traction, especially in mobile games. With instant delivery, you can let the user test a feature from your app without downloading it. Instant delivery is an excellent tool for showing users the best part of your app and potentially engaging new users.

However, making an instant delivery module requires pre-conditions that may be hard to achieve.

1. The user needs access to the feature you want to instant-deliver plus your app base module.
2. Both of these modules together shouldn't be larger than **10Mb**.
3. Your base module shouldn't use any background services.

Yes, it sounds a little tricky, and it can be. If you want to do this, you have to do a lot of planning and get specific.

The first step to creating an instant module is analyzing your APK, as you did in the previous chapter. Click **Build ▸ Build Bundle(s) / APK(s) ▸ Build APK(s)**. Then, in the same menu, go to **Build ▸ Analyze APK...**. Look at the images below for reference:

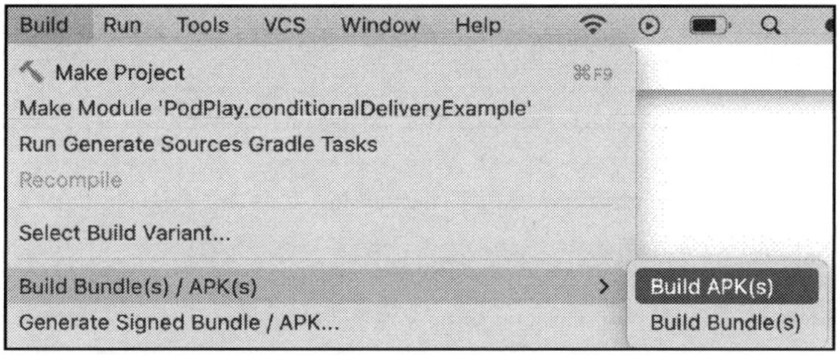

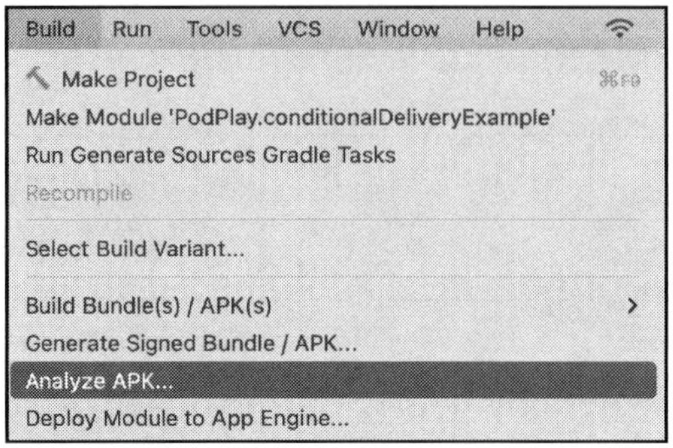

After the analysis finishes, you'll see the results in the main window. **PodPlay** will be around 5-6MB. For a detailed explanation of how to interpret this data, go to the previous chapter.

With these results, you know your main module is below the **10Mb** mark, and you can create an instant module. Yay!

Creating an instant module

As you did in your previous examples, go to **File ▸ New ▸ New Module...**. This time, instead of selecting **Dynamic Feature Module**, choose **Instant Dynamic Feature Module**. As the name explains, this option is for instant apps.

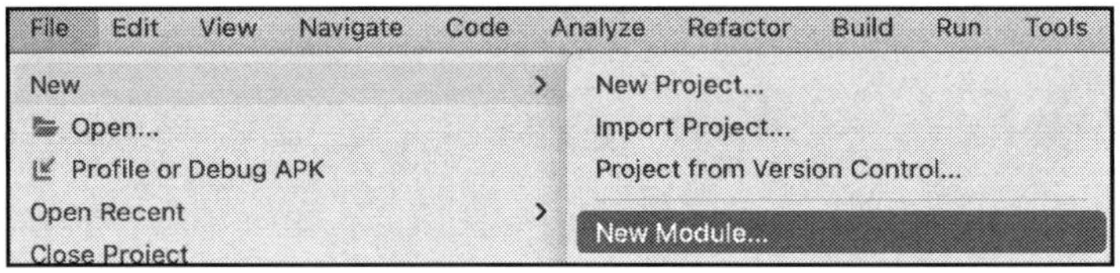

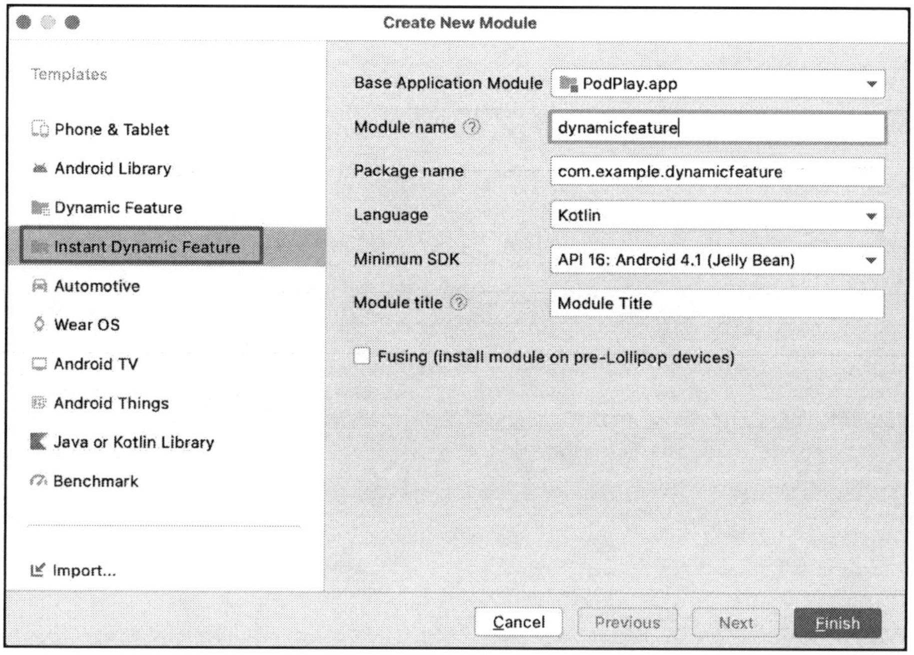

You'll notice the configuration screen is almost the same as the one in **Dynamic Feature Module** except all the options are on one screen instead of two.

By now, you probably know what to put in each option. But, just in case, look at the image below to see what you should add:

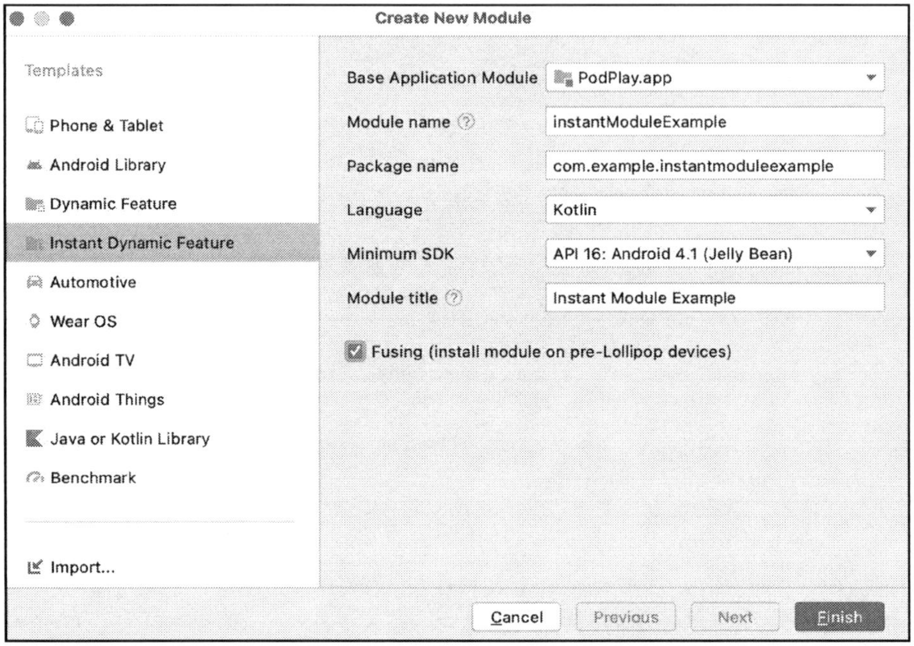

Click **Finish** and, as in the previous examples, wait for the module to appear. Now, you have five modules in your app.

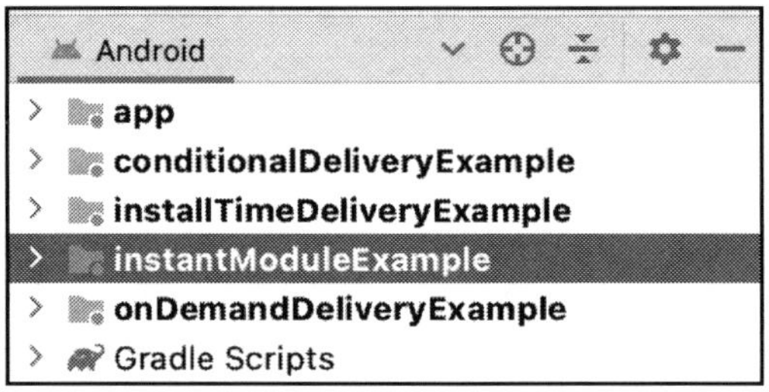

As you learned before, the assistant automatically adds specific properties to your created module's **AndroidManifest.xml**. In the case of instant apps, you'll notice this line:

```
dist:instant="true"
```

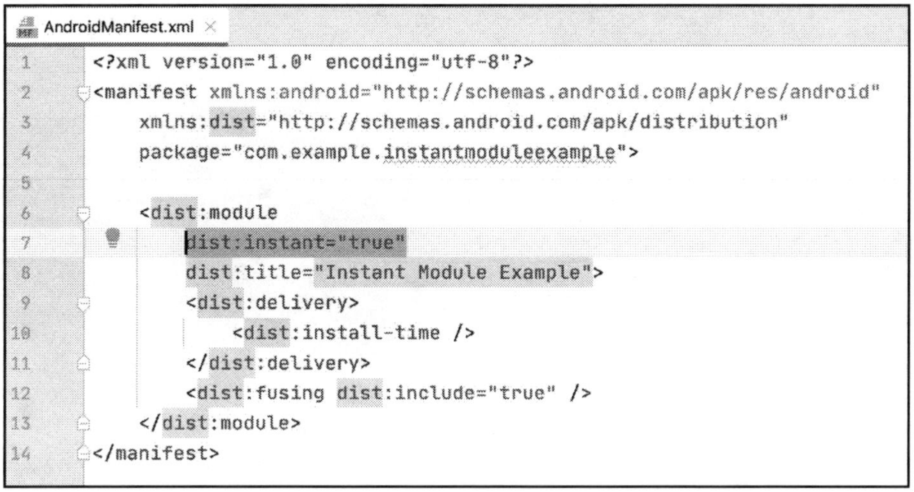

With the above you have now enabled a module that will appear when the app is downloaded as an "instant" experience. To test this on Android Studio, follow this steps:

1. Delete previous versions of your app from the device or emulator you are currently using to test.

2. Go to **Run ▸ Edit Configurations**

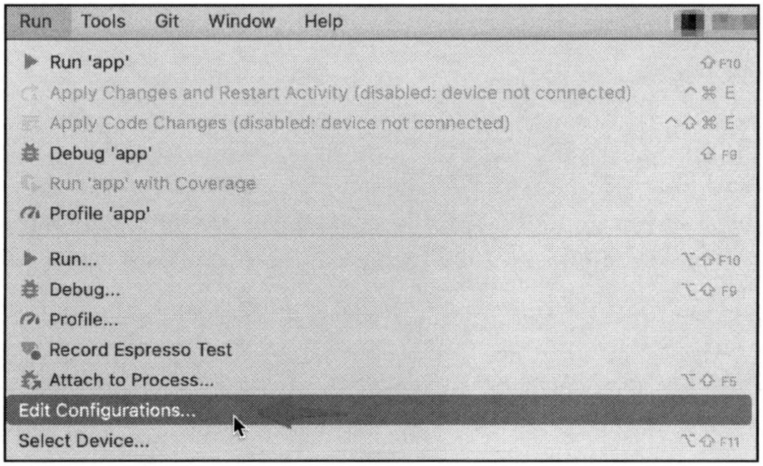

3. Select the checkmark next to **Deploy as Instant App**.

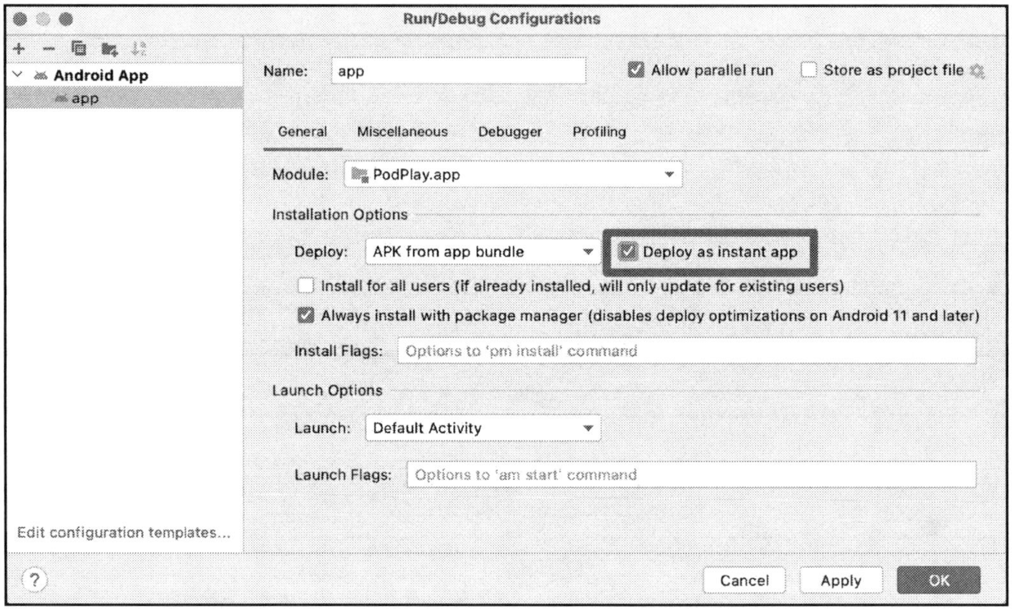

4. Now you can run that module as if you were running your full app.

Once you are running an Instant App test, ensure you are seeing only that module and that you can't accidentally access other modules or the app will crash.

You've learned everything you need to build dynamic modules with your AAB. Now you can choose which one to add to your app or make a mix of them. Adding this will provide a great user experience!

Feature flagging

Besides AABs' capabilities, **Feature flagging** is a software development term that's been around for a long time. Feature flagging refers to enabling or disabling features depending on a specific condition. Ideally, a server would control the flags to enable or disable them depending on the app's needs.

Here's an example. Imagine that in **PodPlay**, you created a module for taking notes about the podcasts.

Once again, go to **menu_search.xml**, which you can find in the main app **module ▸ res ▸ menu**. Switch to the editor's code view and add the following lines before the </menu> closing tag:

```
<item android:id="@+id/write_notes_item"
  android:title="@string/notes"
  android:icon="@android:drawable/ic_menu_edit"
  app:showAsAction="always"/>
```

Look at the preview in the editor. The menu will look like this:

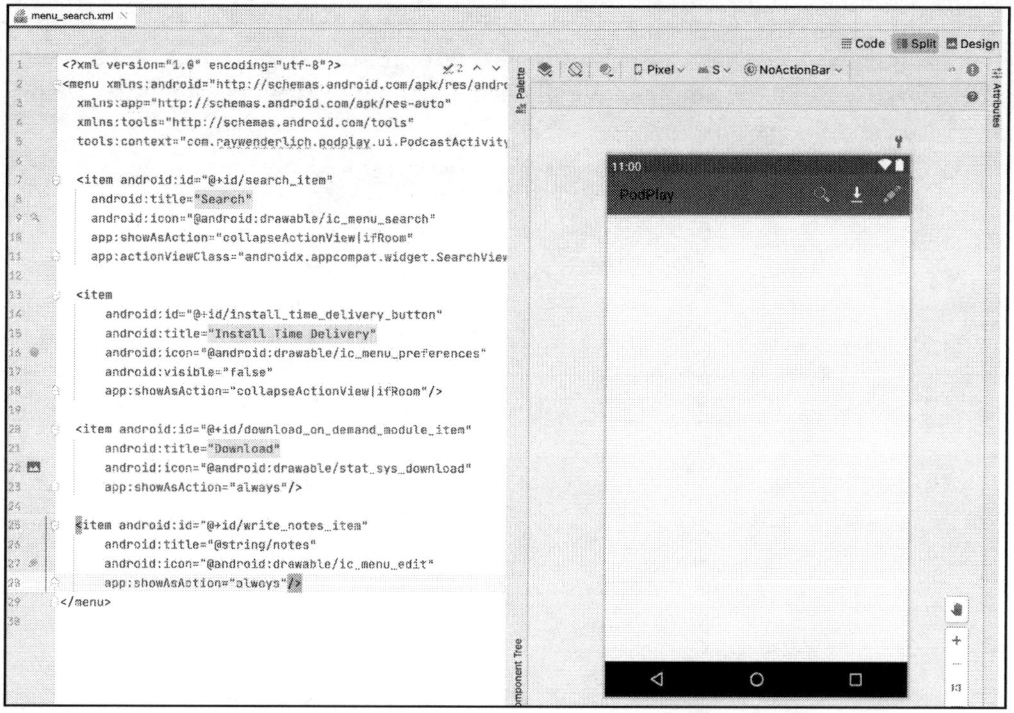

In **app ▸ java ▸ ui ▸ PodcastActivity**, open **PodcastActivity.kt**. There, you have a function called `onCreateOptionsMenu`, which is a function you can add in any activity for storing all the code related to your menu items. At the bottom of this function, before the `return true` statement located above the closing bracket, add:

```
notesMenuItem = menu.findItem(R.id.write_notes_item)

visibilityOfNotesFeature()
```

You want to test the feature. So, put a flag on it with the following code:

```
private fun visibilityOfNotesFeature(): Boolean {
 notesMenuItem.isVisible = areNotesEnabled
 return true
}
```

Now, you need the `areNotesEnabled` feature flag. At the top of your class, where you initialize all variables, create a new variable with:

```
private var areNotesEnabled = true
```

Run the app twice: Once with the Boolean `areNotesEnabled` set to true and the other with it set to false. You'll notice the pencil icon only appears when the variable is true, like in the image below:

In a real case scenario a backend service would pass a parameter in a service call that the app would use to determine the state of the feature flag. Depending on the returned state, your app can show or hide this option.

Why would you want to implement a feature flag?

There are several reasons for implementing a feature flag. Some examples include:

1. While developing, you want to control which modules to view to make your testing more efficient.
2. Marketing teams can make user tests to see user engagement with or without a feature.
3. You can release unfinished features when you have a Continuous Delivery pipeline and add all your code without enabling access to those unfinished parts. You'll learn about Continuous Delivery pipelines later in the book.

Key points

- **Android App Bundles** provide dynamic delivery options to make your app lighter and better meet your users' needs.
- You can create **install-time delivery** modules that are added to the app immediately when the user downloads your app.
- Users can request **on-demand delivery** modules, depending on their needs.
- Another option is **conditional delivery** modules, which will download depending on various factors like hardware requirements, version of the device or country.
- **Instant apps** are an excellent option for engaging your users, but you have to ensure your **base module** and **instant app module** are not larger than 10MB.
- **Feature flagging** is a technique used in Software Development for controlling the visibility of features and the functionality of your app. Ideally, the back end of your app would change this data.

Where to go from here?

There's a lot to discover about Dynamic Features. For more on this topic check out Android App Bundles: Getting Started (https://www.raywenderlich.com/9043-android-app-bundles-getting-started) and Instant Apps: Getting Started (https://www.raywenderlich.com/9519-instant-apps-getting-started), which will help you practice the skills you just learned.

Looking forward to seeing the amazing modules you add to your app.

Chapter 9: Build Variants: Implementing Build Types

By Evana Margain Puig

In the following two chapters, you'll learn how to create different versions of your app within the same project. Before you begin, you need to understand three terms: **build variants**, **build types** and **build flavors**. These three terms are often a source of confusion when releasing to the Google Play Store, especially if you haven't played around with them. Time to dive right into learning what these terms mean:

1. **Build types**: In Android apps, build types usually refer to the environment in which you're testing. By default, when you create an app in Android Studio from any of the templates, you get two build types: **debug** and **release**. If you've worked in tech companies, you may know there are usually more than those two. You can customize your build types to include other types such as QA, Release Candidate or RC, Pre-Prod or whatever fits your needs.
2. **Build flavors**: Apps often vary in ways besides environment-based differences. Flavors support these kinds of variations. For example, you can use flavors to handle:

- Having a paid version of your app vs. a free version.
- Having a version for each store you upload to, such as Amazon Appstore, Google Play Store and Samsung Galaxy Store.
- Using the same app for different products and customizing the assets to change the app's look and feel.

3. **Build variants**: Variants are the combination of build types and build flavors. For example, you can have a "dev paid" version of your app, which is a combination of the "dev" build type and "paid" flavor of your app. If you have both flavors and types, you'll release variants when uploading to the Google Play Store or any other store.

Now that you have a clear understanding of what each of these terms means, you'll start by learning how to implement **build types** throughout this chapter.

Why use build types?

By now, you understand build types at a high level. In short, it's a build configuration that lets you differentiate versions of your app depending on the environment you're targeting, such as development, testing or release. But from a high level, this may not sound like something special or different from a flavor. So take a look at precisely what a build type does behind the scenes.

Build types target configurations in your Gradle properties. For example, a build type can:

- Enable or disable debugging in your app.
- Sign the app with a production certificate if needed.
- Shrink or obfuscate your resources. For an in-depth understanding of this topic, take a look at Chapter 7.

Remember, you need at least one build type to build your app. Android Studio templates give you two by default.

Android Studio base build types

Take a look at **PodPlay** to see where you can find those default build types. Open the **PodPlay** project in Android Studio. In the Navigation panel's Android view, navigate to **Gradle Scripts ▸ build.gradle(Module: PodPlay.app)**. Look at the `buildTypes` group inside the `android` declaration.

There you'll find two build types: **debug** and **release**, as shown in the image below:

```
buildTypes {
  debug {
    minifyEnabled false
    shrinkResources false
  }
  release {
    minifyEnabled false
    proguardFiles getDefaultProguardFile('proguard-android.txt'), 'proguard-rules.pro'
  }
```

Also, look at the tag above those build types, named `defaultConfig`. It defines the properties available to all `buildTypes` unless you override them inside the specific `buildType`.

```
defaultConfig {
  applicationId "com.raywenderlich.podplay"
  minSdkVersion 23
  targetSdkVersion 30
  versionCode 1
  versionName "1.0"
  testInstrumentationRunner "androidx.test.runner.AndroidJUnitRunner"
}
```

If you create a project from scratch with an Android Studio template, you'll only see the **release** build type defined, like in the image below:

```
buildTypes {
  release {
    minifyEnabled false
    proguardFiles getDefaultProguardFile('proguard-android-optimize.txt'), 'proguard-rules.pro'
  }
}
```

Although you can't see it, the debug type also exists by default. It isn't mentioned since it uses all the configurations from the `defaultConfig`. If you want to change something in the debug build type beyond what you have by default, you can add it, as in the **PodPlay** example.

Switching build types in Android Studio

Android Studio has a **Build Variants** panel. Usually, you'll find it at the bottom left of your screen as a closed tab. Tap it and you'll see the panel. If you can't see the panel there, go to **View ▸ Tool Windows ▸ Build Variants** as shown below:

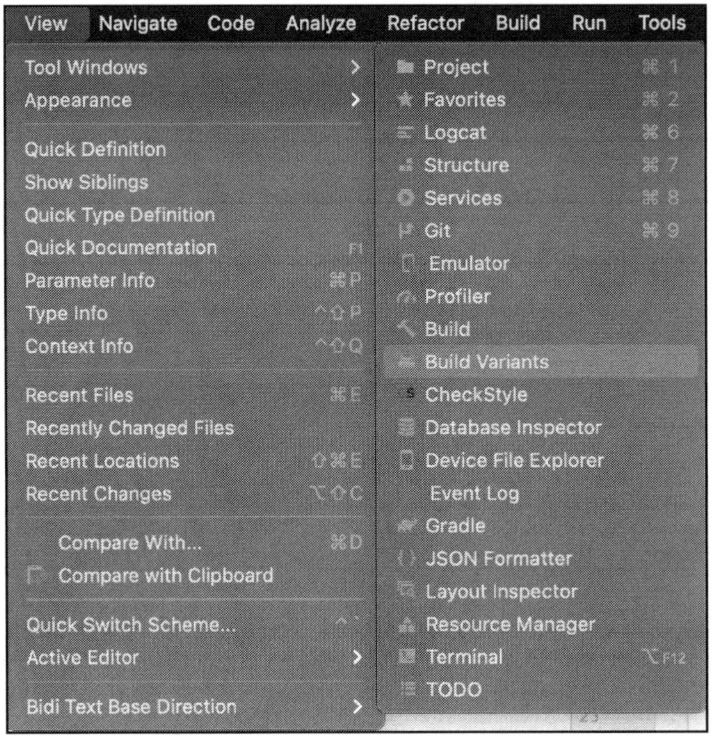

You'll find this panel:

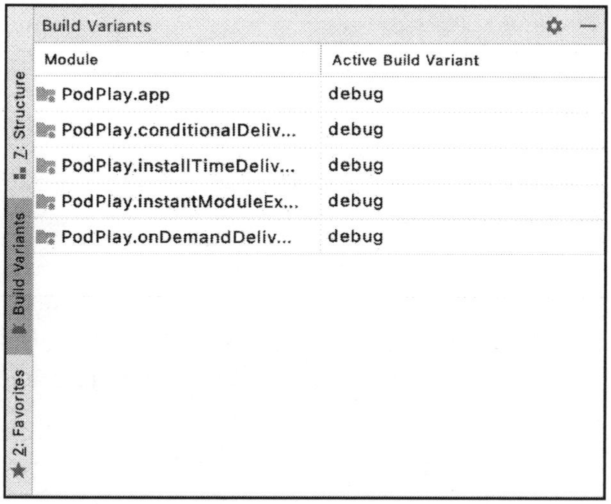

Here, you'll see a list of all the app modules with their current build variant. All the previously defined modules in **PodPlay** have the default release and debug build variants. Changing from one build variant to another requires a Gradle Build.

> **Note**: In most projects, different modules within a single app all need to point to the same environment to compile. For example, if you select a *release* version on a module, you may also need to change all the other modules to *release* in the *Build Variants* window. Otherwise, you may get compile errors.

Implementing build types in your app

Now it's time to put what you've learned into practice and create a new build type. Open your app module's **build.gradle** located in **Gradle Scripts ▸ build.gradle(Module: PodPlay.app)**. Below the release version closing bracket, add a build variant named **qa** with:

```
qa {
  initWith debug
  applicationIdSuffix ".qaTesting"
  signingConfig signingConfigs.debug
}
```

For this new config, you define three parameters:

1. **initWith**: This parameter has the value debug, which means this version has all the properties the debug build type has, plus the ones defined inside the brackets.
2. **applicationIdSuffix**: This parameter has the value `.qaTesting`, which, as the name implies, adds the suffix to your app's installed package name. Adding this suffix facilitates installing more than one version of your app for testing on the same device.
3. **signingConfig**: In this case, you set it to use the debug build's signing configs because you aren't uploading this version to a store. If you use a third-party service to distribute your app to testers, you may need to include another type of signing here.

Click **Sync Now**. Once Gradle finishes syncing, open **Build Variants** and choose **qa** for **Podplay.app** as shown below:

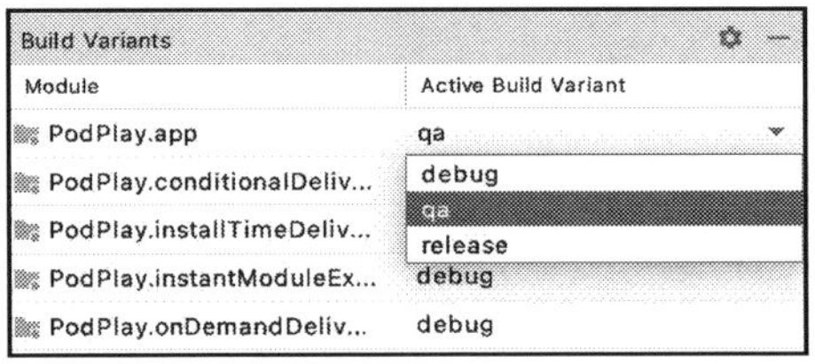

Once you change the build variant, Gradle will take a few seconds to sync. Build and run the app. Open the **Logcat** tab, and you'll see the app's package of is now **com.raywenderlich.podplay.qaTesting** in the logs.

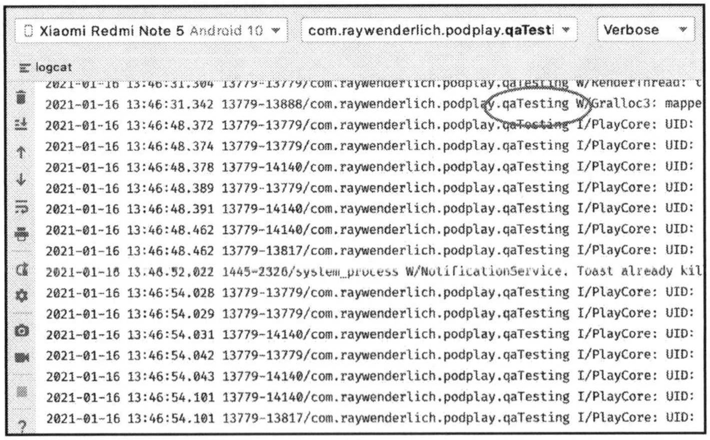

As simple as that! No need to add anything complicated at all.

If you get errors (Optional)

If you had no trouble running the previous step, skip this section. Otherwise, keep reading.

If you didn't download the starter project, there are a couple of lines that may cause a conflict in the build because you need to add the `buildType` to each of the modules defined in the app. You have two options for fixing this issue:

1. Go through each Module **build.gradle** and add the same build type you added.
2. Go to your **Android Manifest** and delete `<dist:module dist:instant="true"/>`. In the app's module **build.gradle**, where you added the build type, remove or comment the line with: `dynamicFeatures = [':installTimeDeliveryExample', ':onDemandDeliveryExample', ':conditionalDeliveryExample', ':instantModuleExample']`.

If you're following along with this chapter's 'starter', these lines are no longer there.

Now run a Gradle build to make this **build type** available by clicking the icon shown below.

Re-open the **Build Variants** panel. You'll see the new build type and can change it, as in the image below.

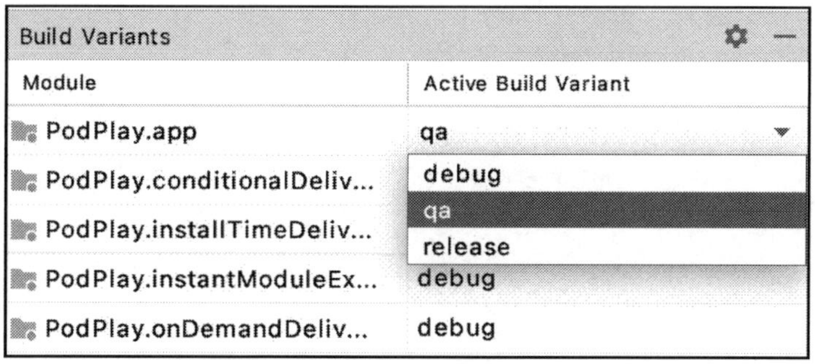

Gradle DSL reference

PodPlay's Gradle files are in a Groovy-based DSL. Groovy is a Java scripting language and DSL stands for Domain-Specific Language. You may find other apps have Kotlin based Gradle files. Either way, the configurations are similar.

The properties available for configuring your build type depend on the **Android Gradle Plugin** version you use. At the time of writing, the current release is 4.2.2. You can find the reference of Gradle files in the Android documentation at https://developer.android.com/docs by navigating to **Reference ▸ Other Libraries ▸ Android Gradle Plugin**:

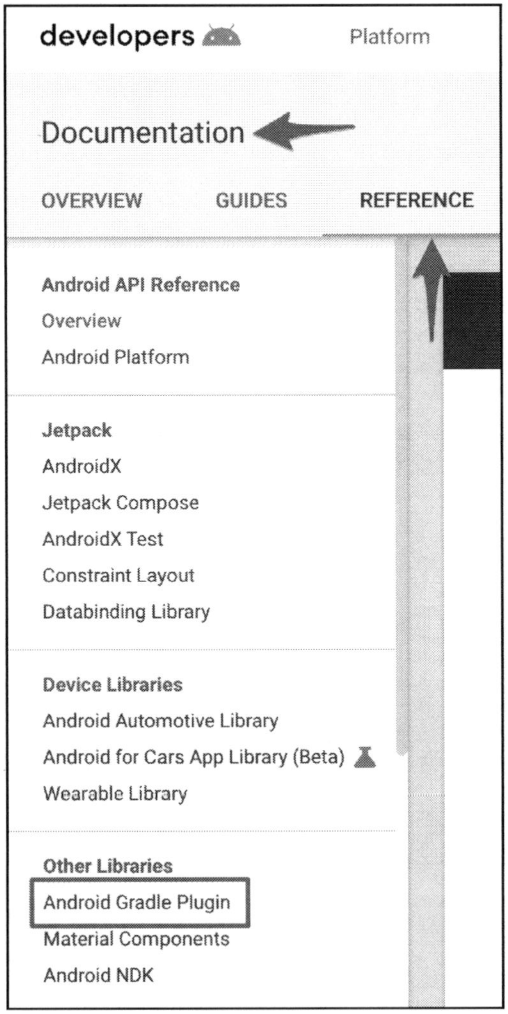

You'll see a page where they indicate the latest **Android Gradle Plugin** version.

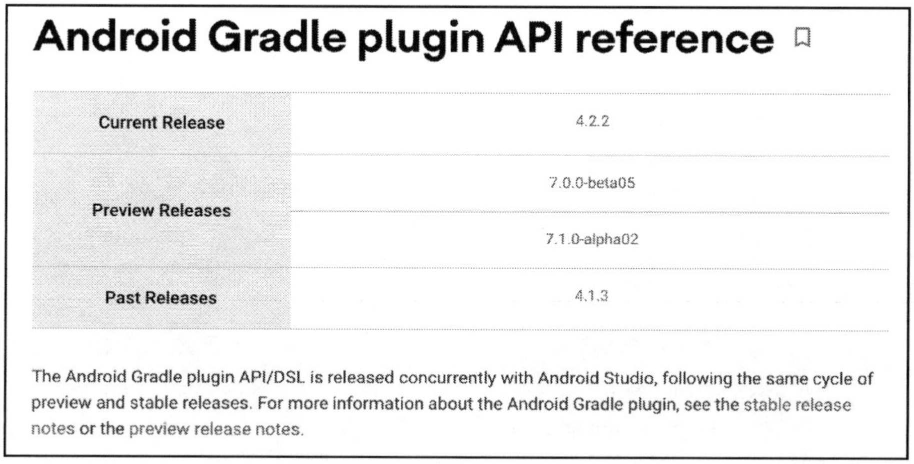

Android Gradle plugin API reference

Current Release	4.2.2
Preview Releases	7.0.0-beta05
	7.1.0-alpha02
Past Releases	4.1.3

The Android Gradle plugin API/DSL is released concurrently with Android Studio, following the same cycle of preview and stable releases. For more information about the Android Gradle plugin, see the stable release notes or the preview release notes.

Click **Current Stable Release** as shown in the image above. You'll see a page that displays all the classes available in the plugin. Select **BuiltType**, and you'll see the documentation for the BuildType class.

On this page, you can find all of the build variant's properties. For example, **isMinifyEnabled** specifies whether to enable code shrinking for this build type. Code shrinking is important for your build types because while it makes debugging harder, it also optimizes code for distribution versions.

You may notice only a few properties listed in the documentation, and they don't match the ones in **PodPlay's** Gradle files. This is because there's an inheritance. BuildType has access to all the properties in **VariantDimension** because, as you learned earlier, build types paired with flavors form variants. So, you can put the listed properties in the VariantDimension reference either in your **build types** or **flavors** depending on the app's needs.

You can view all of VariantDimensions' properties at https://developer.android.com/reference/tools/gradle-api/4.2/com/android/build/api/dsl/VariantDimension.

Release build type

It's important to understand release type because it's the version you'll upload to the Google Play Store. Choose the release variant in the **Build Variants Panel**, and wait for the Gradle sync to finish.

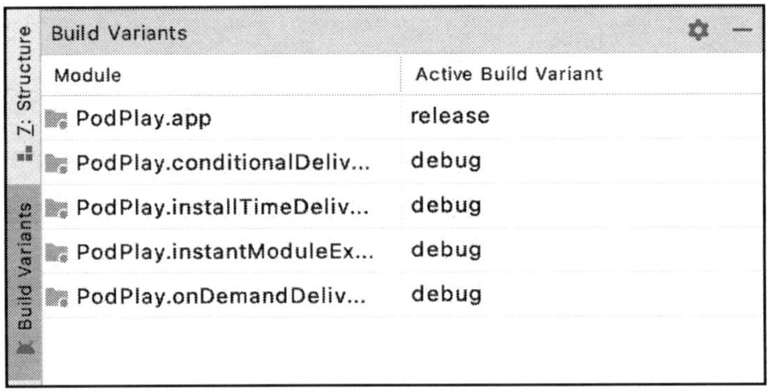

You won't see any errors when the build finishes but that doesn't mean you're done. Try to run the app with the Run button at the top of Android Studio. You'll see an **Edit Configurations** dialog. You'll also see the app version in the top bar has a small red x sign next to it:

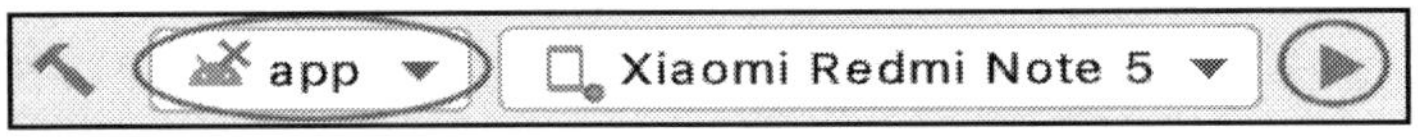

That x means Android Studio still doesn't know how to sign your app. In chapter 2, you learned how to create signing certificates. You need to add some here. The **Edit Configurations** dialog offers an option to **Fix** the problem. But you need to create the certificate first if you don't have it.

Creating a release certificate (Optional)

Before doing this let's review how to create the certificates for signing a release build as you learned in previous chapters.

In the top bar of Android Studio go to **Build ▸ Generate signed bundle / APK**, as in the image below.

In the dialog shown select **Android App Bundle**. Technically you can choose either, but Android recommends using Bundles and they will be soon the only accepted format in the Google Play Store, so go for this option. Click **Next**.

In the next screen supposing you don't yet have a certificate for the app, click on the **Create New** button under the **Key Store Path** label.

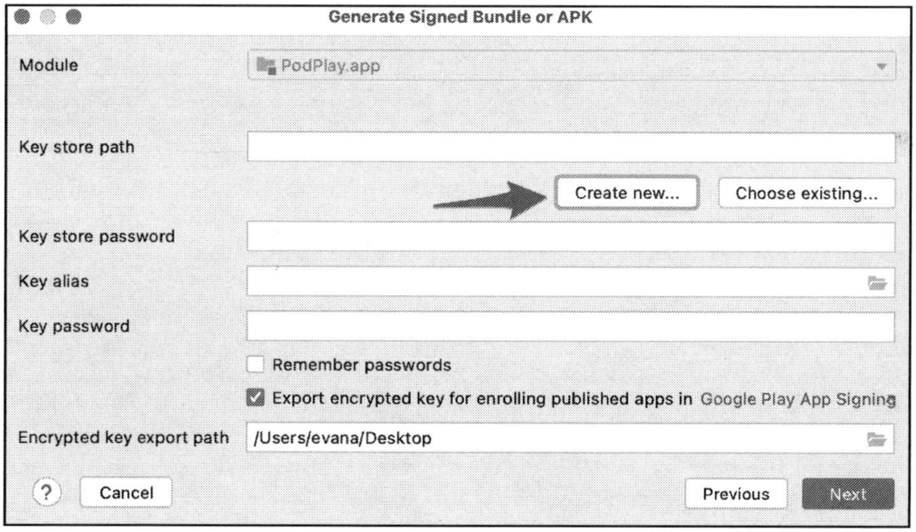

Now fill in the fields one by one and save the information you input there because you will need it later:

1. **Key Store Path**: Where in your local storage you want to save your certificate. I selected: **../Desktop/pod_play_key_example**.
2. **Password**: The pass of that key store. Always be sure to save both the keystore and this password in a safe place, if you lose them you won't be able to update your app on the Google Play Store. For the purpose of this example and just so you don't forget I suggest using **pass123**.

> **Note:** Remember to always use safe passwords in any certificate, someone with unauthorized access could damage users devices through your app.

3. **Alias**: A name with which you will identify the key, for example: **pod_play_key**.
4. **Password**: Another, preferably different, password for the key itself. For the purpose of the example again use **pass123**.
5. **Validity**: Just leave the default.
6. In the fields below you only need to fill in one field, fill in the one that says **First and Last name** with your own.

Leave the rest of the fields empty. Take a look at the image below to see how the data should look now.

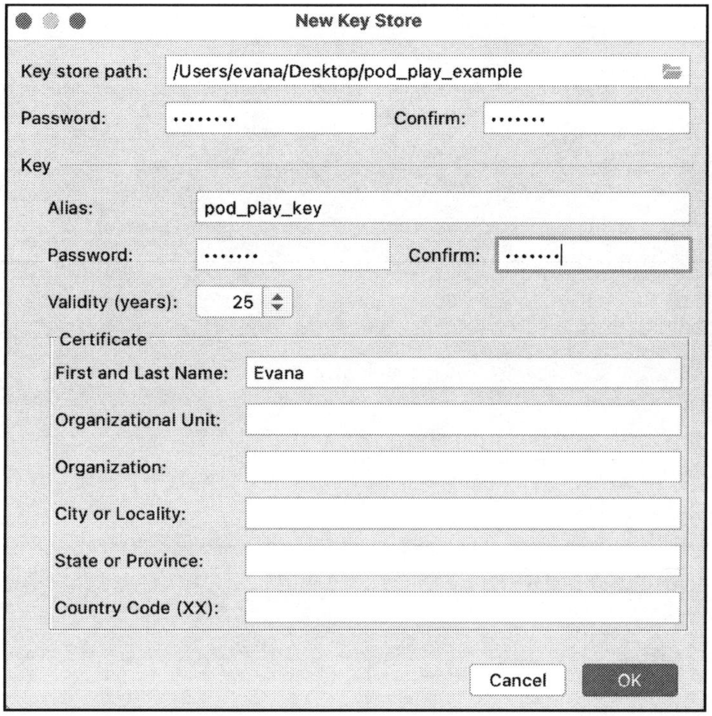

Click **OK** and the **Key** related fields should automatically have the information filled in as in the image below.

Click **Next** and you will see a list of your app's **Build Variants**.

Select the **release** variant and click **Finish**.

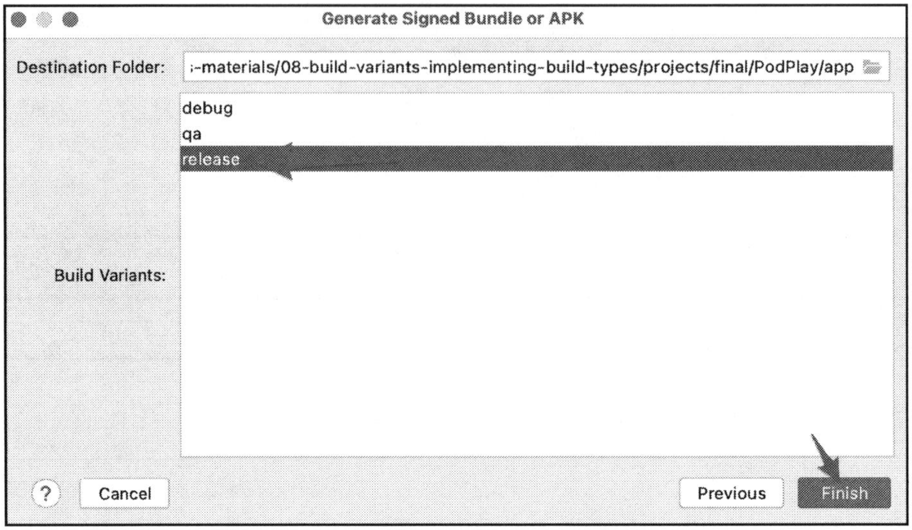

Right after clicking the button a Gradle Build will start, wait until it finishes.

Fixing the release build problem

Now try to run the app again with the Run button at the top of Android Studio, with the release version selected. You'll still see the app version in the top bar has a small red x sign next to it:

That means Android Studio still doesn't know how to sign your app, even though you already created them. You now need to add them to the project.

Click on the icon with small red x, choose **Edit Configuration** and a dialog will come up with an option to **Fix** the problem.

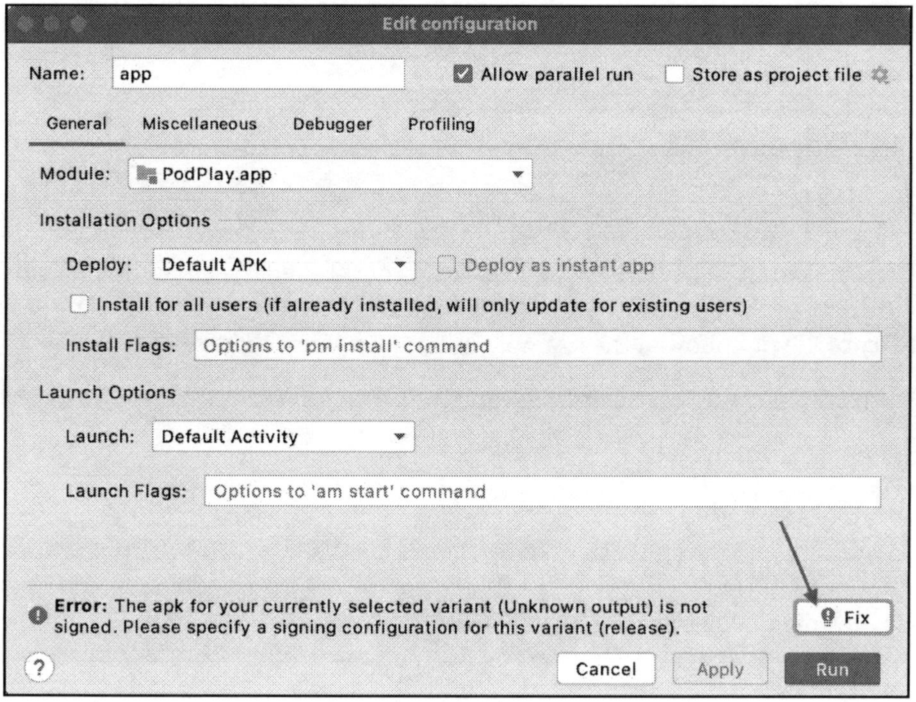

Click on the **Fix** button.

With that, you'll see a **Project Structure** dialog appear and a **Signing Configs** tab selected. The compiler will take them every time you choose that release build. Click on the + sign shown in the image below.

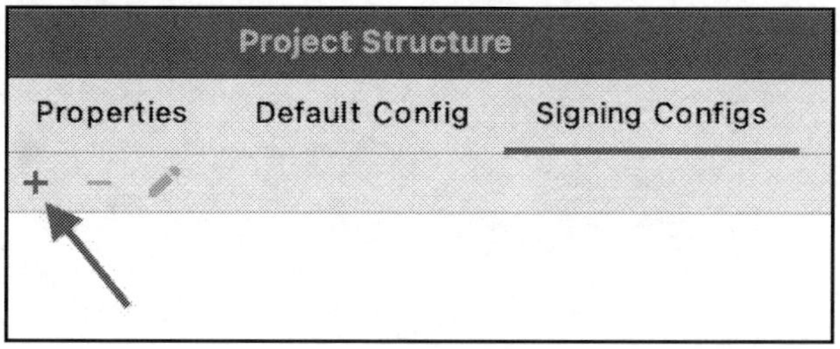

A small dialog with a text input will appear now, write **release** as the name of the build config.

Click **OK** and you will be back in the **Project Structure** dialog. Fill in the information with the data of the certificate you created in the last section **Creating a Release Certificate**. If you followed the example above then you will have:

1. Store File: The file location of the certificate
2. Store Password: **pass123**
3. Key Alias: **pod_play_key**
4. Key Password: **pass123**

This is how the dialog should look like now:

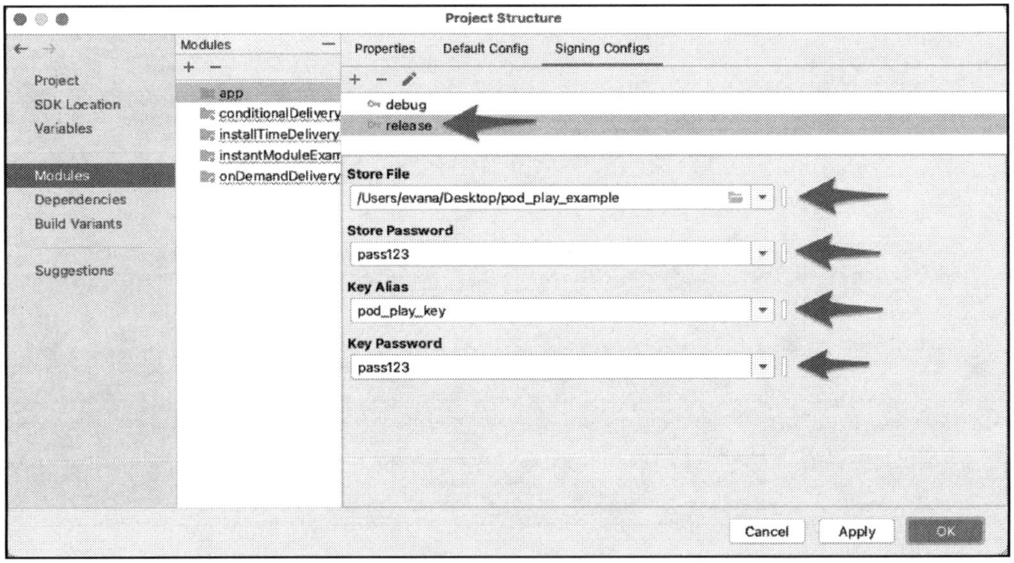

Then you can click **OK** and you will be back in the first dialog called **Project Structure**. Change to the tab called **Default Config** and locate the field called **Signing Config** and in the dropdown select the option **$signingConfigs.release**. Look at the image below for guidance.

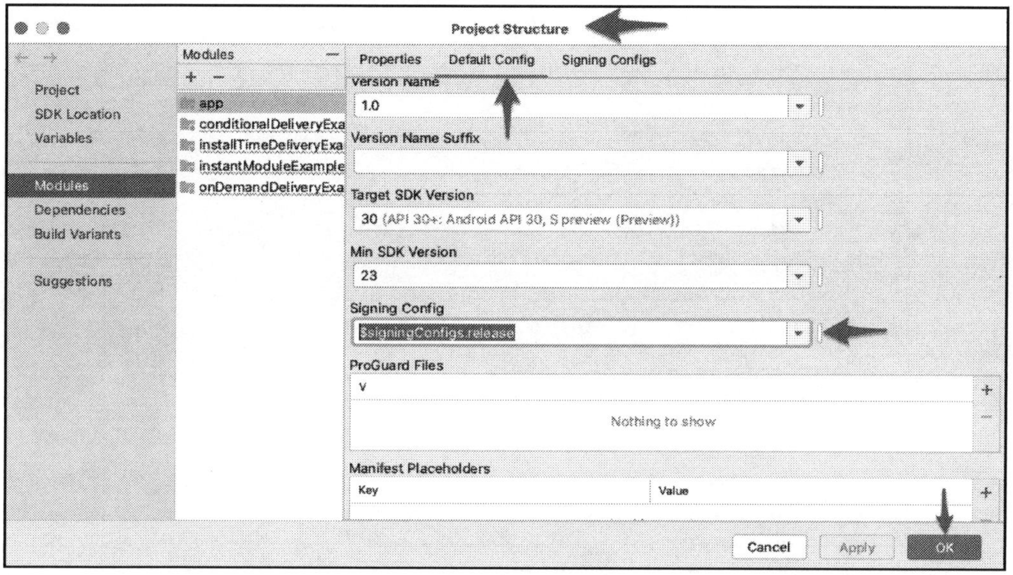

With those changes, now you can run the app. Verify the app is working as expected.

Now navigate to **Gradle Scripts ▸ build.gradle(Module: PodPlay.app)**. In this file you will notice some lines were added in order to have the certificate and credentials added automatically every time you build a release version. In the image below you will see the sections of the code that Android Studio added for you through the configuration steps.

```
android {
  signingConfigs {
    release {
      storeFile file('/Users/evana/Desktop/pod_play_example')
      storePassword 'pass123'
      keyAlias 'pod_play_key'
      keyPassword 'pass123'
    }
  }
  compileSdkVersion 30
  buildToolsVersion = '30.0.3'
  defaultConfig {
    applicationId "com.raywenderlich.podplay"
    minSdkVersion 23
    targetSdkVersion 30
    versionCode 1
    versionName "1.0"
    testInstrumentationRunner "androidx.test.runner.AndroidJUnitRunner"
    signingConfig signingConfigs.release
  }
```

Note: In the code above you are using a hardcoded path to the keystore. This is not a good practice because in the example above you are referencing a path that is specific to one developers machine, which will be different from developer to developer. Later in the book you will learn techniques to store this key safely and make it accessible for larger teams. In the meantime, keep in mind that you should not put it in a public repository because that will make it easy for a bad actor to get it, which will create a security issue for your app.

That's all you need to know about build types! In the next chapter, you'll build on this knowledge to create flavors that'll make your build variants complete.

Key points

- Build variants are a compound output of **build types** and **build flavors**.
- Build types take care of your app's Gradle configurations.
- You can create as many **build types** as your app needs.
- Most Gradle files are in a **Groovy Based DSL**, but some are written in Kotlin.
- The release build type requires a signing configuration that includes the release certificates.

Chapter 10: Publishing in the Real World

By Evana Margain Puig

In the previous chapter, you learned about **build types**, the first step in creating build variants. You also learned that **build flavors** are the second group of components you need to create a build variant.

This chapter will teach you all about build flavors. They'll help you manage different versions of your app without having separate code bases.

We call this chapter "Publishing in the Real World" because most developers build different versions of their apps through build flavors.

What can you do with flavors?

Flavors let you add different resources, assets or items to your app while still using the project's core functionality. You can have the same app using the same code but with a different look and feel.

In the past, you may have copied all of your code into a separate repo and changed the assets. You don't need to do that when you have flavors. Flavors give you the advantage of a single code base and let you apply bug fixes in a single app without synchronizing all versions.

In the previous chapter, you saw some use cases for flavors. If you need to refresh your memory, here they are again:

- Having separate free and paid versions of your app, where the free version makes certain parts available to the user but restricts others.
- Having a version for each store you upload to. Such stores include Amazon Appstore, Google Play Store and Samsung Galaxy Store. Each store has different requirements for how your assets should look, the app's size and items you may need to attach on compile time. With different flavors, you can follow each store's requirements.
- Using the same app for different products but customizing the assets to change the app's look and feel. For example, you may have two companies that sell items. You can have a single app that sells products but customize it with each company's products and brand.
- 'White labeling' is a common practice related to the previous example. With white labeling, you have a base app without any brand labels and can customize it as you want.
- Distributing apps across different countries. Certain parts of your content may not be approved or apply to customers in certain regions. You can customize what they see or don't see based on their specific region.

Flavors are a powerful tool. However, they may add more complexity and build time, so you should keep them focused and targeted.

Default Config and flavors

In the last chapter, you learned which properties build types support. Build flavors also support specific properties. The **Default Config** contains those properties. You'll find the **Default Config** in your apps' **build.gradle** like this:

```
defaultConfig {
  applicationId "com.raywenderlich.podplay"
  minSdkVersion 23
  targetSdkVersion 30
  versionCode 1
  versionName "1.0"
  testInstrumentationRunner
"androidx.test.runner.AndroidJUnitRunner"
}
```

When creating flavors, you need to specify an **applicationId** or **applicationIdSuffix** for each flavor. The **applicationId** defines a different application Id while **applicationIdSuffix** appends something to that specific's flavor application id.

This step is important because the Google Play Store won't let apps have the same app ID. Additionally, since different flavors result in different artifacts, you'll have separate AAB's or APK's for each flavor.

Creating flavors

You're probably reading this chapter to learn how to implement flavors. So, dive right in!

Flavor dimensions

The first thing you need to add when creating a flavor is a **flavor dimension**. Dimensions are a way to group flavors. Look at the examples you saw earlier in this chapter and develop names you'd give each group.

Here are some dimension name examples in the same order as the examples above:

1. Pricing
2. Store
3. Product_name
4. White_label
5. Country_localizations

Of course, the name can be anything suitable for your app. However, if you don't specify a flavor dimension, the compiler will ask you to with this message:

"Error: All flavors must now belong to a named flavor dimension. The flavor 'your_flavor_name' is not assigned to a flavor dimension."

Build flavor example

Now that you know you need a flavor dimension to create flavors in your app, it's time to put this into practice. You'll follow the **pricing** example and create a 'demo' flavor and a 'full' flavor.

Demo vs full version

Open **PodPlay** in Android Studio. In the Navigation panel's Android view, navigate to **Gradle Scripts ▸ build.gradle(Module: PodPlay.app)**.

First, specify a flavor dimension by adding the following line of code right after the **buildTypes** block:

```
flavorDimensions "version_type"
```

The previous code adds a new flavor dimension named `"version_type"`.

Then define the two flavors: one for the 'free' version and another for the 'full' version. Add the following code after the `flavorDimensions`:

```
productFlavors {
  free {
    dimension "version_type"
    applicationIdSuffix ".free"
    versionNameSuffix "-free"
  }
  full {
    dimension "version_type"
    applicationIdSuffix ".full"
    versionNameSuffix "-full"
  }
}
```

In the code above, `applicationIdSuffix ".free"` creates the application ID **com.raywenderlich.podplay.free**. `versionNameSuffix "-free"` creates the version name **1.0-free**. Ensure the dimension inside the flavors is exactly the same as the one defined above using `flavorDimensions`.

Whenever you make changes in Gradle files, Android Studio will ask you to do a Gradle sync. Do it and ensure the app compiles and runs without problems.

You won't see any changes yet. Make sure nothing happens when the app runs.

Switching between versions

In the previous chapter, you learned Android Studio has a **Build Variants** panel. Usually, you can find it at the bottom left of your screen as a closed tab. If you tap it, the panel displays.

If you don't see the panel there, go to **View ▸ Tool Windows ▸ Build Variants** as shown below:

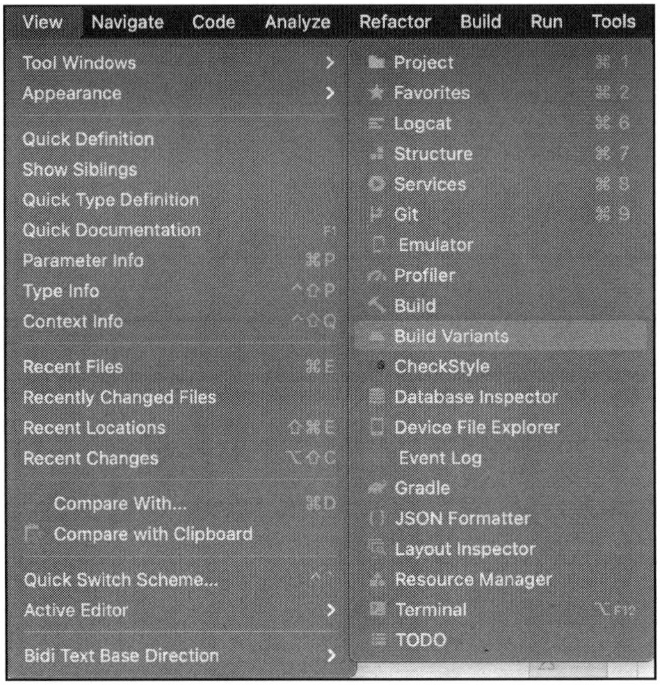

Open **Build Variants**. You'll see the panel shown below:

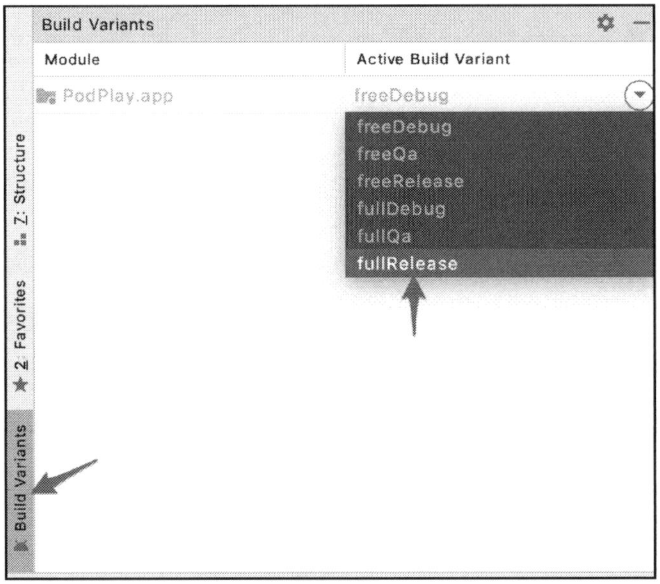

If you followed the previous chapter, you'll notice a change in this panel. The panel displays a combination of each of your build types and each of your build flavors. You'll see one of each of the types 'Debug', 'QA' and 'Release' paired to each of the flavors 'free' and 'full'. Android Studio concatenates the names in camelcase structure. These are build variants!

> **Note**: If you run the 'release' version of the build variants, Android Studio will probably require a signing key for your app. If you've forgotten how to do that have a look at chapter 2.

Adding a second flavor dimension

As you add build flavors and build types, Android Studio creates combinations called build variants. You can create a more complex structure by adding multiple flavor dimensions.

To better understand this concept, look at one of the build variants you already have: **freeQa**, a combination of the **Qa** build type and the **free** flavor.

Next to the first flavor dimension, create another dimension named **store** by separating both with a comma. This new dimension defines the store to which you upload, say Amazon and Google. Now the dimensions code will look like this:

```
flavorDimensions "version_type", "store"
```

Next, define the two flavors that'll belong to that dimension, under the first pair you created, using the code below:

```
productFlavors {
  google {
    dimension "store"
    applicationIdSuffix ".google"
    versionNameSuffix "-google"
  }
  amazon {
    dimension "store"
    applicationIdSuffix ".amazon"
    versionNameSuffix "-amazon"
  }
}
```

You'll see a prompt to perform a Gradle sync. Wait for it to complete. Open the **Build Variants** panel. Now you have several variants. The number of build types and flavor dimensions create combinations:

Three Build Types * Two Flavors of version_type dimension * Two Flavors of store dimension = Twelve Build Variants

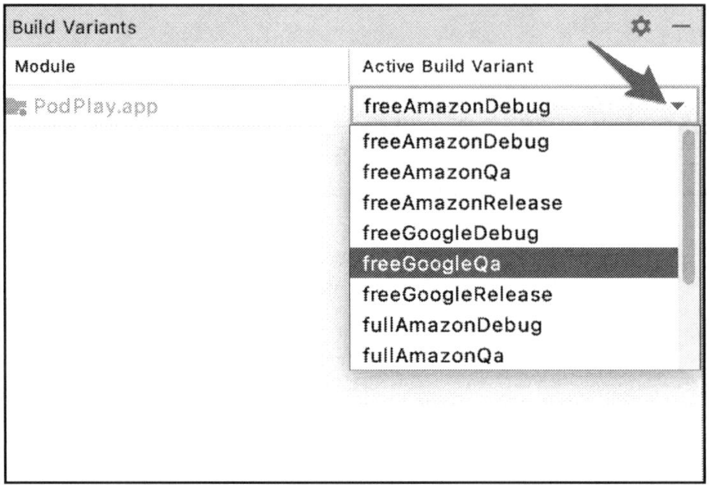

Now you can see why you should create a limited amount of flavors. This number can grow large with so many combinations.

Variant filters

Now that you have so many variants, you may notice some are part of the resulting combinations you don't need. Imagine you don't want to upload the free version of your app to the Amazon store. **Variant filters** let you use filters to exclude build variants that meet certain conditions.

After your `productFlavors` block, add:

```
variantFilter { variant ->
  def names = variant.flavors*.name
  if (names.contains("free") && names.contains("amazon")) {
    setIgnore(true)
  }
}
```

In the preceding code, you check if the flavor name includes the words **free** and **amazon** for each variant. If any flavor name contains both words, you filter out the variant by calling `setIgnore(true)`.

Perform another Gradle sync as prompted by the notification above the file. Recheck the build variants dialog. You'll see the one that met the conditions, **freeAmazonBuildType**, disappeared. Now you have a less cluttered group of choices.

Common build flavor properties for configuring

Earlier, you created some flavor dimensions and added a basic configuration. You learned about `applicationIdSuffix` and `versionNameSuffix`, but there are more properties. In this section, you'll review the most common ones.

Signing configs

As you learned in earlier chapters, any version you upload to a store, like the Google Play Store, will need signing for security and identifying your app.

In the past, you may have manually added the signing process. But you can define the signing configs inside your build flavors and avoid adding them every time.

You'll add the signing keys next. But first, see what happens if you run a release version in the emulator or a physical device without defining signing configs.

In the **Build Variants** dialog, select one of your release versions, such as **fullAmazonRelease**. After the Gradle build completes, look at the area in the top bar where you run the app. It'll look like this:

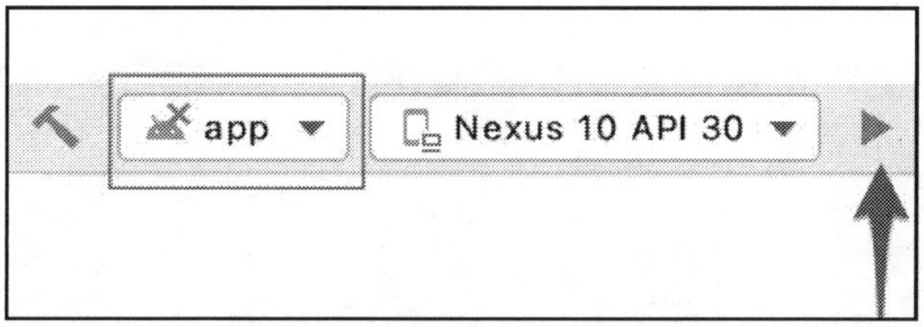

First, you'll notice the little 'android' logo mentioning the name of the app you're about to run has a small **x** sign. Now try to run the app with the green **play** button. A dialog like this will appear:

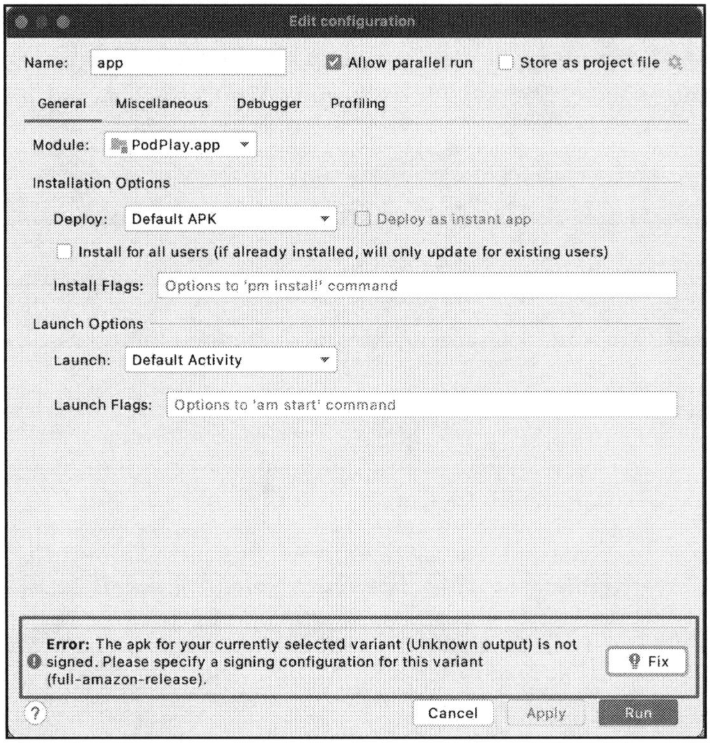

Look at the error at the bottom of the dialog. Click **Fix**, and you'll get another dialog. In the new dialog, click the small + sign at the top left to add a new signing config. Choose a name for it, as shown below:

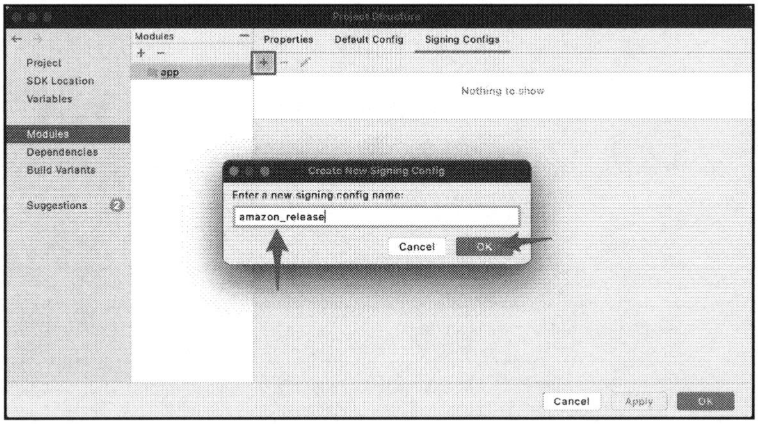

In the example above, you see a config named **amazon_release** since that's the one you chose in the build variants window.

Click **Ok**. Android Studio will ask you to enter your app's credentials:

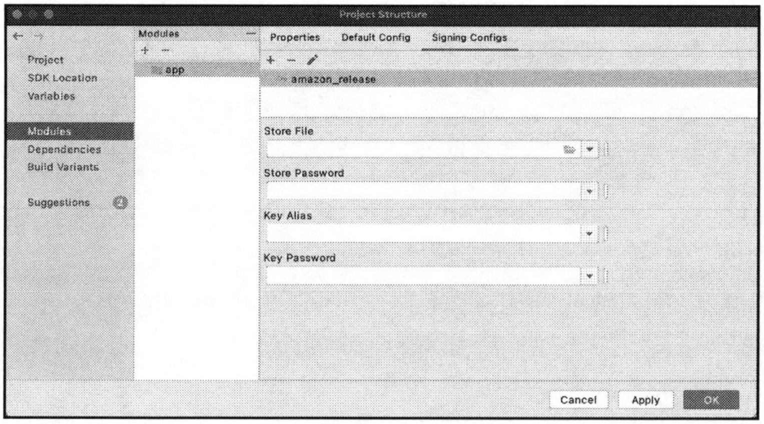

Note: This section assumes you already created the necessary files for signing your app. If you haven't and need a refresher, you can find one in chapter 2.

After you enter the appropriate information, click **Ok** in the first dialog and **Cancel** in the second one. You'll be back in the Gradle file.

Take a close look. Notice Android Studio created a piece of code for you at the top of the file like this:

```
signingConfigs {
  amazon_release {
      storeFile file("myreleasekey.keystore")
      storePassword "password"
      keyAlias "MyReleaseKey"
      keyPassword "password"
  }
}
```

Note: For security reasons, I won't display any of the app's information. You should also be careful of uploading any credentials to public places where they could fall into the wrong hands.

You could also add the code snippet above manually without going through the dialogs. It's a matter of personal preference.

Once you have the credentials, add the signing config to your build variant using the following:

```
amazon {
  ...
  signingConfig signingConfigs.amazon_release
}
```

In the code above, you specify that whenever you build the amazon flavor, Gradle should use the signing config name **amazon_release**.

Build and run. If you added the correct credentials, you can run your app without problems.

Build config fields

Build variants have another powerful property: **buildConfigField**. It's a property that lets you create static constants available at runtime. The values you put there usually flag your app content. Take a look at an example.

Imagine you wanted to only show a menu for the builds that aren't in production. In **build.gradle(Module: PodPlay.app)**, inside **defaultConfig**'s brackets, add the following:

```
buildConfigField "boolean", "IS_PRODUCTION", "false"
```

The code above creates a static variable that lets you distinguish whether the app is a production build. You can also create fields for other data types such as string.

Now switch to the 'Project' view in Android Studio and navigate to **PodPlay ▸ app ▸ build ▸ generated ▸ source ▸ buildConfig ▸ fullAmazon ▸ release ▸ com ▸ raywenderlich ▸ podplay ▸ BuildConfig.java** .

Look at the image below for reference on the folder structure:

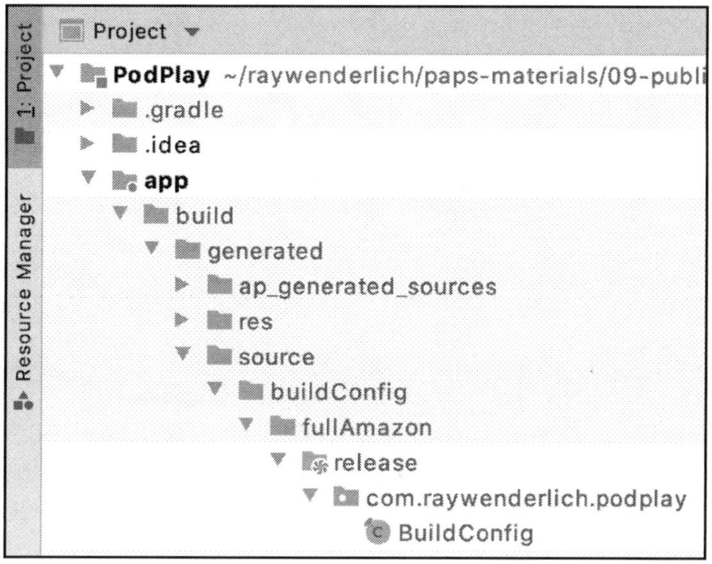

> **Note**: Never change any of the files inside the build folder. You'll notice the code is in a different color, usually yellow, but it can vary depending on the color mode of your computer. Those files regenerate every time you build, so any changes you make here will be overwritten every time you rebuild and are of no use.

Once you open the **BuildConfig** file, you'll see many of the variables you have in your Gradle file. However, if you haven't re-built the project, the added field won't be there. If you haven't done so, perform a Gradle sync and build the project.

After the build, you'll see the variable appear in **BuildConfig.java**, like this:

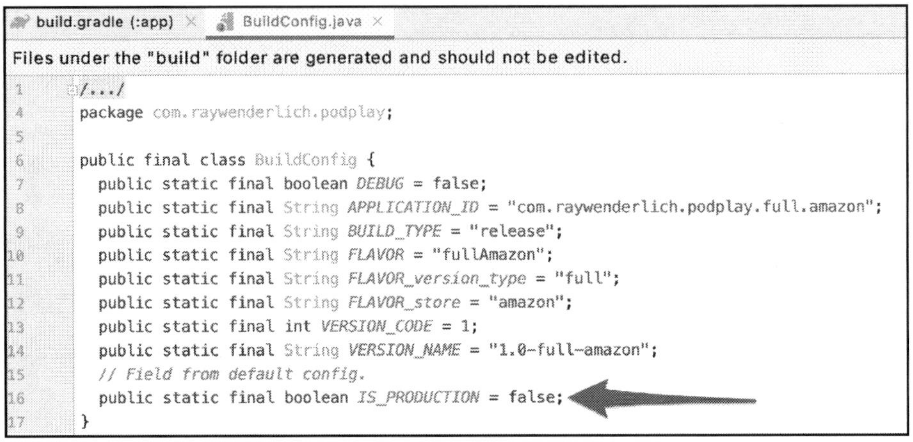

Now you can use that variable, and any others you add, across your app. If you add one of those variables with a different value to a specific flavor, it'll be different for that flavor.

Creating source sets for different variants

Build variants let you customize each variant's assets.

All your files and resources are under **app ▸ src ▸ main ▸ res** by default. You can verify this by opening the 'Project' view in Android Studio and going through **PodPlay**'s folders. Look at the image below for reference:

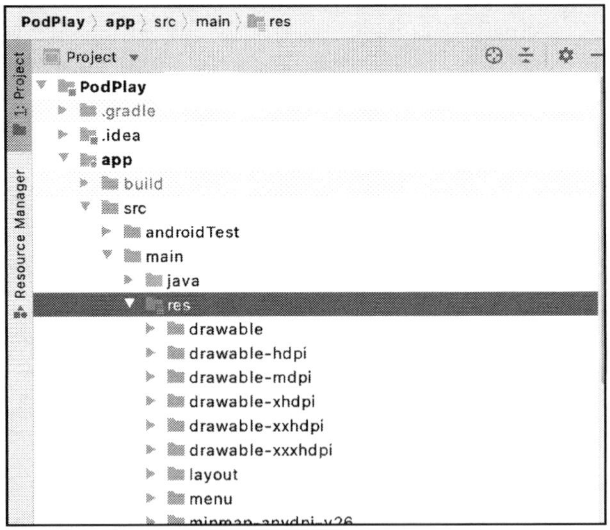

Manually creating folders for specific build variants

To create specific files that are only available for one build variant, you can create another folder at the same level as **main**. Test it out by creating a new folder named 'debug'.

Right-click **src** ▸ **New** ▸ **Directory** and type the name 'debug' in the prompt.

Now your folder structure looks like this:

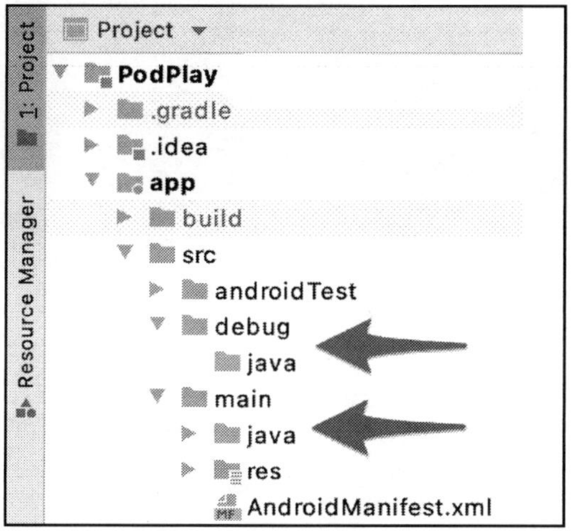

The Gradle plugin can help you when you're unsure which folder structure you need to add files to for a specific flavor. To the right of Android Studio, click **Gradle** and expand **Podplay** ▸ **Tasks** ▸ **android**. Then double click **sourceSets**.

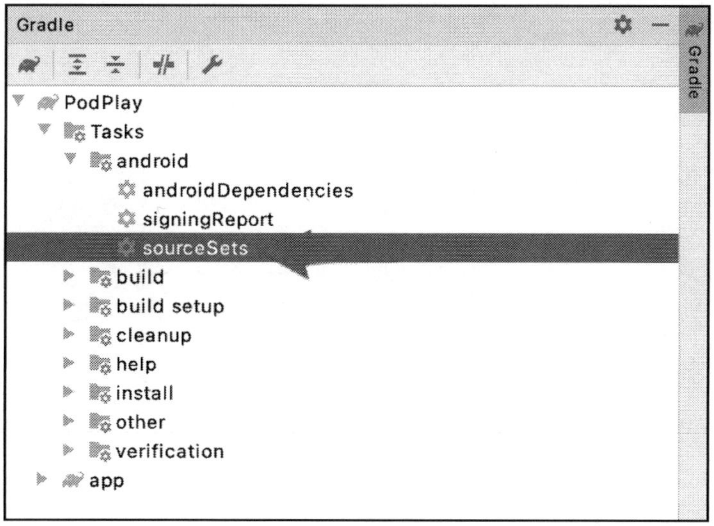

Then a build will run. The results will emerge in the **Run** panel at the bottom of Android Studio. As in the image below, they'll show you all the possible combinations of build Variants you can create specific files for.

Scroll down until you find the **debug** version. Verify the folder you created in the previous step matches the one below:

`Java sources: [app/src/debug/java]</code>.`

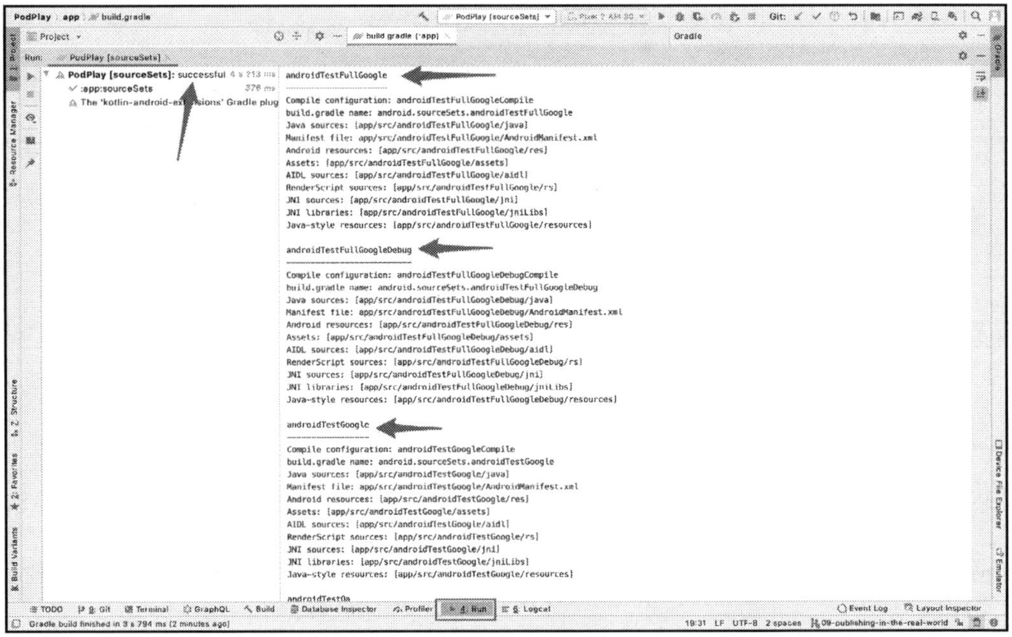

Using Android Studio to create folders for specific build variants

Of course, Android Studio wouldn't leave you hanging without a tool for this process. Right-click **Project**'s **src**. Then select **New ▸ Folder ▸ Java Folder**.

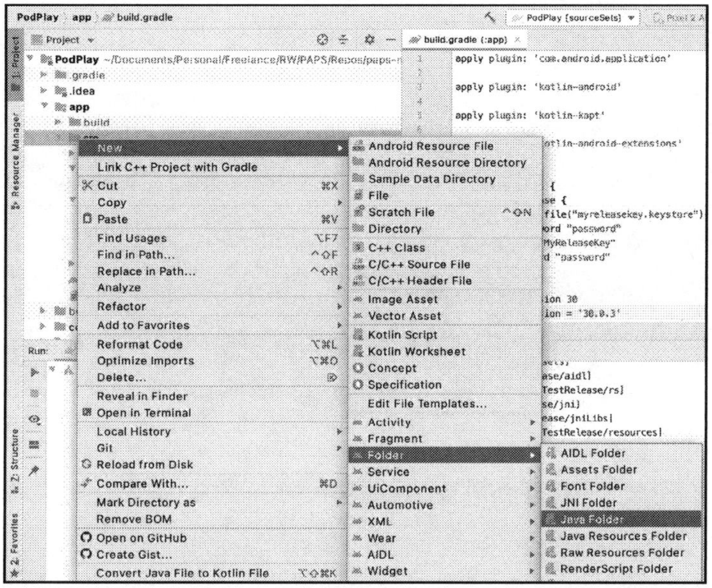

You'll see a pop up asking you to choose which build variant you want to target. Choose **google**, and click **Finish**. You can see an image of the dialog here:

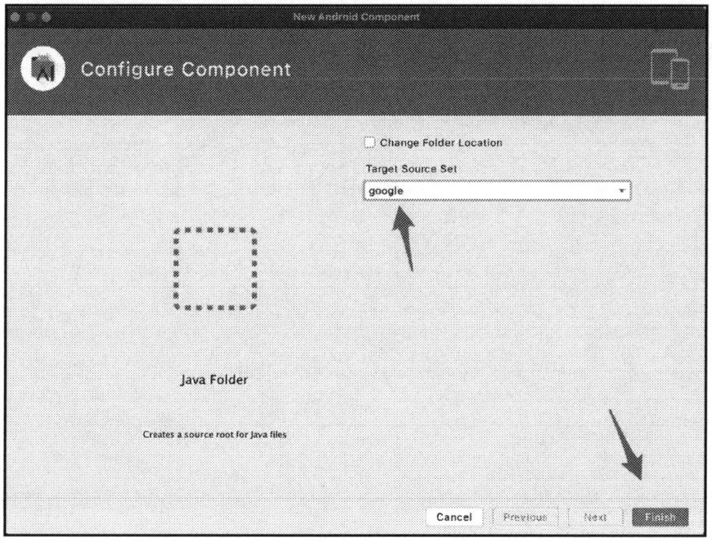

Just like the manual process, you'll see two folders: one labeled **google** and another nested inside it labeled **java**.

Depending on the version you selected on the Build Variants panel, you'll notice the java folder may be blue or gray. Blue means the files inside that Java folder apply to the version you're going to build. Gray means it isn't included. Here are some examples:

1. Select *freeGoogleQa*. You'll see the *main* and *google* Java folders in blue.
2. Now, select *fullAmazonDebug*. The *main* and *debug* Java folders will turn blue.
3. Finally, select *freeGoogleDebug*. The three folders will turn blue.

These colors are useful when you lose track of which files apply to a version and want to debug a feature that isn't applied to one of your build variants.

Creating files to target a build variant with Android Studio

You can also create these folders by creating a file that targets one of your build variants and letting Android Studio handle folder creation.

Say you want to create a fragment that only appears on the free version of your app, for example, a checkout screen. Then right-click **src** and select **New ▸ Fragment ▸ Fragment (Blank)**.

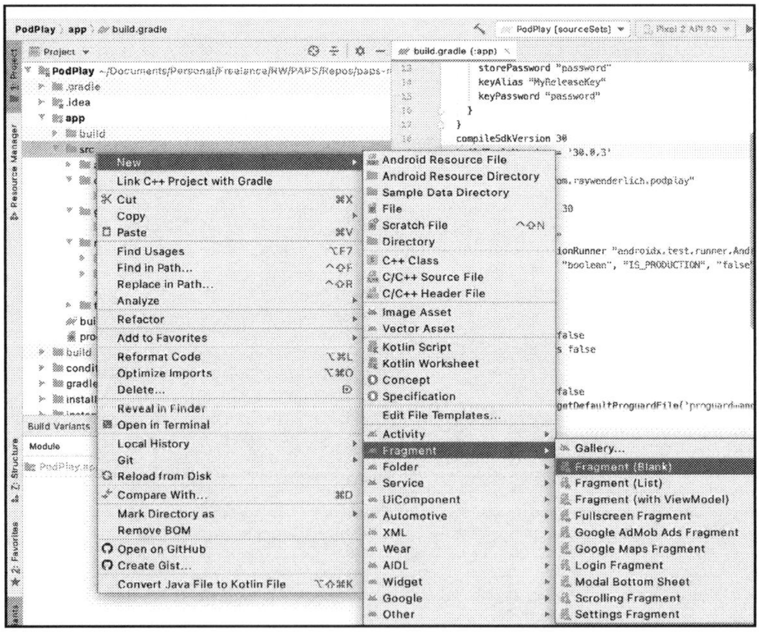

As in the folder creation, a dialog will appear. Leave all the default fields. Modify the **Target Source Set** by selecting the free option from the dropdown.

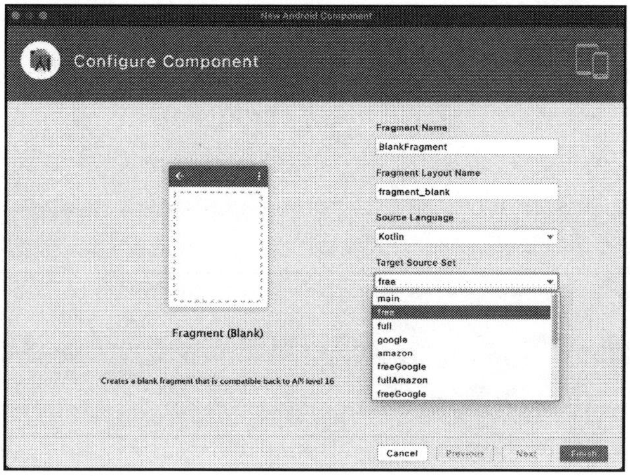

Click **Finish**. Wait for the Gradle sync to finish. You'll see it created various folders for you.

Look at the image below. Notice Android Studio created all the files and folders enclosed in the red rectangle:

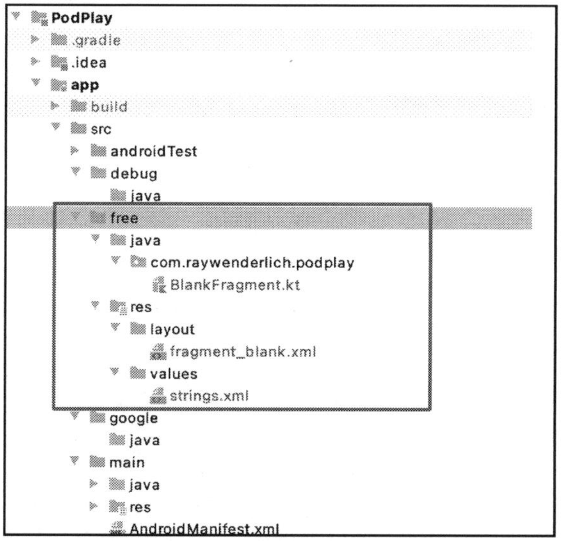

Note: You can apply all the previous procedures to either build variants, build flavors or build types depending on your project's needs.

Key points

- Build variants are the combination of build types and build flavors
- Use build flavors to customize various versions of the same code where you get separate builds that share code but have key differences.
- You need to specify an applicationId or applicationIdSuffix for each flavor you create because two apps can't have the same application id when uploaded to any store.
- You need to assign each flavor to a flavor dimension.
- You create build flavors in your Gradle files, similar to how you create build variants. Each has its purpose.
- Use variant filters to avoid a clutter of build flavors and build types that you won't use.
- You can add any assets or classes to a specific build variant by navigating to Android Studio's Project view, creating a folder with the same name as the targeted variant and placing a Java file inside.

Section III: Automation: Continuous Integration & Delivery

Manually building and releasing your app can quickly become time-consuming and error-prone. Chapter 11 guides you through tools and steps to help automate the process. It's also important to have reliable builds that can build on multiple machines and to constantly integrate code so that releases don't become a big, error-prone, merging event. Chapter 12 shows you some tips and tricks to get CI set up for your project.

Chapter 11: Automation Tools for Your Local Environment

By Evana Margain Puig

In the previous chapter, you learned about **build flavors** and how you can combine them with **build types** to create **build variants**. You also reviewed the process of creating build certificates and signing your app for release.

Those processes are crucial to publishing your app to the **Google Play Store**. The not-so-great news is that repeating them every time can be a tedious and a time-consuming task.

This chapter will teach you all about **automation**. You'll learn how to automate your release process, so you don't waste time and avoid errors in every release you make.

What is automation?

Before diving deeper into the topic of automation, you need to learn what it is. Far from a mobile-only concept, automation refers to any system that reduces human intervention and executes processes by itself.

If you take a closer look at the Android world, automation is everything that happens once the developer finishes coding and the app is ready to go to the next steps, including:

- App Signing
- Testing
- Uploading to the store
- Validating code

Think of any process you repeat over and over every time your team finishes a feature.

Why automate my process?

Teams often choose not to automate processes because they think it's challenging or the tools might make mistakes that humans could avoid. The truth is that automating an Android app is an easy and safe process.

Here are some of the benefits of automating your app:

- Time savings
- Avoiding human errors
- Detecting bugs sooner
- Re-running tests often

Building the app via command line

Before integrating any automation tools, it's important to know how to build your app from the command line. Understanding this process will give you some insight into what automation tools do under the hood.

> **Note**: We are showing you how to run your terminal from Android Studio, but if you are experienced with using the command line you can use your favorite terminal as well.

Gradle Wrapper

The **Gradle Wrapper** is a command-line tool available to all projects you create with **Android Studio**. Usually, the terminal is at the bottom of Android Studio, with other windows like Logcat and Run. Take a look at the image below for reference:

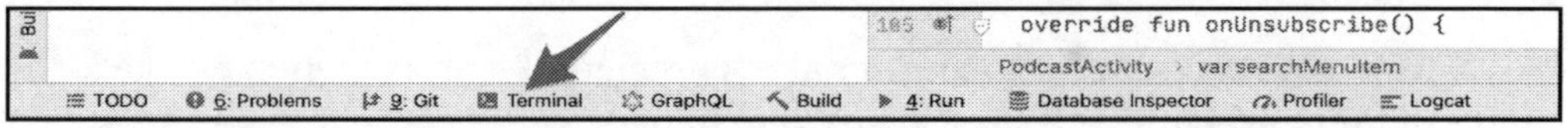

If you can't find it there, you can also navigate in the top bar to **View ▸ Tool Windows ▸ Terminal** or tap **F12** on your keyboard.

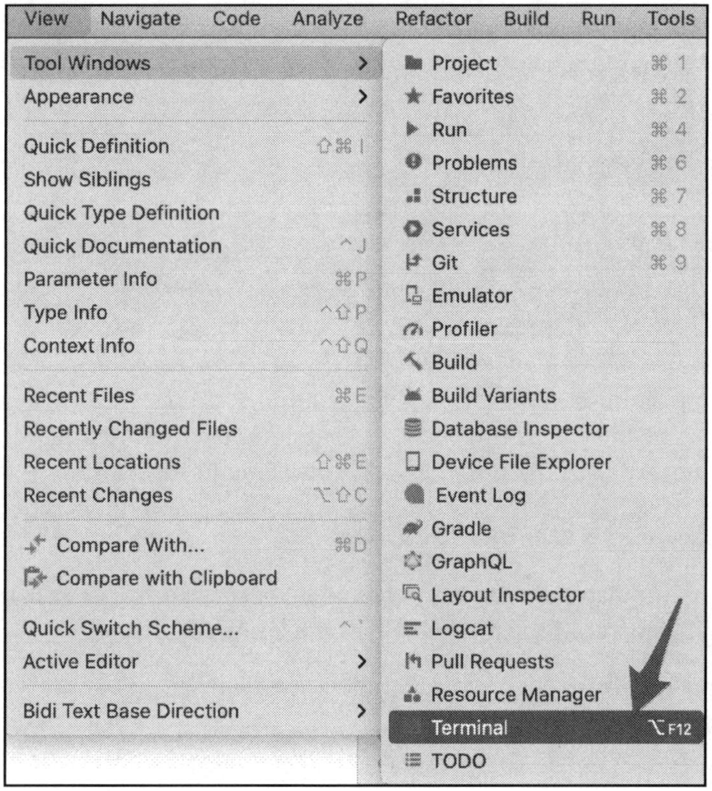

All the commands you'll use in the terminal start with **'gradlew'**, which stands for **Gradle Wrapper**. It varies a little from one OS to another. In Windows, you use:

```
gradlew instruction-to-execute
```

While in Mac or Linux, it's:

```
./gradlew instruction-to-execute
```

For your terminal test, you'll build a debug apk. In the terminal, write:

```
gradlew assembleDebug
```

Press **enter** and then wait for the terminal to complete the process. It may take a couple of minutes, but you'll see the progress in percentage at the top of the terminal. Once it finishes, use your file explorer app to navigate to **PodPlay ▸ app ▸ build ▸ outputs ▸ apk**. You'll see three folders, one for each of the possible debug apps outputs:

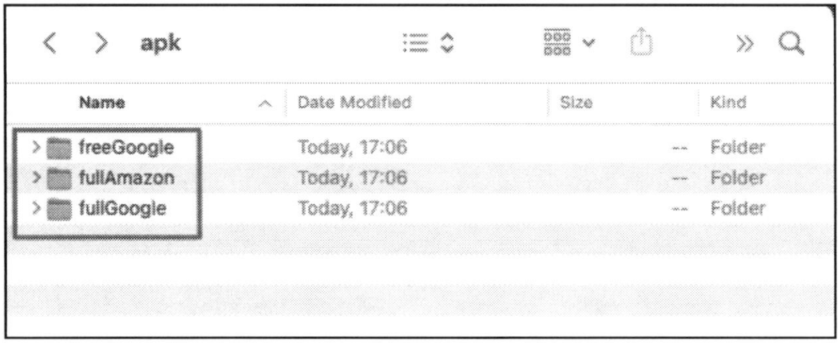

Navigate to any of those folders. Inside the subfolder debug, you'll see an apk. Now say you want to install the *freeGoogleDebug* version in your emulator. Make sure an emulator is running and type the following command in the terminal:

```
gradlew installfreeGoogleDebug
```

The app won't automatically run as it does when you run it from the **Run** button on Android Studio, but you'll see it available in the emulator.

You can do much more in the terminal. In fact, you can do almost everything Android Studio enables through the UI.

For more information on the topic of terminal commands, take a look at the **Where to go from here?** section at the end of the chapter.

Introduction to Fastlane

In this section, you'll learn about **Fastlane**, one of the most popular automation tools out there. Fastlane is an open-source platform aimed at Android and iOS deployment. Although developers use it more on iOS than on Android, it's still the most powerful tool out there.

Some of the most notable features of Fastlane are:

1. Taking automated screenshots for the Play Store.
2. Distribution to beta testers via Firebase App Distribution.
3. Deployment to the Play Store.

Installing Fastlane

Before using Fastlane, you need to download and install it. The installation will vary depending on your OS.

MacOS or Linux

The most common way is to install it in macOS is through homebrew. Open a terminal and type the following command:

```
brew install fastlane
```

Windows

For this OS, there are several options. I'll guide you through the easiest one:

1. Navigate to rubyinstaller.org and download an installer for Ruby 2.5 or newer.
2. Once you install it, confirm which Ruby version you have by running the following in a terminal:

```
$ ruby --version
```

Your output will be something like: `ruby 2.7.2p137 (2020-10-01 revision 5445e04352) [x86_64-darwin19]`

3. Install **Bundler** by running the following command in the terminal:

```
gem install bundler
```

4. In the root directory of your Android project, create a file named **Gemfile**. Add the following lines to it:

```
source "https://rubygems.org"

gem "fastlane"
```

5. Save the file and go back to your terminal. Then run:

```
bundle update
```

6. Add ./Gemfile and ./Gemfile.lock to your version control repository if you're using it.

> **Note**: This process may vary a lot depending on your OS. If you have any problems, refer to the Fastlane Documentation at https://docs.fastlane.tools/getting-started/android/setup/ for a more comprehensive explanation of the install process.

Creating a Fastfile

By now, hopefully, you've installed **Fastlane** without further trouble.

In your terminal, navigate to the root of the **PodPlay** project and run:

```
fastlane init
```

The terminal will display a lot of text and stop at certain points to ask you for information. Add the information as shown below:

1. The package name: **com.raywenderlich.podplay**.
2. A JSON secret file: Leave empty. Press enter.
3. Download existing metadata and setup metadata management: **y**, indicating you do want to download that information. The metadata is the information you enter when uploading the app, such as the app name, version code and description. You can manually manage those, but as the purpose of this chapter is automation, you want Fastlane to do it for you.

Here are two screenshots of the terminal output in case you need to reference any of the information:

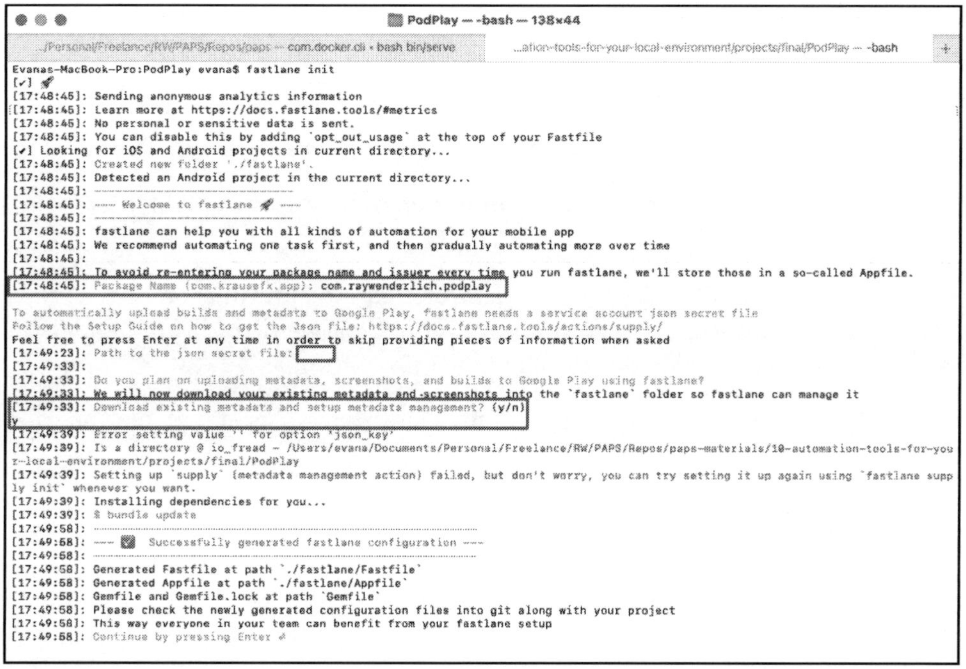

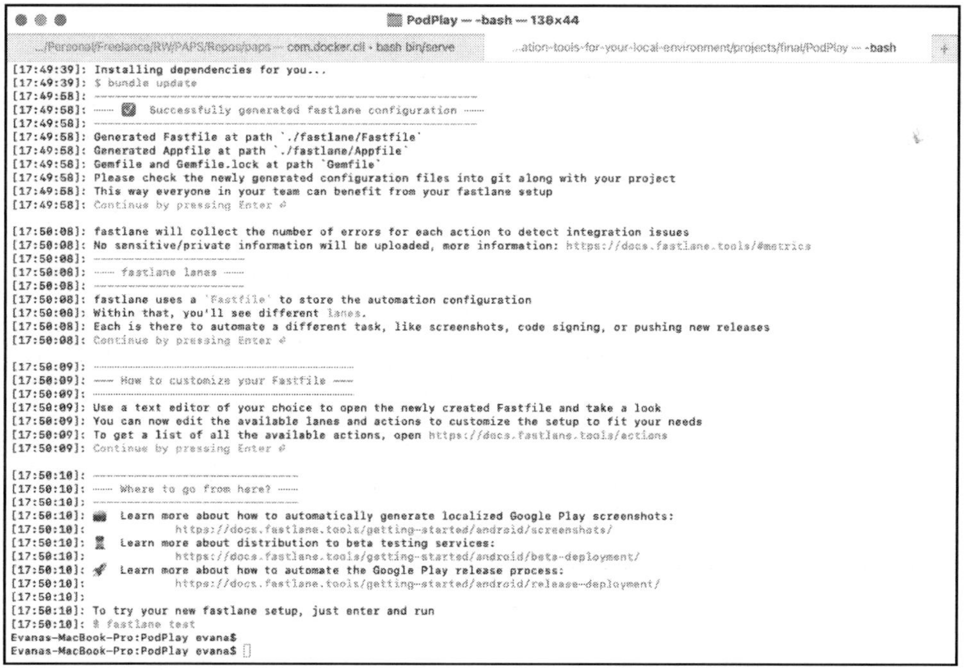

Once this finishes, in your file system, navigate to the root of the **PodPlay** project. You'll see this command created a *fastlane* folder. If you navigate inside that folder, you'll notice two files: **Appfile** and **Fastfile**.

Open **Appfile** from the project view of Android Studio. You'll see it has two lines pre-filled with the information you added in the terminal above.

1. json_key_file: Contains two open quotes because you just pressed enter to skip it.
2. package_name: **com.raywenderlich.podplay**, the same as you added in the terminal.

Now open **Fastfile**. You'll notice it's a longer file than the previous one. This file contains the **automation** instructions. It may look a bit weird, but you'll understand what each line is trying to do if you follow the information.

- Lines 1-14: These are comments providing you with sources of information to edit the file.
- Lines 16 and 18: Both of these lines specify that your platform is Android and signal the start of the *automation* instructions.

After that, you'll see three blocks of instructions which start with **desc**, standing for description, and end with **end**. You'll learn about each of these commands, using an example, in the next section.

Running tests

As mentioned throughout the book, tests are a fundamental part of delivering robust and successful apps. Running tests is an essential part of an automation pipeline.

The first block, shown in the Fastfile, runs tests. Take a look at the image below to see which block it is.

```
19    desc "Runs all the tests"
20    lane :test do
21      gradle(task: "test")
22    end
```

Take a closer look at each line of code:

- 19: **desc** explains that this lane runs all the tests in the app and is purely for documentation.
- 20: Now pay attention to the second line, named **lane**. The name of this lane is **test** followed by a keyword **do**.

- 21: Then the body, which has only one line, instructs to run a gradle task named **test**, which of course runs the app tests. The body can contain more than one instruction.
- 22: The end keyword signals the end of the lane's instructions.

Executing a lane

In the command line where you installed Fastlane, type:

```
bundle exec fastlane test
```

The terminal will now show instructions related to testing your app, which will take up to a couple of minutes. Be aware that this is dependent on your app size. In the end, you'll get a summary of the tests.

In the above case, the terminal executed tests successfully.

Using Screengrab

Another great feature of Fastlane is automatically taking screenshots using a tool named **Screengrab**. This is useful both for UI tests and for the screenshots required for the store listing.

Setting up Screengrab

Screengrab is a tool that doesn't come bundled in the base Fastlane package, so you need to install it to use it.

In the same terminal where you ran your tests, run the following command to install Screengrab:

```
sudo gem install screengrab
```

It may take a while to run. Be patient because, in the long run, your automation pipeline will make your life way easier.

Unlike previous steps in this chapter, you need to add a line of code to your Android Studio project to take the screenshots. Go to the app level **build.gradle**. Locate a TODO for adding the screengrab dependency and replace it with:

```
androidTestImplementation "tools.fastlane:screengrab:2.0.0"
androidTestImplementation 'com.jraska:falcon:2.2.0'
```

Make a gradle sync as the IDE requests in the banner at the top. Then wait for the project to integrate screengrab.

Now navigate to the debug version of **AndroidManifest.xml**. Both manifests are the same, but you only want to enable permissions for screengrab on the debug version. Otherwise, someone may misuse the permissions in your production app.

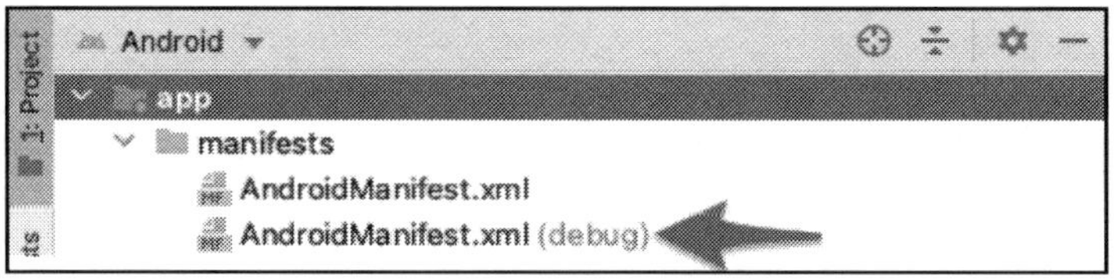

At the bottom of the manifest file, you'll find a TODO showing you where to put the following permissions:

```
<!-- Allows unlocking your device and activating its screen so
UI tests can succeed -->
```

```
<uses-permission
android:name="android.permission.DISABLE_KEYGUARD"/>

<!-- Allows for storing and retrieving screenshots -->
<uses-permission
android:name="android.permission.WRITE_EXTERNAL_STORAGE" />
<uses-permission
android:name="android.permission.READ_EXTERNAL_STORAGE" />

<!-- Allows changing locales -->
<uses-permission
android:name="android.permission.CHANGE_CONFIGURATION"
  tools:ignore="ProtectedPermissions"/>
```

You may notice the bottom permission has a **tools:ignore** directive. This is because you're sure it's safe since you're only using it in a debug version of your app. You may need to add the tools to your top `manifest` tag like this:

```
<manifest
  ...
  xmlns:tools="http://schemas.android.com/tools"
  ...>
```

Using Screengrab for screenshot tests

Now that you have everything ready for Screengrab to work, you'll create screenshot tests. If you're new to the term, screenshot test refers to a test when the testing tools take screenshots and then compares them with older ones to ensure no unintended UI change occured.

Create a new Kotlin file in: **PodPlay ▸ app ▸ java ▸ com.raywenderlich.podplay (androidTest)** and name it **AutomatedUITests**.

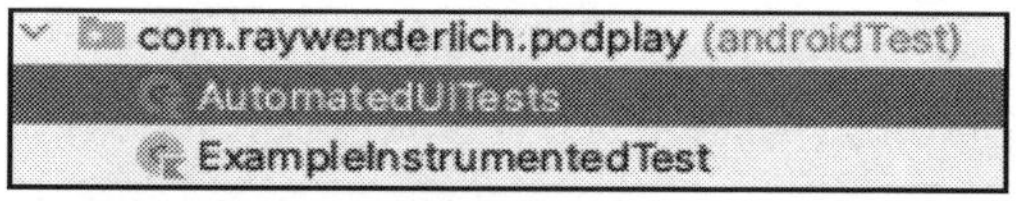

Replace the boilerplate code with:

```
package com.raywenderlich.podplay

// 1
import androidx.test.core.app.ActivityScenario
import androidx.test.ext.junit.runners.AndroidJUnit4
import com.raywenderlich.podplay.ui.PodcastActivity
import org.junit.Before
import org.junit.Test
import org.junit.runner.RunWith
```

```
import tools.fastlane.screengrab.Screengrab
import tools.fastlane.screengrab.UiAutomatorScreenshotStrategy

// 2
@RunWith(AndroidJUnit4::class)
class AutomatedUITests {
  // 3
  @Before
  fun setUp() {
    ActivityScenario.launch(PodcastActivity::class.java)

Screengrab.setDefaultScreenshotStrategy(UiAutomatorScreenshotStr
ategy())
  }
  // 4
  @Test
  fun captureScreen() {
    Thread.sleep(500)
    Screengrab.screenshot("podcast_activity")
  }
}
```

Inspect the code above to see what it's doing in each part:

1. Imports needed for the code to work.
2. You add this annotation to tell the compiler this is a JUnit test class.
3. A function that executes before the test. First, you tell it which Activity to launch and then which strategy to use.
4. Finally, the test itself. You add a sleep of 500 milliseconds to wait for the screen to launch and then take the screenshot. The screenshot will save with the name **podcast_activity**.

That's about it for the test.

Now initialize Screengrab in Fastlane. Go to your terminal and run:

```
bundle exec fastlane screengrab init
```

When this finishes running, you'll notice a new file named **Screengrabfile** in the fastlane folder.

As you did with the other files, open this one with a text editor. Replace the contents with:

```
# 1
android_home('$PATH')
```

```
# 2
use_adb_root(true)

# 3
app_package_name('com.raywenderlich.podplay')

# 4
app_apk_path('app/build/outputs/apk/freeGoogle/debug/app-free-
google-debug.apk')
tests_apk_path('app/build/outputs/apk/androidTest/freeGoogle/
debug/app-free-google-debug-androidTest.apk')

# 5
locales(['en-US'])

# 6
clear_previous_screenshots(true)
```

In the code above, you:

1. Use the environment variable `PATH` to set the directory for the Android SDK.
2. Grant root privilege to ADB. This lets Screengrab store screenshots on the Android device.
3. Set the app's package name.
4. Set the directories to find the app APK and the instrumentation test APK.
5. Set the locale to **en-US**. This function takes an array of locales you can use to take screenshots of the app in different locations.
6. Clear screenshots from previous executions of Screengrab.

Now you want Fastlane to run this test automatically. So, add a new block of code containing a lane to the fastfile.

Open your Fastfile located in **Podplay ▸ Fastlane**. Then, below the first test lane, create another lane with:

```
desc "Screen Grab tests"
lane :screenshot_main_screen do
  gradle(task: "clean assembleDebug assembleAndroidTest")
  screengrab
end
```

Save your **Fastfile** and close it. Launch an emulator since the tests require a virtual device to use root privileges.

Also, make sure you have environment variables for Android tools set up correctly. You generally set them when installing Android Studio, but just in case, you can run the following in the terminal.

```
# Path to Android SDK
export ANDROID_HOME=$HOME/Library/Android/sdk

# Path to Android platform tools (adb, fastboot, etc)
export ANDROID_PLATFORM_TOOLS="$ANDROID_HOME/platform-tools"

# Path to Android tools (aapt, apksigner, zipalign, etc)
export ANDROID_TOOLS="$ANDROID_HOME/build-tools/29.0.3/"

# Add all to the path
export PATH="$PATH:$ANDROID_PLATFORM_TOOLS:$ANDROID_TOOLS"
```

Test the setup with:

```
bundle exec fastlane screenshot_main_screen
```

After the test executes, the screenshots appear in an HTML file and most likely open in your browser as shown below:

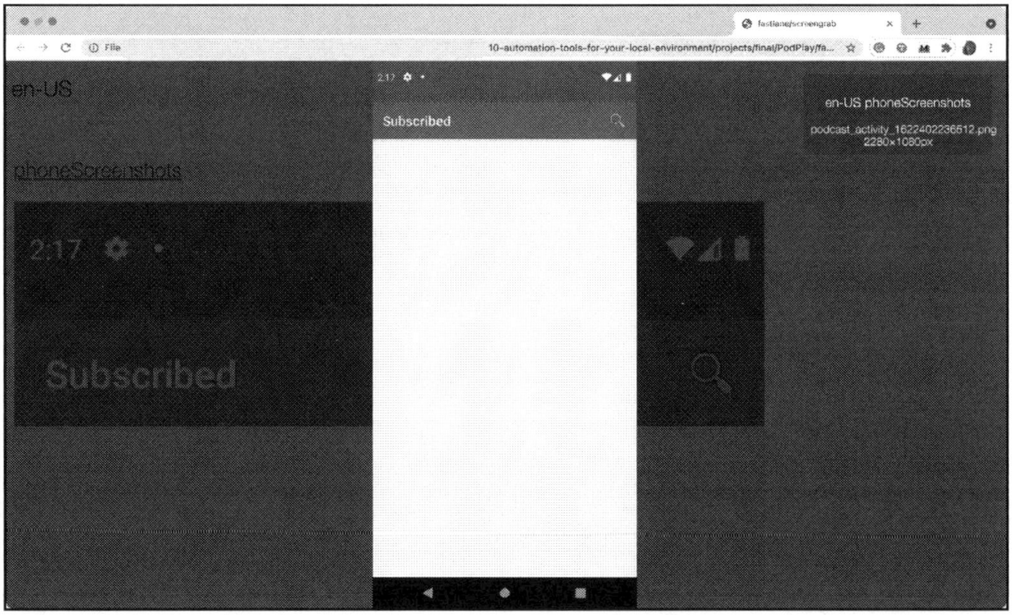

Congratulations! You've created screenshots for PodPlay with Screengrab and created a lane to execute them in one step! This is the beginning of your automation journey.

Deploying beta builds

Fastlane isn't only about testing and building your app. It also lets you upload your app to the store. Once you have this setup, you can release as many versions of your app as you want with minimal intervention.

Once you finish an app release, the first thing you usually want to do is release it as a "Beta". This is a common practice, and there are lots of users willing to participate in beta testing.

Fastlane supports many services that upload Beta versions of Android apps. But in this chapter, you'll focus on uploading to Firebase. For an extended list of other providers, check the Fastlane documentation at https://docs.fastlane.tools/actions/#beta on beta testing actions.

Firebase App Distribution

You may have noticed when you opened your **Fastfile**, the provided code had an action to upload to **Crashlytics**. Android has replaced that tool with **Firebase App Distribution**.

Go to the Firebase Console at https://console.firebase.google.com/. It may ask you for credentials to your Google Account. Provide them, and you'll log into the console. Click the first tile with the text **Add project**.

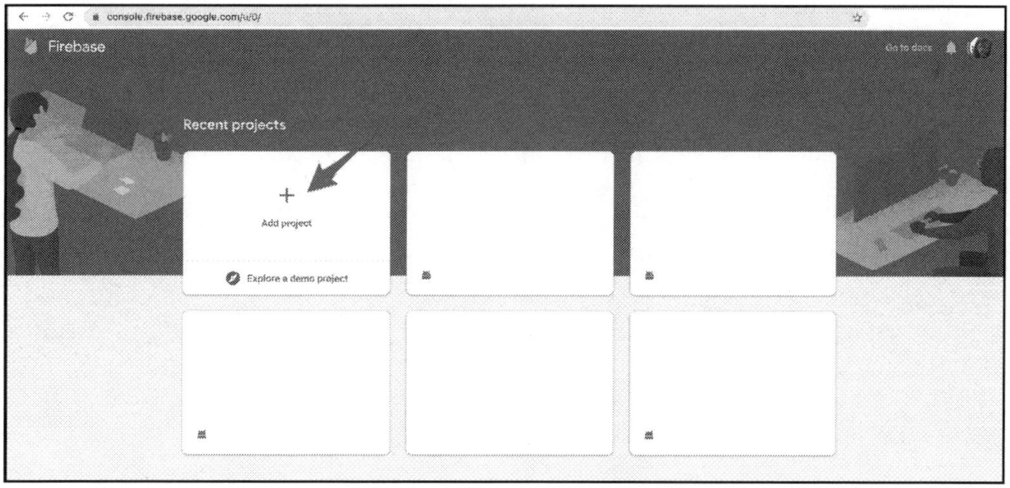

Then add the name of the project **PodPlay** and click **Continue**, like in the image below:

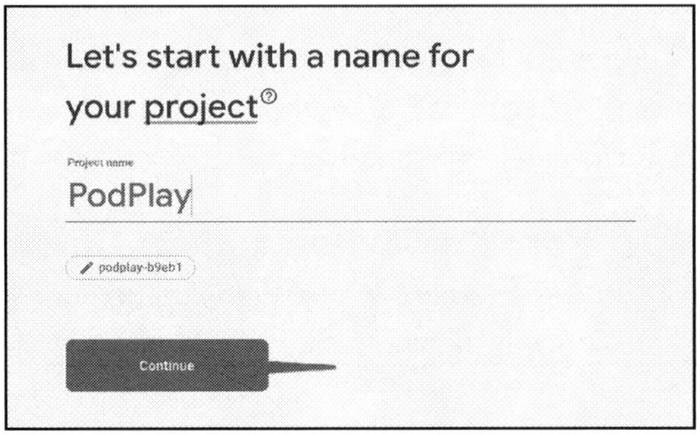

Don't enable Google Analytics since you won't need it for this project. Click **Create Project**. Wait until it finishes, and then click **Continue** again.

Now you'll find yourself in the project dashboard.

Installing Firebase CLI

After creating the project in the Firebase Console, you'll need to install **Firebase CLI** in your local environment. The instructions vary depending on your computer's OS. You can read them at the Firebase CLI docs https://firebase.google.com/docs/cli. There are instructions that work for both cases. If you are on a MacOS of Linux machine you can install them in your project base path by runnning:

```
curl -sL https://firebase.tools | bash
```

The code above downloads a script from the given URL and runs it using `bash`.

After the installation is complete, log in to the Firebase console through your terminal by entering:

```
firebase login
```

It'll open a browser window asking you to select your google account and then show you a success message like in the image below.

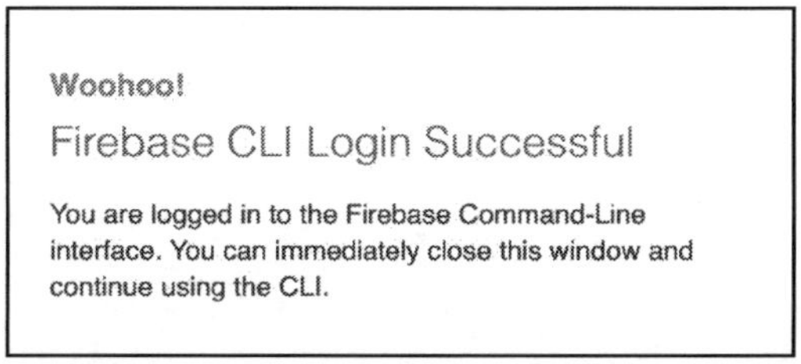

Installing the Fastlane plugin for Firebase Distribution

With that configured, you're ready to install the Firebase Distribution plugin in Fastlane. Go back to your terminal and run:

```
bundle exec fastlane add_plugin firebase_app_distribution
```

The code above adds the plugin named **firebase_app_distribution** to Fastlane.

It'll take a while to run and then ask you a question regarding modifying the GemFile. Type **y** and press **Enter** to continue.

Once you get a success message, go back to the Firebase console. Select **PodPlay**. On the main screen, select the little Android logo shown in the image below.

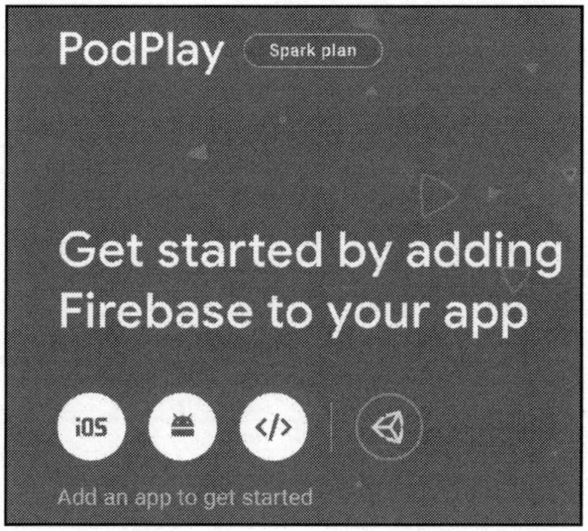

On the next screen, add **PodPlay**'s package by entering **"com.raywenderlich.podplay"** and **PodPlay** as the name. Click **Register App**.

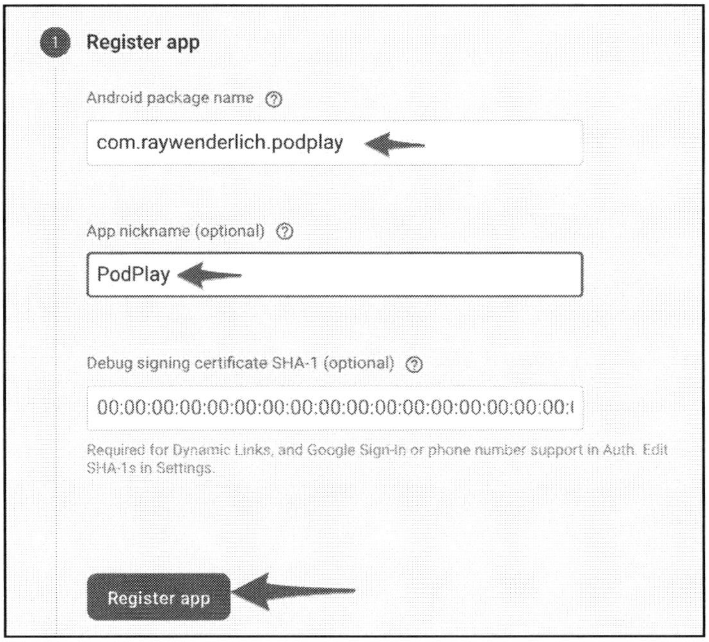

After a couple of seconds, the screen will show step two and give you instructions to add a JSON file to the project in Android Studio. Follow those instructions and put the file in the project as shown in the image below:

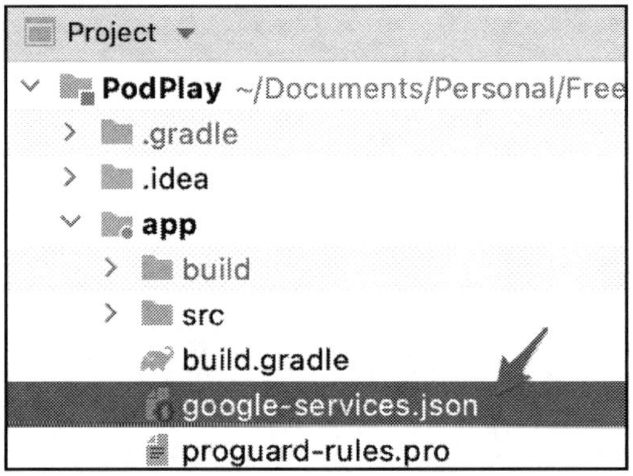

Click **Next** to go to step three in the Firebase console, and you'll see instructions to add the Firebase SDK to the project. Follow the steps there and run Gradle sync. Ensure the app is still working and unchanged after those steps.

Click **Continue to console**. Then you'll land on the project page in the Firebase Console. On the menu to the left, click the settings button at the top and then choose **Project Settings**. Scroll to the bottom, and you'll see an App ID. Save it somewhere handy because you'll need it soon.

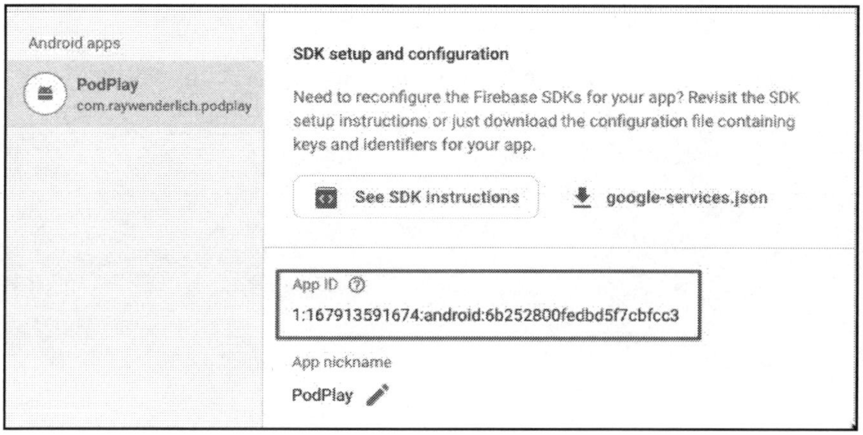

Distributing your beta build

In the menu at the left of the Firebase console, you'll see an option named **App Distribution**. Click it. You'll see the title App Distribution and a small dropdown with the name of the app you just added in the top banner.

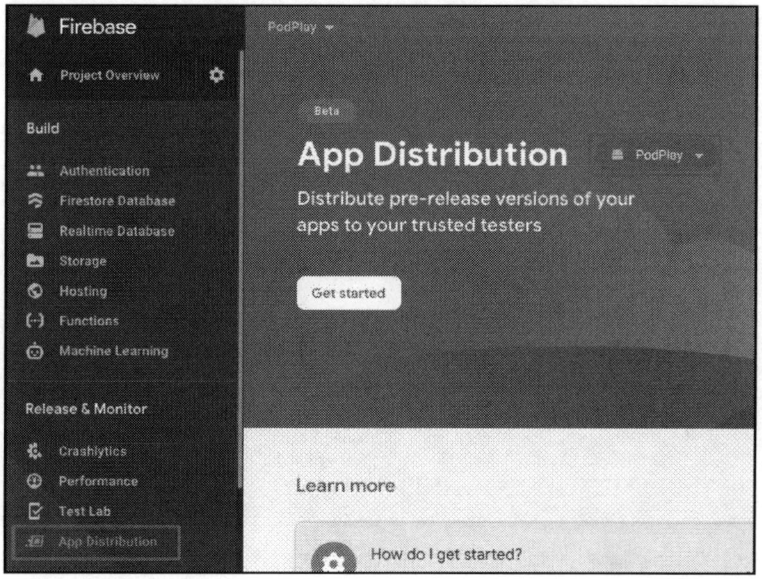

Click **Get Started**, and you'll see where your builds will appear after you upload them through Fastlane.

Before configuring Fastlane, you need to create a tester group that will receive the beta builds. There are three tabs on the screen. Currently, you're in the one called **Releases**. Open **Testers & Groups** and click **+ Add group**.

Add the group name **PodPlay Beta Testers** and click **Save**. Look at the image below for guidance.

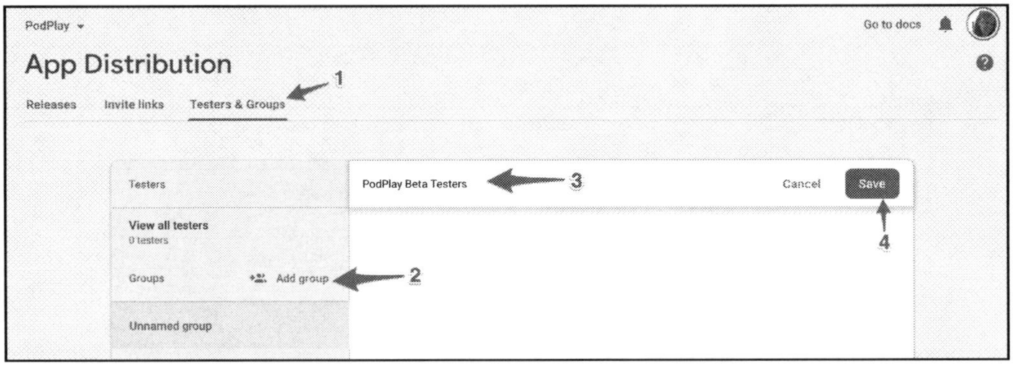

Then add your email to the testers group so you can verify betas are being sent.

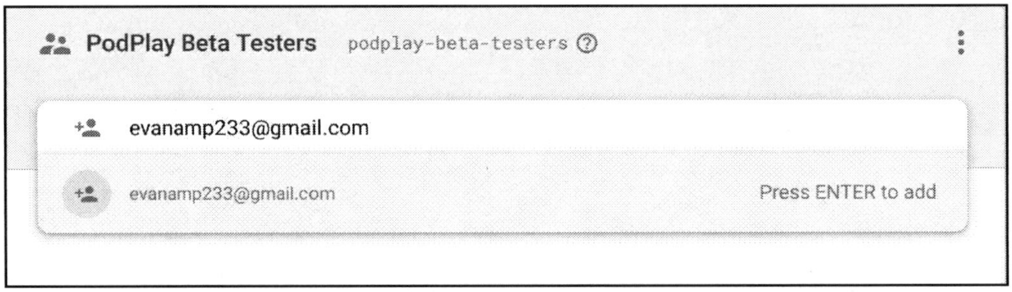

Go back to the **PodPlay** project in Android Studio and open **Fastfile** by opening the project view of the file explorer and navigating to **PodPlay ▸ fastlane**.

Previously in this chapter, you explored this file and noticed a lane for beta builds. Google originally intended it for Crashlytics but later deprecated it and replaced it with Firebase Distribution. So, change that lane in lines 30-37 of the Fastfile with:

```
desc "Submit a new Beta Build to Firebase App Distribution"
lane :beta do
  gradle(task: "clean assembleFreeGoogleDebug")

  firebase_app_distribution(
      app: "1:167913591674:android:6b252800fedbd5f7cbfcc3",
```

```
        groups: "podplay-beta-testers",
        release_notes: "First Podplay Beta!"
    )
end
```

In the code above, you generate a build using the `assembleFreeGoogleDebug` Gradle task and upload the same build with the release notes specified in `release_notes`.

Replace the app id with the one you copied previously from the console. Now execute this lane as you did with the others by running the following command in the terminal:

```
bundle exec fastlane beta
```

The console will output a lot of text. To verify that you successfully generated and uploaded your build, look at the following part:

```
[18:04:18]: Authenticated successfully.
[18:04:19]: Uploading the APK.
[18:04:28]: Uploaded the APK.
[18:04:29]: Posted release notes.
[18:04:29]: Added testers/groups.
[18:04:29]: App Distribution upload finished successfully.

+------+------------------------+-------------+
|               fastlane summary              |
+------+------------------------+-------------+
| Step | Action                 | Time (in s) |
+------+------------------------+-------------+
| 1    | default_platform       | 0           |
| 2    | clean                  | 17          |
|      | assembleFreeGoogleDeb  |             |
|      | ug                     |             |
| 3    | firebase_app_distribu  | 12          |
|      | tion                   |             |
+------+------------------------+-------------+

[18:04:29]: fastlane.tools finished successfully
```

Go back to the Firebase console, and you'll see the apk appears there as in the image below:

That's all you need to know about distributing betas. At this point, anyone added to the selected group will get an email and can download and test your app.

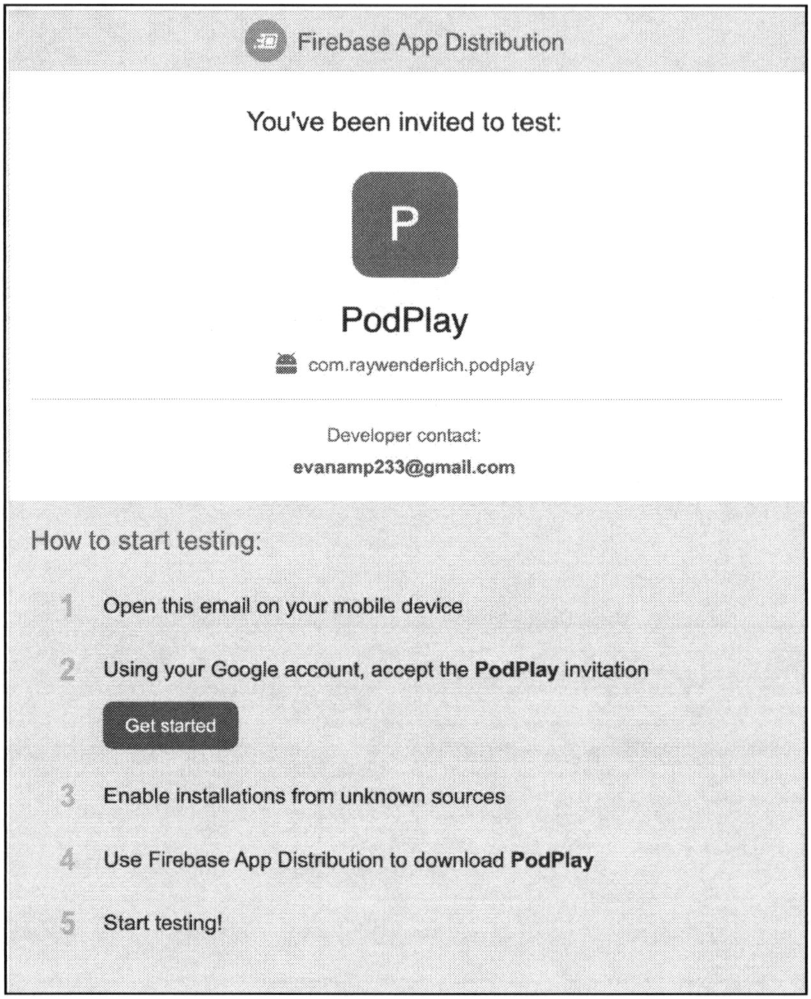

Deploying to production

Once you're sure your app is mostly bug-free and has been beta-tested enough, you'll want to get your app into production so everyone can enjoy it. To do this, once again, you'll get help from Fastlane.

Before anything else, you'll need an API key, which comes from a service account. A service account is like an identifier for your app to communicate with Google Cloud Services.

> **Note**: If you haven't done so already, you may need to create a developer account in the Google Play Console and pay the required $25 fee.

Go to the Google Play Console at https://play.google.com/console. In the left menu, scroll to the bottom. Under **Setup**, click **API Access**. You may see a screen prompting you to select a Google Cloud Project or create a new one. Select the option to create a new project and click the button at the bottom to continue. Once you see the screen below click **Create new service account**.

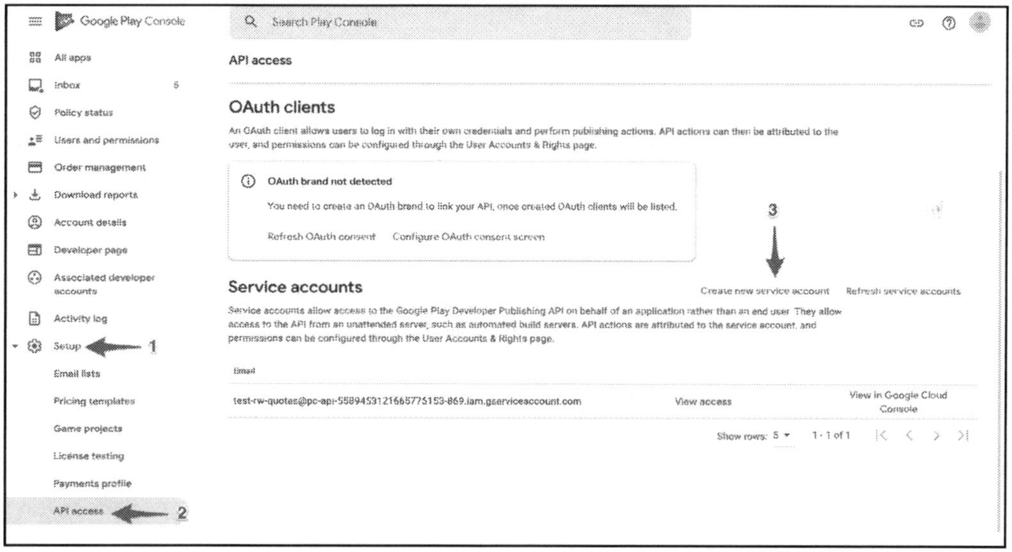

Creating a service account

Google Cloud Platform now manages a service account. This process will take place in that admin console. The **Google Play Console** will prompt you to go to **Google Cloud** and create the **Service Account**. Click the hyperlink to access the **Google Cloud Platform**, and your screen will look like the image below. Click **+ Create Service Account** at the top.

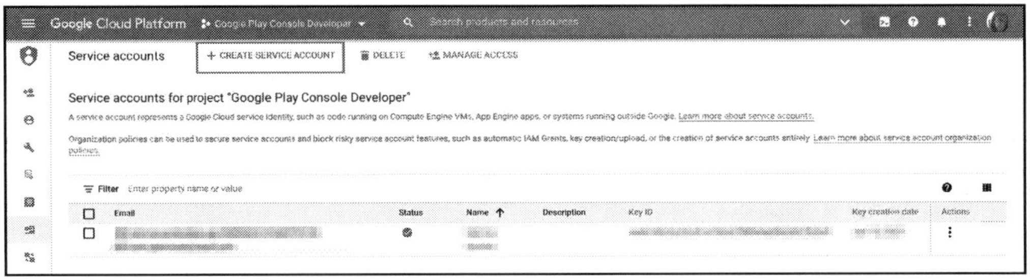

On the form that appears, add only the **Service account name** by writing **fastlane-podplay** and clicking **Create and continue**. Then in the role, search for **Service account** and **Service account user**.

Click **Continue**. Leave the next section empty and click **Done**.

At this point, you've created a Service account but still need the API Key. Notice there's a Key ID column, and the newly created service account has no keys. To the right of that row, you'll see a menu called *Actions* with three vertical dots that you can click for more options. Click **Manage Keys** from the menu shown.

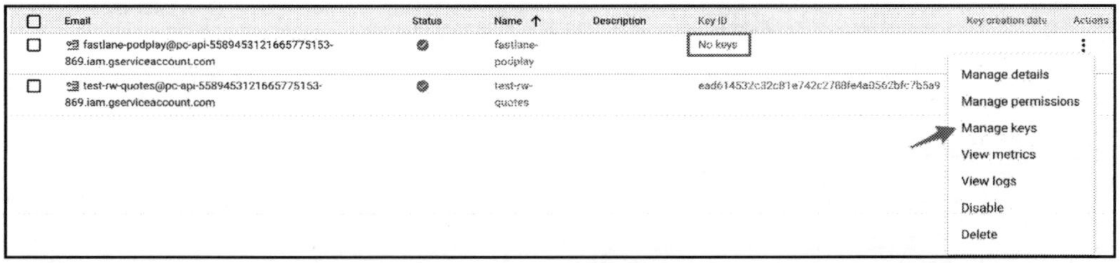

This redirects you to the keys screen, where you'll add your key. Click **ADD KEY**. Then select **Create New Key**. In the options, select **JSON** and click **Create**. Then, it'll prompt you to download the file to your computer.

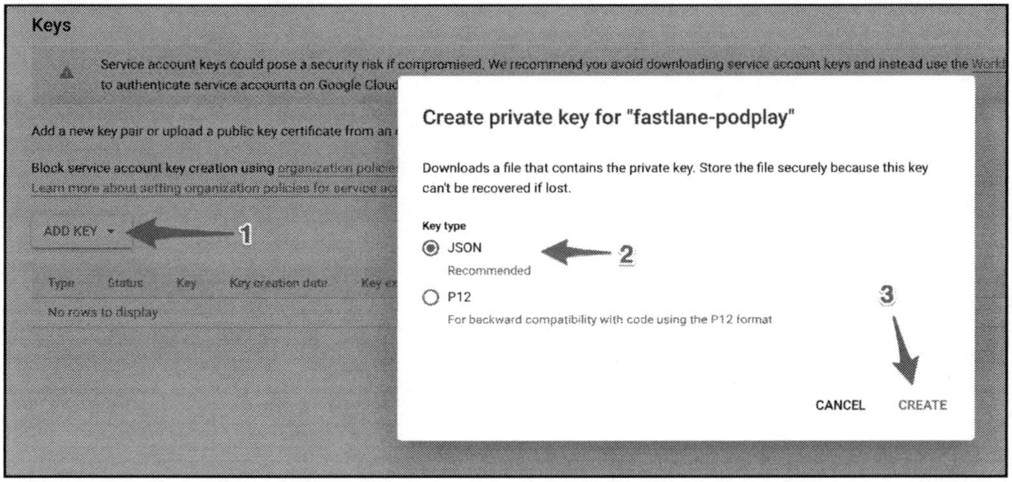

Note: Please create your own keys. The one in the example project isn't valid because of Google's security policies.

Adding your service account to the Google Play Console

Go back to the **Google Play Console**, where the last thing you saw was the popup requiring the service account. Click **Refresh service accounts** as shown below.

Once you see your service account in the list, click **Grant Access**. Be careful when granting these kinds of permissions, as someone with unauthorized access who may get control of a service account could make harmful changes to your app. For testing, grant the **Admin** permission but remember you won't do that in a production app.

Then click **Invite user** and confirm by clicking **Send invite** in the alert shown to finish the process.

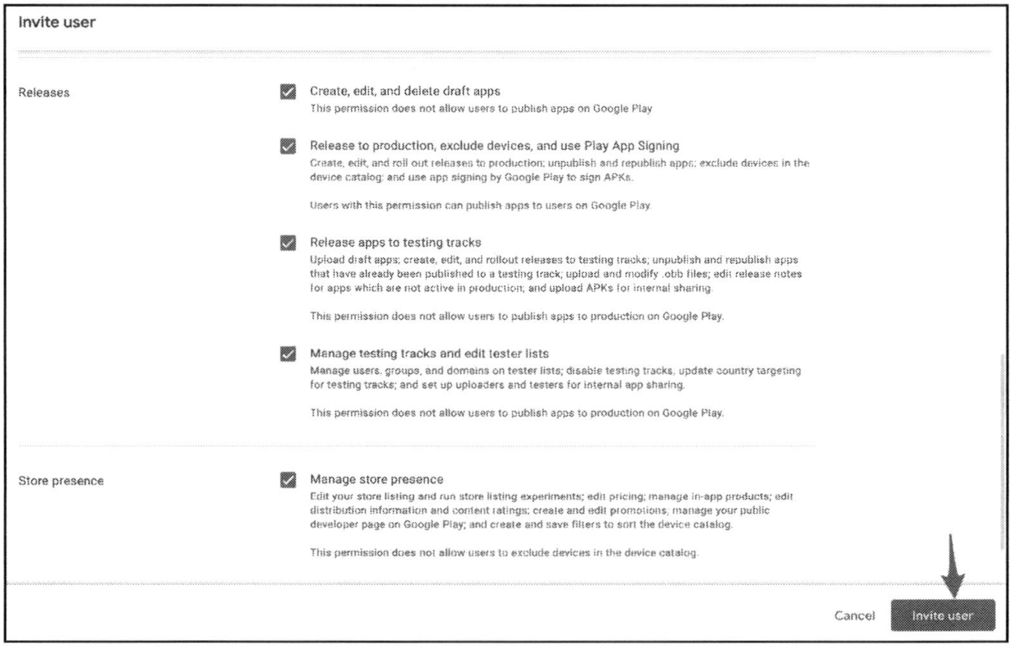

Good job! With that set, Fastlane can now release the project for you.

Uploading your app to the Play Console

Finally, with all those validations, you can upload to the store. There are a few more points to take into consideration. Take a moment to go through each of them.

Which Build Variant do you want to upload to the store?

If you've followed the book, you may know that at this point, you have several **Build Variants**, and each generates a separate APK. To tell Fastlane which one you want to upload, navigate to your fastfile in the Project View of Android Studio under **Podplay ▸ fastlane**. In the last lane, change the code between do and end to:

```
gradle(task: "clean assembleFreeGoogleRelease")
upload_to_play_store(release_status: 'draft')
```

With the lines above, you tell Fastlane the app you want to upload is the 'Free Google Release' build variant. You also indicate this is a **draft** app, so it doesn't go live right away.

Validating the JSON key with Fastlane

As with many other services, you need to authenticate your Fastlane setup with the **Google Play Console**. You already generated the key in the previous step. All you need to do now is authenticate with it by running the following command at the root of your project through the terminal:

```
bundle exec fastlane run validate_play_store_json_key json_key:/
path_where_you_downloaded_the_json_key
```

If you followed the steps in the previous section correctly, you'll see a success message in the terminal, as follows:

Then you need to add the JSON file path to your project and Appfile. Rename the file you downloaded to **podplay-playstore-key.json** and copy it to the root of the Android project structure. Then open the Appfile, located in the project view of the Android Studio PodPlay project, under **Podplay ▸ fastlane**. Add the following line:

```
json_key_file("./podplay-playstore-key.json")
```

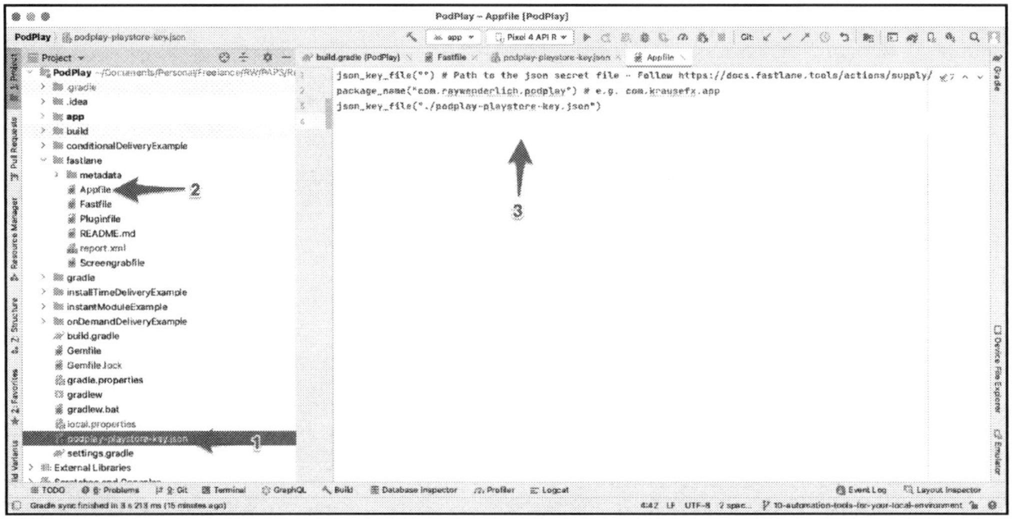

The Application ID has to be unique

At this point, if you tried to upload the app with the release lane in Fastlane by running `bundle exec fastlane deploy`, you would get an error saying you don't have permissions. That's because in the **Google Play Store** every app has to have a unique identifier.

The **Application ID** located in the app-level build.gradle file is currently defined as `com.raywenderlich.podplay`. Since there's already an app with that same app id in the **Google Play Store**, you get a permission error. To fix this, change that identifier to something unique.

In my case, I changed it to `com.raywenderlich.podplay.evana`. So, change it in the second line of the **Appfile** and the app level **build.gradle**, by changing the `applicationId`.

Having the app listed in the Play Store

Before you can upload your app, you need to have it listed in the Play Store. That topic is too long to cover in this chapter. If you still haven't done that, go back to Chapter 2 and look at the **Creating your first app** section.

In summary, go to the Google Play Console at https://play.google.com/console and click the top right button, **Create app**, and fill in the information with the requested data like in the images below.

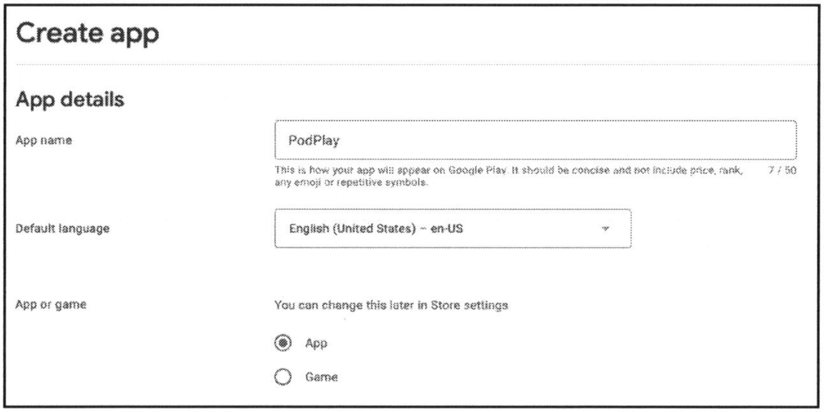

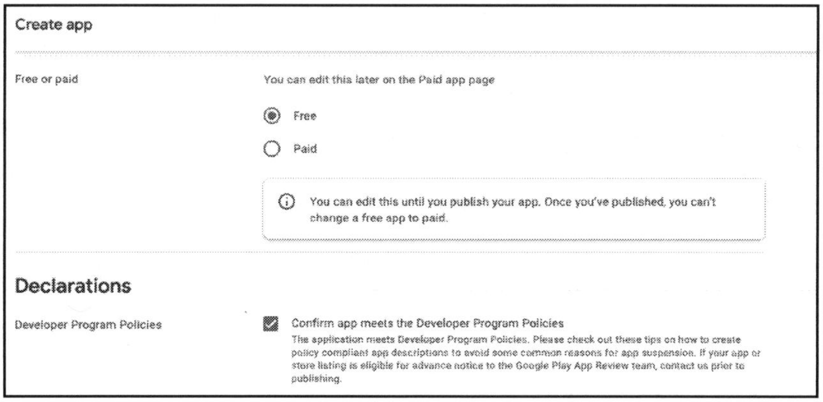

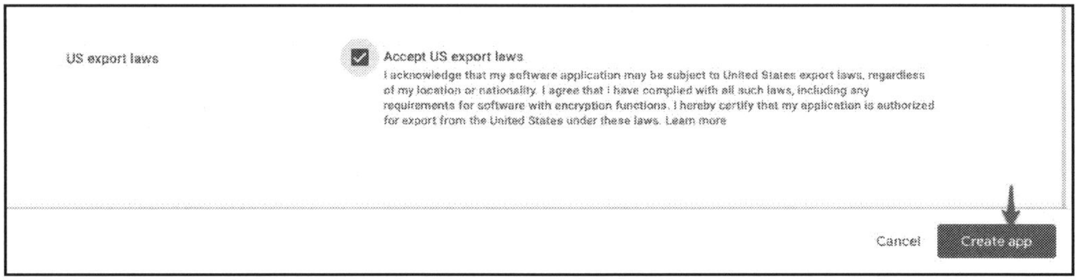

Then the console will drop you on the app's **Dashboard** page.

You need to upload the first version of your app manually, so the **Google Play Store** recognizes the app identifier, thus enabling Fastlane to do releases later.

In Android Studio, create a signed apk in the top menu **Build ▸ Generate signed Bundle/APK...**. You can find it by clicking the **locate** hyperlink at the bottom right.

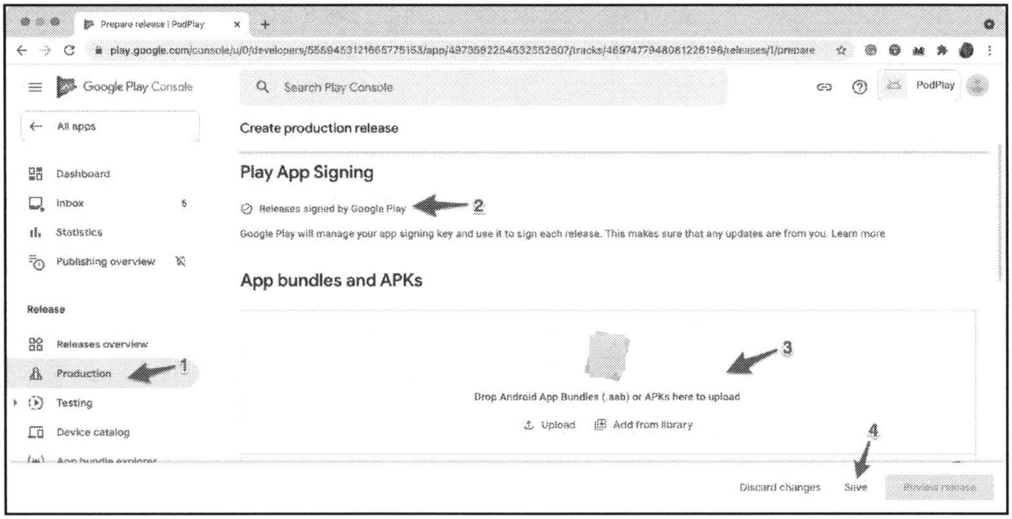

Back in the **Dashboard**, click in the menu to the right in the option and click **Create new release**. Then, let google make the signing for you and drag the APK you just created into the square for it, as in the image above.

Finally, click **Save**, and you're ready to go. There's a button in the top left of the page to go back to **All apps**. Click it, and you'll see a list of apps that includes **PodPlay** with its App ID at the bottom.

Now, Fastlane knows where to upload the app! Awesome job!

Running the lane

Open the Android Studio Project once again and go to the app module **build.gradle**. In the `version code`, increment it to **2** since you uploaded 1 manually.

If you correctly set up everything above, you can now run the lane in the terminal. Run the deploy command again:

```
bundle exec fastlane deploy
```

It'll take a couple of minutes for the whole process to execute, but you'll eventually see a success message in your terminal like the one below. You did it!

```
[16:57:38]: Uploading all changes to Google Play...
[16:57:40]: Successfully finished the upload to Google Play

+------+------------------------+-------------+
|               fastlane summary              |
+------+------------------------+-------------+
| Step | Action                 | Time (in s) |
+------+------------------------+-------------+
| 1    | default_platform       | 0           |
| 2    | clean                  | 27          |
|      | assembleFreeGoogleRel  |             |
|      | ease                   |             |
| 3    | upload_to_play_store   | 14          |
+------+------------------------+-------------+

[16:57:40]: fastlane.tools finished successfully 🎉
Evanas-MacBook-Pro:PodPlay evana$
```

Go back to the **Google Play Console** and verify the apk you uploaded is there by clicking **Releases Overview** in the left menu. The upload will be there with the version number **2**.

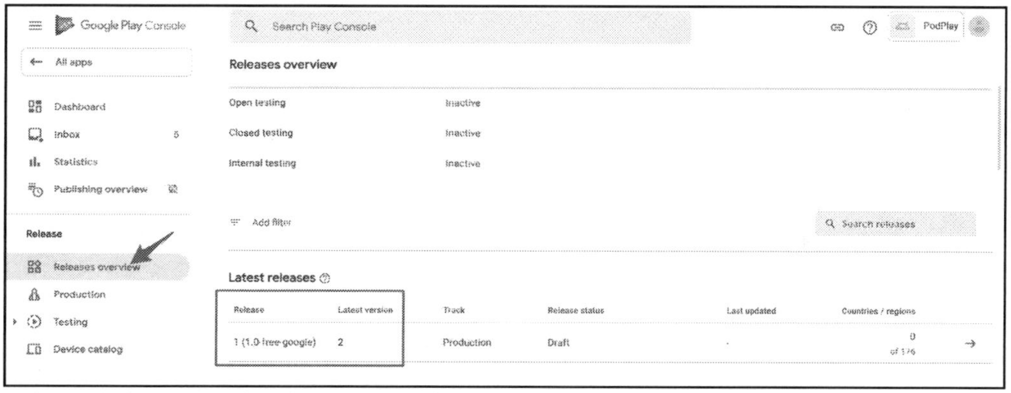

Great job! You now have an automated release pipeline! That's quite an achievement. Many senior devs out there have never done this process.

Key points

- **Automation** reduces the number of manual tasks you need to do after developing your app, and **Fastlane** is a great tool to help with mobile automation.
- Automation tools use commands you can run by yourself in the **Terminal**.
- **Fastlane**'s most important files are the **Fastfile** and the **Appfile**.
- A **Lane** is a group of instructions that execute together in an automated command.
- You can create lanes for testing, taking screenshots, releasing your betas and uploading to production.

Where to go from here?

- If you want to practice what you just learned, check the Fastlane Tutorial at https://www.raywenderlich.com/10187451-fastlane-tutorial-for-android-getting-started on our site.
- Check out the Fastlane Android Documentation at https://docs.fastlane.tools/getting-started/android/setup to learn more things you can automate with it.
- Read the documentation at https://developer.android.com/studio/build/building-cmdline about using the terminal in Android Studio.

In the next chapter, you'll learn about **Continuous Integration and Build Servers** to go beyond your local environment.

Chapter 12: Continuous Integration & Build Servers

By Evana Margain Puig

In the previous chapter, you learned about **Fastlane**, one of the best automation tools for your local environment used by developers worldwide. You also learned how to build, test, take screenshots and release your app with Fastlane.

Fastlane is a great tool and one that you'll often encounter in your Android development career. But most companies take it one step further. Instead of making developers do automation tasks on their local machines, they delegate them to **build servers**.

This chapter will teach you how to use a free and open-source build server hosted by **GitHub** called **GitHub Actions**. With its help, you'll take your automation skills to the next level. Even better, you'll free your computer from executing tasks locally so you can continue developing while the server does its job.

The benefits of CI

Before diving into build servers, it's important to understand two common terms: **Continuous integration** and **Continuous delivery**, also known as **CI/CD**. These two terms are often a source of confusion, and many developers have trouble understanding the difference between them.

- **Continuous integration**: A development practice where you **continuously** merge code into the main repository. Once you merge the code, a series of automated tasks occur, such as testing or linting the code.
- **Continuous delivery**: The process of delivering useful and working code to the final user in a consistent timeframe. Depending on the project and number of developers, a company can choose a CD pipeline that runs as often as once a day or infrequently as every two weeks.

Finally, take a look at build servers.

- **Build servers**: Dedicated instances of virtual machines that can build, test and run your code. In Android, the server you use will compile Android code on a version you specify when configuring it.

Advantages of using a build server

At this point, you may be thinking there's not much of a difference between build servers and what you learned in the last chapter. Here are some examples of the advantages build servers provide:

- They don't run on your computer, so you can keep working while the remote server validates the code.
- All developers on a team can commit their code to the server and then ensure all the code is working. Have you ever been in a situation where a developer swears the code is working on their computer, but there's no way to run it on another computer? Continuous integration solves this important problem because the build server acts as the single source of truth.
- Build servers can have higher specs than many local machines, especially laptops. These specs put less pressure on development machines and give you stable build times. If you've ever worked on a large app that takes more than ten minutes to build, it is easy to appreciate how this is an advantage.

You'll notice many other characteristics as you learn how to use build servers. Keep reading to level up your CI/CD skills.

Which CI/CD provider to use?

There are many CI/CD providers out there. Like most things in tech, and life, each has its advantages and disadvantages. Here's a list of the some of the most commonly used CI/CD providers in the Android platform. This list is not exhaustive, but a good starting point when looking for a provider.

GitHub Actions

- **Advantages**: If you have your project repository on GitHub, this is a great option. The best part is that the free plan is generous, and for that reason, you'll use it for this tutorial.
- **Disadvantages**: For larger business critical projects, you may want to get a paid service so you can get support. Since the community creates actions in **GitHub Actions**, they may have more errors, bugs or limitations than a paid service.

Bitrise

- **Advantages**: Bitrise has become popular in the mobile world. It's stable and has a free tier, so you can use it for small projects and start paying as you grow your app. The interface is easy to use, so new users can get used to working with it quickly.
- **Disadvantages**: Some tests are problematic to run, and updates can break your tests.

CircleCI

- **Advantages**: CircleCI is another commercial platform like Bitrise. It also has a free tier and custom pricing for self-hosted projects.
- **Disadvantages**: It's a bit more technical and can be harder to use if you're newer to the platform.

Jenkins

- **Advantages**: Jenkins comes from the historical roots of Android in Java. It's been in the software industry for several years. Many developers have used it at some point. For the same reason, it has a large development community that provides many plugins and maintenance while still being free and open source.

- **Disadvantages**: It requires the most technical knowledge. Jenkins has to be self-hosted or administered by someone on your team in a cloud provider through a Docker machine. If you're just getting started, the learning curve can be a very frustrating experience.

GitHub Actions

You are going to use GitHub Actions as the CI tool for this chapter. Before using GitHub Actions, you need to upload the project to GitHub. If you already know how to do this, create a repo with PodPlay and skip the next section. Otherwise, follow along.

Uploading PodPlay to GitHub

You didn't come to this chapter to only read theory, and at this point, you're probably eager to create your own CI/CD pipeline. To work through this part of the chapter, you'll need a GitHub account and to upload your **PodPlay** code to a repository there.

If you don't have one already, start by creating a new account on their site by visiting http://www.github.com in your favorite browser and clicking **Sign Up**. They have a very interactive interface. Follow the steps until you have an account.

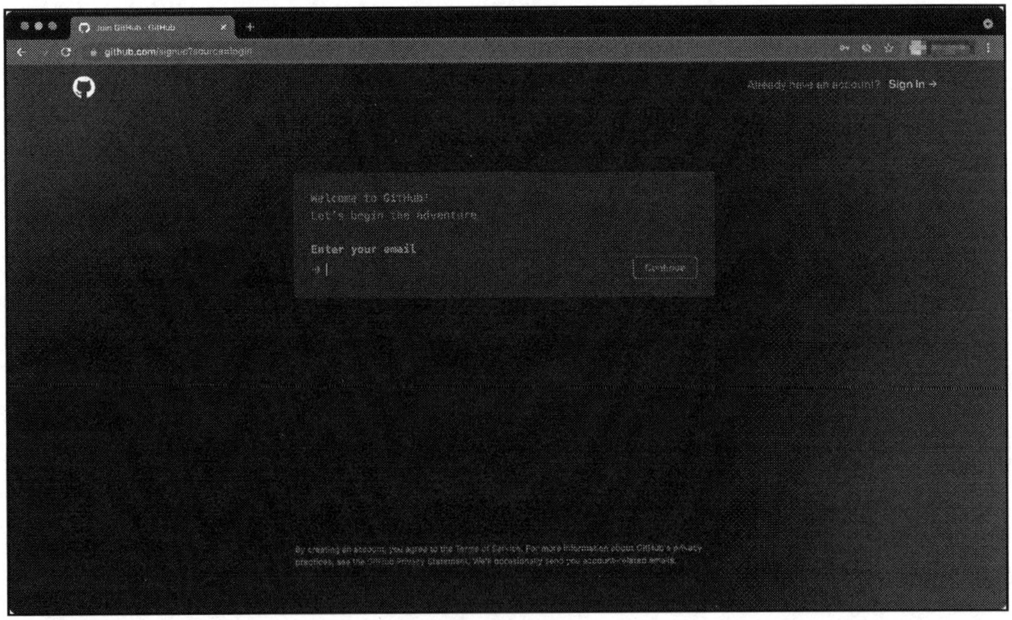

Once you have your account, log in. Copy the starter project of this chapter to your computer's Desktop, or some other location where you can work with it. Open it in Android Studio and click the top menu **VCS ▸ Share Project on GitHub**.

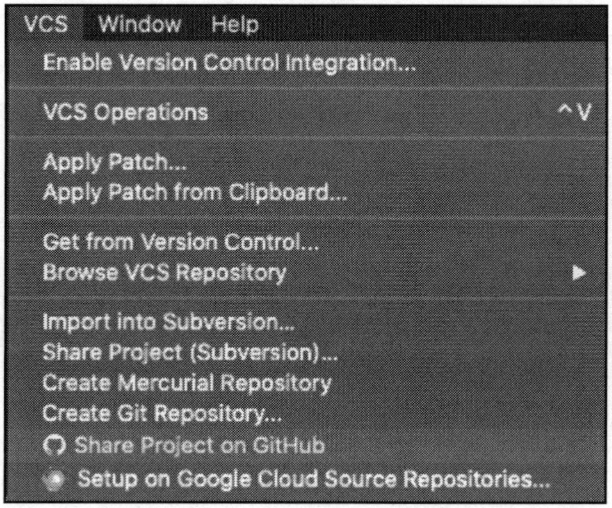

If you've already set up Git in your Podplay project, you'll have to use **Git ▸ GitHub ▸ Share Project on GitHub**.

If you haven't already logged in to GitHub through Android Studio, do so by using **Add Account ▸ Log In via GitHub**. Then leave the defaults in the following dialog and click **Share**.

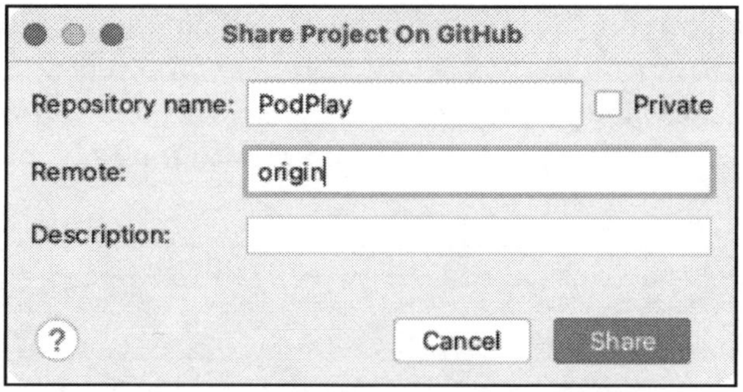

Another dialog will show you all the files it will upload to GitHub. Accept everything as it is and click **Add**.

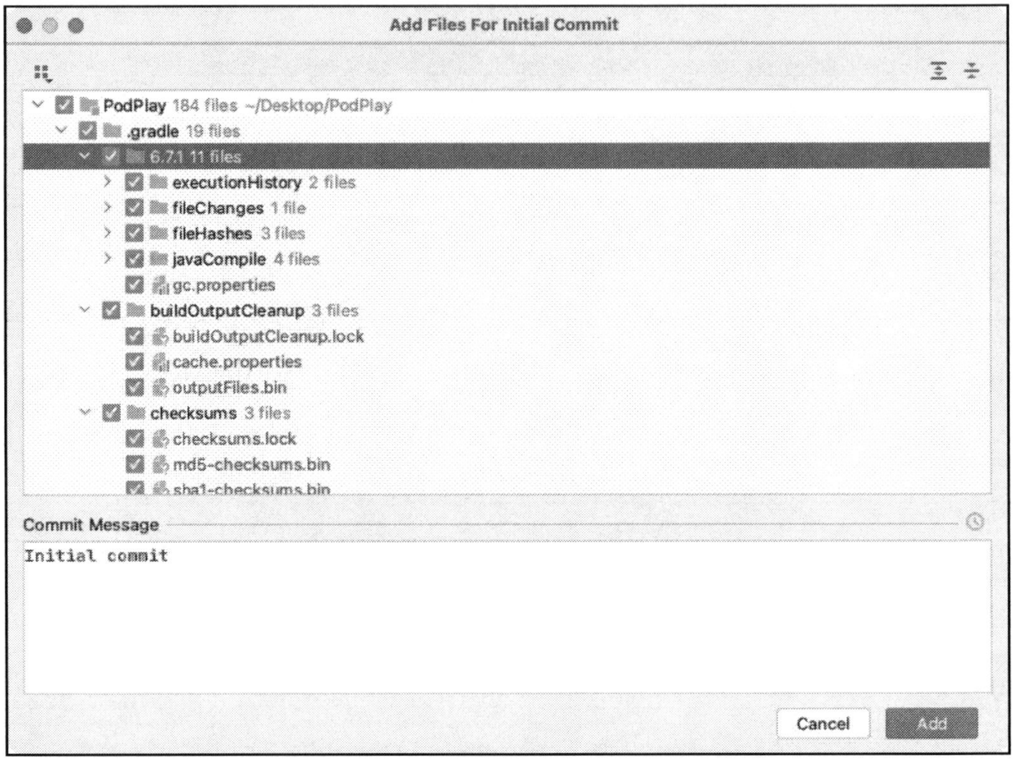

The upload may take a couple of minutes, depending on your internet connection. You can see the progress on the bottom right corner of Android Studio. Once it's done, an alert will show in that same bottom right corner, indicating it was successfully shared. It will also show a blue link named **PodPlay** that will take you to the repo.

Open the repo with the link on the alert and take a look. You'll notice the files you had on your computer are now shared on GitHub.

Getting started with GitHub Actions

Go to the main page of the repository. In the horizontal menu below the repo's name, click the button labeled **Actions**.

The page that opens will give you a brief introduction to **GitHub Actions**. It will also suggest some pre-made flows to get you started right away.

Clicking **Set up a workflow yourself** and **Set up this workflow** suggested for the Kotlin repository gives you the same base script. In case GitHub changes this in the future, make sure to click **Set up this workflow**, as shown in the image below.

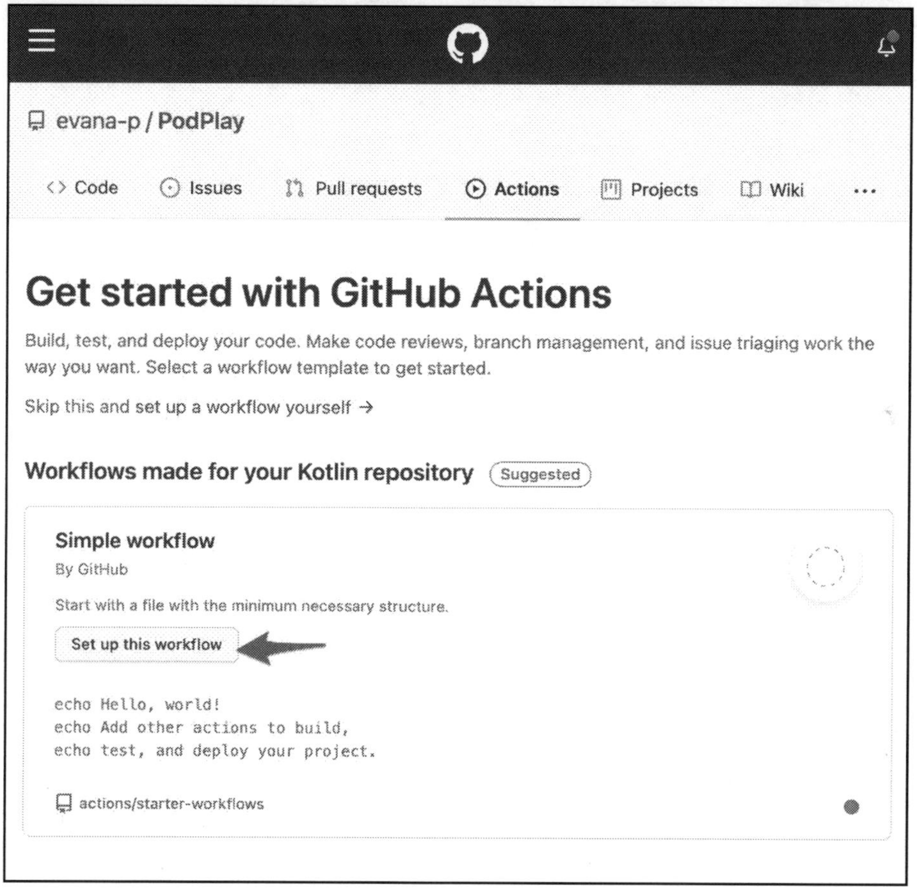

Then you'll get a **blank.yml** for the workflows. **YAML**, the file ending in **.yml**, is the format used by all CI providers. You'll specify the instructions for your different flows in this file.

The template you get is the basic workflow GitHub provides. You can read the comments identified with the # sign to see what each part does. Don't worry if you don't understand it right now. You'll learn everything you need in this chapter.

In the following sections, you'll learn more about what each part means and customize it for **PodPlay**.

Change the name to **dev.yml** and leave the rest of the file exactly as it is. Click **Start commit** to add the new **YAML** file to the repository.

GitHub will ask you for a commit title and description like it does when you commit changes from your local computer to the repository. Leave the default options and click **Commit new file**.

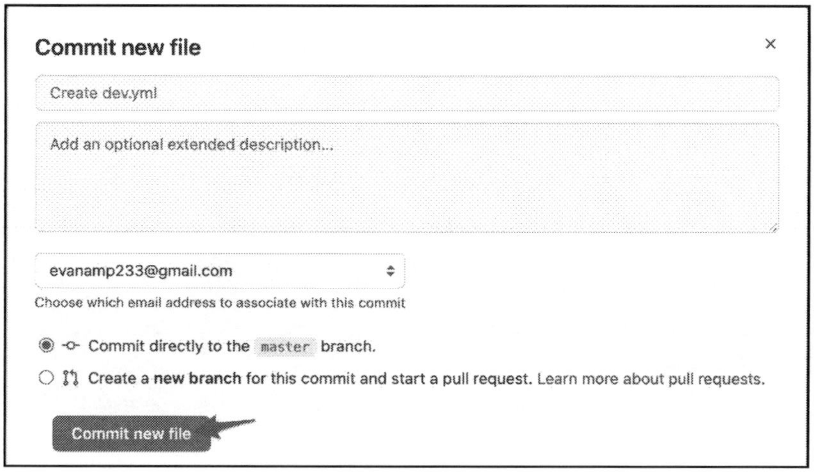

YAML building blocks

A build server can execute many key **actions** through the YAML files. GitHub has a catalog of pre-made actions that you can integrate into your flows.

Before integrating these custom flows, it's important to learn how to create one by yourself.

> **Note**: Although you're learning how to do this with **GitHub Actions**, most of the steps are the same across CI providers.

At this point, you'll edit and change **PodPlay**'s YAML file. Go back to Android Studio and pull the changes in master. Click the top menu **Git ▸ Pull** and clicking **Pull** in the dialog that appears.

Right now, you only have one branch, master, so that will get all the changes.

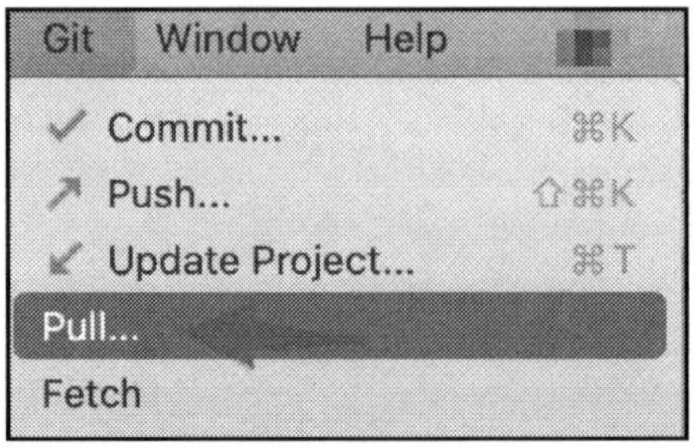

Now switch to the Project view of the file navigator in Android Studio. Navigate to **.github ▸ workflows**. There you'll see your newly added **dev.yml** ready for you to edit.

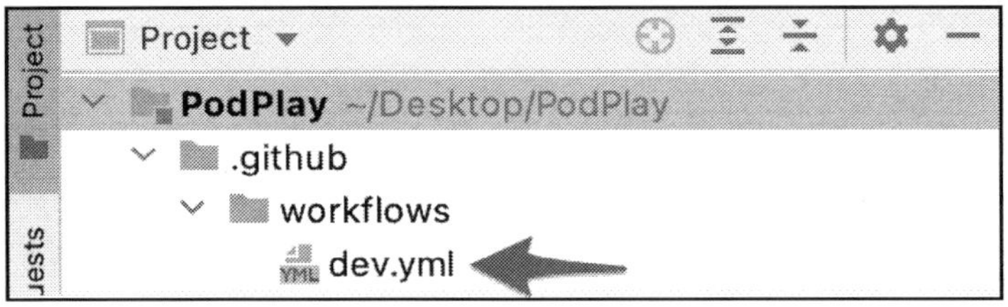

Name

This is the name at the top of the YAML file in line three. You can rename it to anything you want. Preferably, choose a name that will help you identify what that particular flow does.

In a production app, you may have YAML files for your different environments or processes. For example:

- Triggering a build for the QA team to test an added feature.
- Creating a Release Candidate for beta users to test.
- Running automated tests once a day to ensure your new code didn't break anything.

Each of those files should have a name that tells your team what it does.

Triggers

As the word suggests, **Triggers** are situations that cause a workflow to run.

If you're automating a process, you don't want to trigger it manually every time.

With this keyword, you can define triggers that start any workflow every time something happens. Examples include:

- Opening pull requests.
- Merging pull requests.
- Every time someone pushes code in the repository.
- Creating new labels.

You can find a detailed list of other possible triggers in the GitHub Actions documentation at https://docs.github.com/en/actions/reference/events-that-trigger-workflows.

The keyword that identifies triggers is **on:**. Look at the YAML file you created and opened in Android Studio. In one of the first lines, you'll see this keyword, followed by two triggers, **push** and **pull_request**, as shown below:

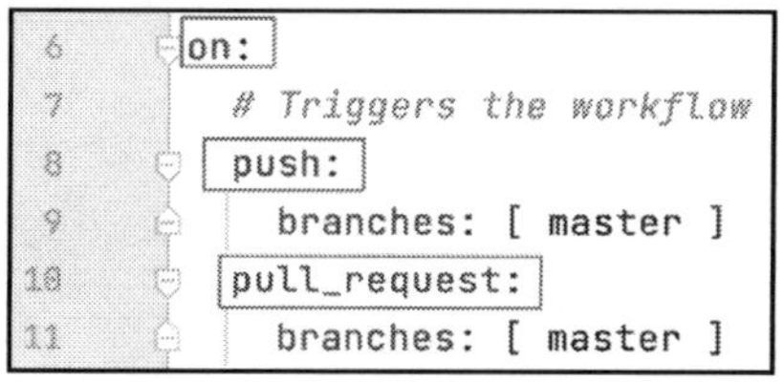

Branch triggers

The most common trigger is when a specific action happens on a branch. In this example, you'll use a **push to the master branch**. This kind of trigger may also occur when you merge a pull request in a branch.

In your **dev.yml** look for the following in your file:

```
on:
  # Triggers the workflow on push or pull request events but
only for the master branch
  push:
    branches: [ master ]
  pull_request:
    branches: [ master ]
```

Replace it with the following:

```
on:
  push:
    branches:
      - 'master'
```

That causes it to trigger every time you **push** to any branch.

> **Note**: Some build server providers that charge based on the number of builds and/or the build duration. A build trigger that is frequently hit under those circumstances could lead to a very large bill. If you have a small or limited hosting budget you may want to choose a trigger that is hit less frequently.

Now, push the changes to trigger your first workflow. In Android Studio's top menu, go to **Git ▸ Commit** and add a commit message as in the image below. Finally, click the small arrow next to the commit button and **Commit and Push...**.

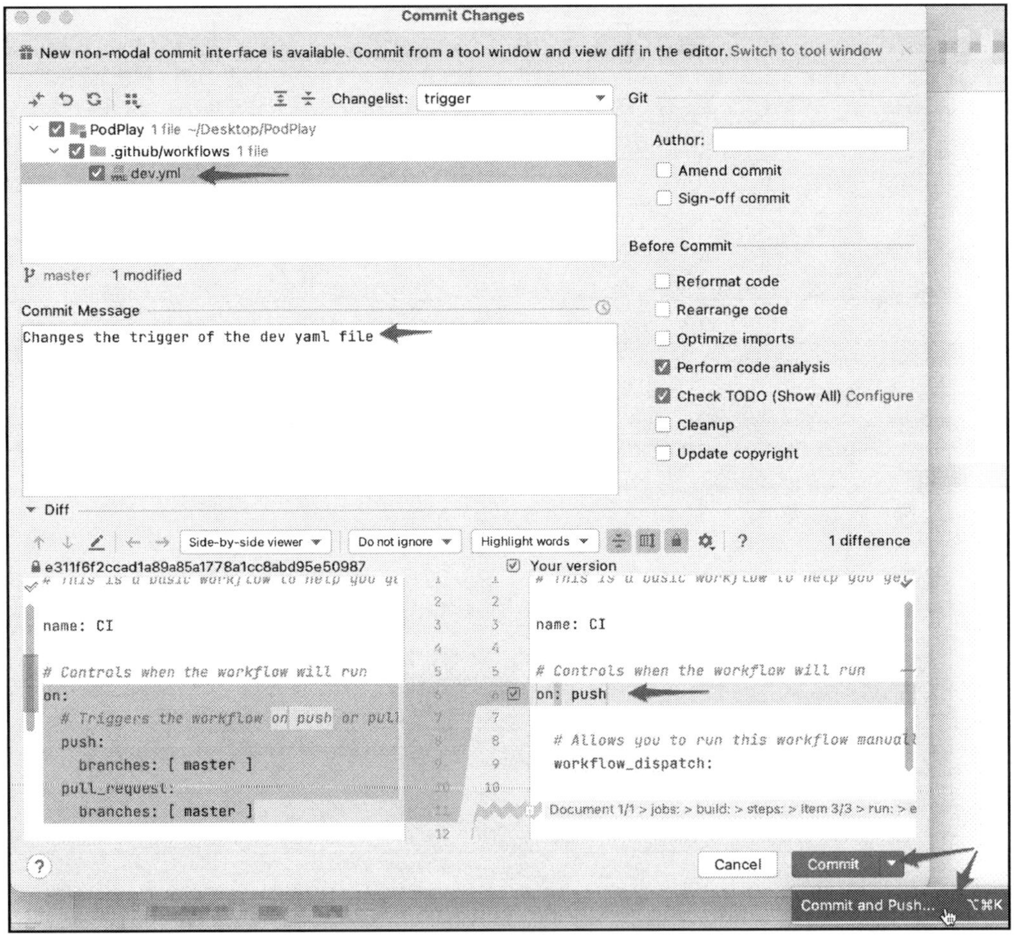

Once you click to go back to the **GitHub Actions** page and look at the flows, you'll see one of three signs:

1. A **yellow dot** if the flow is still running, which happens for a couple of seconds. For some larger apps, it may even take a couple of hours.
2. A **green checkmark** if the flow ran correctly.
3. A **red cross** if you had an error.

Look at the image below for examples of each case:

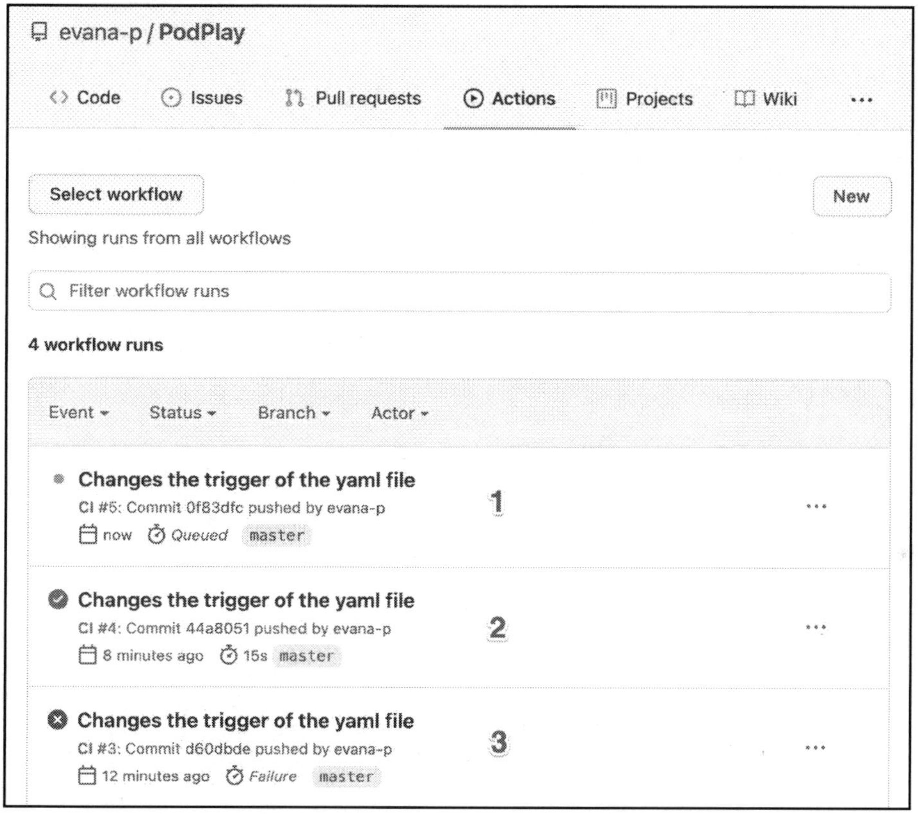

Ignoring branches

In the same way that you can trigger a flow when something happens, you can also ignore branches. Imagine a feature branch where developers are making tons of changes, but none of them is final. You can ignore those branches so developers don't overload the build server with any minor changes they make to their branches.

The syntax is the same as the last example but with `branches-ignore` instead of `branches`.

```
on:
  push:
    branches-ignore:
      - 'feature/**'
```

Since you don't have any feature branches, you don't need to add the above code to your YAML file.

Workflow dispatch

In the YAML file GitHub Actions generated for you, the next line reads `workflow_dispatch:` with nothing else. This line tells GitHub Actions that you want to run the flow manually directly from their site.

On the same page where you looked at the results, you'll notice a column titled **Workflows**. Click the one named **CI**.

A light blue square will appear showing a message, **This workflow has a workflow_dispatch event trigger.**, with a button to **Run workflow**. Click it to manually trigger the workflow like it gets triggered when you push something to master.

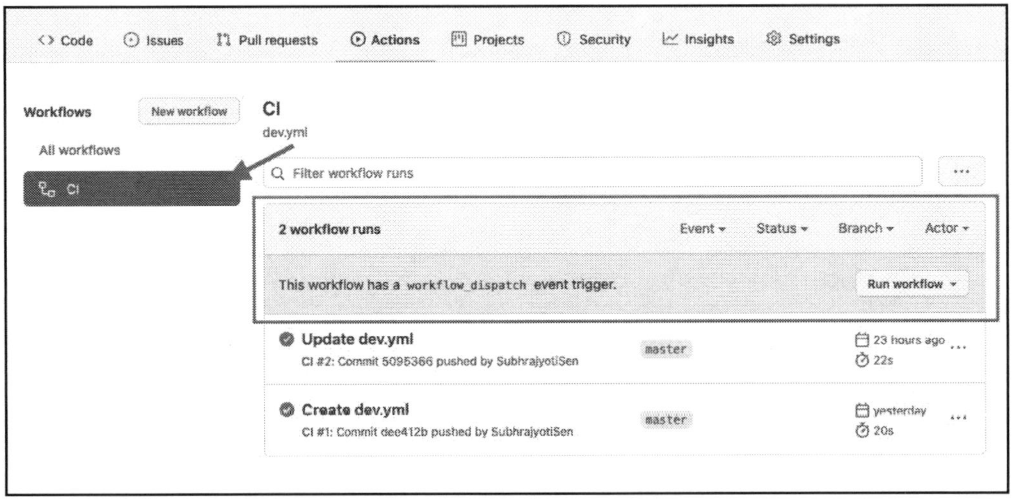

In some special cases, you'll want to trigger the build manually. Here are two examples when you might do this:

1. You want to validate a build is working without opening Android Studio.
2. You need to re-rerun a build that failed for something out of your control, like network availability, a timeout or an error downloading a plugin.

In other cases, you may want to prevent someone on your team from running a build unless something very specific happens, so you don't add the `workflow_dispatch` step. This is particularly important when you're dealing with flows that push to production under certain circumstances. You don't want to risk someone manually triggering that build and pushing code to production.

Jobs and steps

The next part of the code is `jobs`. Jobs are a group of actions that run together independently of other jobs to complete a particular action.

You can have as many jobs as you want, but try to keep it short and simple. Otherwise, it becomes complicated for other developers to contribute to the workflow.

Jobs can be anything you like, but as most build flows are similar, you'll likely have these jobs:

1. **Setting up the project.**

- Checking out the code from the repository.
- Installing the dependencies on the remote machine.
- Downloading assets from your app's repository.

2. **Building the app.**

- Basically, the same things you do on your local machine when testing. This can be either for a debug, release or any other build variant you have defined.

3. **Running tests.**

- As mentioned, developers often overlook this important step. You can run any type of test, but automated and unit tests are the most common.

4. **Depending on the flow, creating a beta, internal or public release.**

- You can release the app to a testing service that will distribute it to your desired testers. Testing services include App center, TestFlight and TestFairy.
- Releasing directly to the Google Play Console and creating an open, closed or internal test.
- Releasing to the Play Store to all your users, as long as you're sure this is a tested and working version.

In the sample project, you'll notice a line called `jobs`. Look at the image below to see what each of the following lines means. The numbers correlate to numbered explanations below:

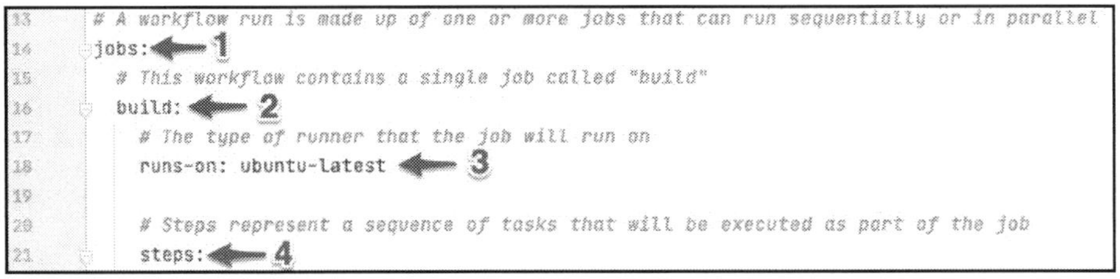

```
# A workflow run is made up of one or more jobs that can run sequentially or in parallel
jobs: ← 1
  # This workflow contains a single job called "build"
  build: ← 2
    # The type of runner that the job will run on
    runs-on: ubuntu-latest ← 3

    # Steps represent a sequence of tasks that will be executed as part of the job
    steps: ← 4
```

1. The start of the `jobs` definition.
2. You have a job named `build`. Unlike other lines in the YAML file, you can give `build` any name you want. You'll have more than one in most projects, but the sample only provides `build` as a starting point.
3. Next, the YAML file specifies what type of remote server the build `runs-on`. For Android builds, you'll commonly use `ubuntu-latest` or `macos-latest`. Note that you can switch the word **latest** with a specific version like `macos-11`.
4. With those two things defined, you can start listing the steps of that specific job by inputting the line of code `steps`.

Creating a job

Your current sample file only has one job. To practice, you'll now create another job that will run your tests.

First, create the job below the final step of the existing `build` job at the end of the file. Name this new step `test`.

```
  test:
```

Make sure to ident the job name with two spaces, so it's at the same level as the other job `build`. Indentation is very important in YAML files, and your whole workflow will break if an item is incorrectly indented. You can use a tool like http://www.yamllint.com/ to validate your YAML files.

Setup tasks, commands & actions

As mentioned earlier, jobs run several steps. If you look at the sample file, each step starts with a hyphen and can consist of one or more lines. They continue until you encounter the next hyphen, a new job or the end of the file.

Steps can be one of three types: setup tasks, commands and actions. Take a look at each in detail.

Setup tasks

If you have a complex workflow, setup tasks will help you define a specific job's dependencies and other technical aspects. You already learned about one setup task, the `runs-on` keyword. As you learned before, this tells the virtual machine what kind of environment you want your flow to run on.

Another useful setup task is the keyword `needs`, which tells a job to wait until the server finishes the named job.

In the job you created, set up the environment as `ubuntu-latest` by pasting the following below `test:`:

```
    runs-on: ubuntu-latest
```

Note: The indentation for this item is four spaces.

This is a setup task because it happens before the actual steps and gets everything ready for your job to run seamlessly.

Commands

Commands are instructions you give to the build server's terminal and run in an automated way. Whenever you run a manual Android build, as shown at the beginning of the chapter, you give instructions to the terminal to execute things.

A command is precisely that: You give the terminal an instruction, but the server automatically does it.

Some common examples include:

- Printing log messages so you can customize the output after you review how the build went. Log messages can be: debug, warning and error messages.
- Making the workflow start or stop depending on specific conditions.
- Setting environment variables.
- Creating paths in the virtual machine for files your build may need to create.

Now, create a command in your new `test` job, with the code below:

```
    steps: #1
      - name: Run a log message #2
        run: echo This is my job for running tests! #3
```

Here's a code breakdown:

1. Unlike the setup tasks, commands and actions start with the `steps` keyword. There are four spaces of indentation.
2. The hyphen that indicates a step is starting, followed by the keyword `name`. The name itself can be any string of your choice. In this case, you chose `Run a log message` as the name for that step. Be sure to use simple and understandable names to label what your flow is doing in each part. There are six spaces of indentation before the hyphen.
3. The keyword `run` without a hyphen because it's still part of the previous step. This keyword indicates what the step will do. In this case, it will print `This is my job for running tests!` in your output. There are eight spaces of indentation.

Actions

Explaining what an action is might seem redundant, but think of it this way. Action is a single command in your workflow. It's the smallest unit in your YAML file: Workflow > Jobs > Steps > Actions.

An action is similar to a method in programming. It contains a series of commands you can reuse as a single unit.

Take a look at an example by using the checkout action in your test. Add the following code to your YAML file:

```
      - uses: actions/checkout@v2 #1

      - name: set up JDK #2
        uses: actions/setup-java@v1 #3
        with:
          java-version: 11 #4

      - name: Unit tests
        run: ./gradlew test #5
```

There is a lot going on here, so let's break it down:

1. You'll use the `checkout` action often because most of the time, you need to check it out in the remote machine to do anything with your app. `@v2` refers to version 2 of the action. This designation is useful when there are multiple versions of an action, and you want to use a specific version.
2. The name of the step that you'll run once you check out the code.
3. `setup-java@v1` installs the correct version of Java on the build server.
4. You specify the Java version to use with the `with` keyword.
5. A command in gradle to run tests.

Your complete job is as follows:

```
  test:
    runs-on: ubuntu-latest
    steps: #1
      - name: Run a log message #2
        run: echo This is my job for running tests! #3

      - uses: actions/checkout@v2

      - name: set up JDK #2
        uses: actions/setup-java@v1 #3
```

```
        with:
          java-version: 11 #4

      - name: Unit tests
        run: ./gradlew test
```

With this code added, you're ready to see your new job in action. Commit and push your code with the commit message `Adding a new job for running tests`. Go to your GitHub repository to the actions section.

It will take up to an hour to run because of the many build variants you created throughout the book. Since this is not a service you're paying for, servers are not as fast. As long as you see the yellow dot to the left of the run, it's still in progress.

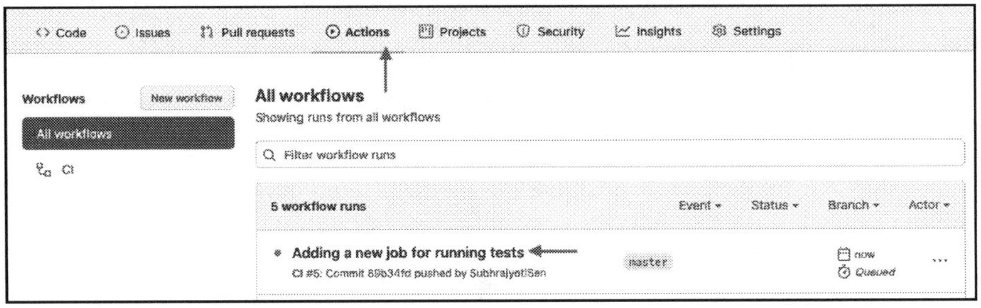

While you wait, look at a couple of the details inside the workflow run. Click the bold text of the build as shown above, and you'll see the details page as follows:

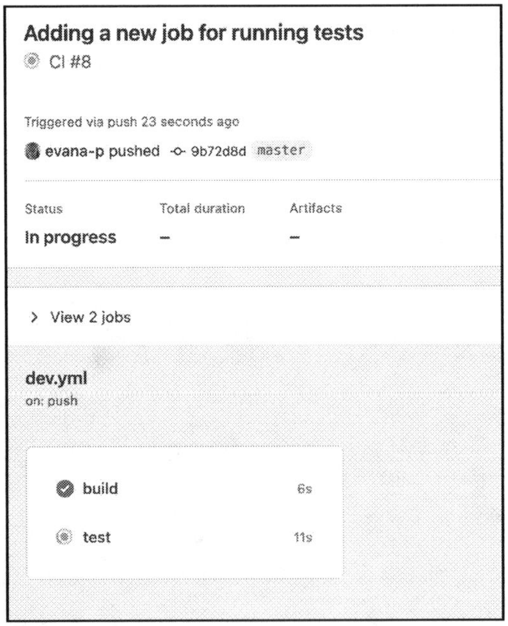

Click each of the jobs to see the execution's details. In the image above, the build job is already finished, and the test job is still ongoing.

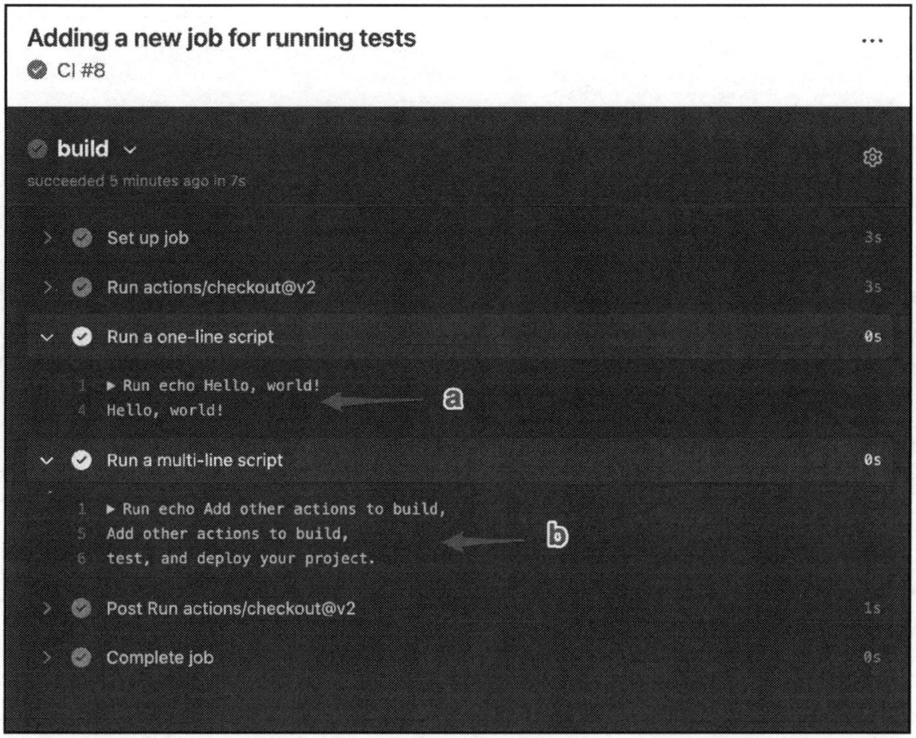

You can see the inspection of the build job and each of the steps signaled by an arrow and their corresponding name. See if you can identify the relationship of the steps with your yaml file. Look at the image below to identify where the a and b steps come from.

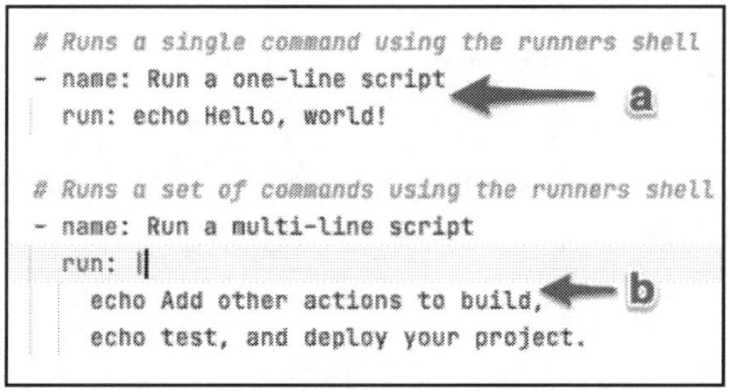

Great! Now you have your first workflow running on Github Actions. These build servers are powerful, and you can customize them to do many of your everyday tasks.

Key points

- CI is short for **Continuous integration**. It refers to the process of continually merging your code into a repository. The server takes care of testing, linting and other helpful things in your code.
- CD is short for **Continuous delivery**, the process of delivering to production as often as possible with the help of a build server. This process is not covered in detail here because it's a topic on its own, but the same build server can take care of it.
- **Build servers** are powerful machines that release your time and resources while saving your project from human error when automating tasks.
- There are many **CI/CD** providers with their own advantages and disadvantages.
- In this book, you tried **GitHub Actions** as your build server because it's free and easy to use.
- You need to upload a project to a GitHub repo to use GitHub Actions in it.
- GitHub Actions provides pre-made workflows that match your needs and get you started with a YAML template.
- **YAML** files are the base of Continuous Integration Servers, and the language and commands are very similar across build servers.
- You can set up **triggers**, such as when you create a pull request or push code to the repository, to automatically start your workflows.
- **Workflow Dispatch** refers to manually triggering a workflow without the trigger happening automatically.
- YAML files require a series of keywords to work. The most important are **jobs, steps** and **actions**.
- It's easy to monitor and debug your workflows through the GitHub Actions tab on the repository's webpage.

Where to go from here?

Congratulations! You just created your first CI pipeline.

In this chapter, you learned the basics you need to continue mastering CI and even dive into CD. Don't be afraid to get deeper into the topic.

Reinforce your CD knowledge by taking a look at this tutorial: https://www.raywenderlich.com/19407406-continuous-delivery-for-android-using-github-actions.

Also, check out this amazing tutorial if you want to learn about continuous Integration if you want to learn how to sign and deploy your Android Apps with GitHub Actions: https://www.raywenderlich.com/10562143-continuous-integration-for-android.

Section IV: Beyond Publication

In an ideal world, you could release an app and, without doing anything, have it be wildly successful and generate money while you relax in the tropics. However, in the real world, an app is a living thing that needs continuous care and feeding.

App ratings can make or break an app's success in the store. Chapter 13 talks about techniques for cultivating good reviews and addressing negative ones. Two common causes of bad app reviews are app crashes and poor performance. Chapter 14 dives into monitoring and improving your app's performance to proactively address issues before they turn into poor reviews.

Chapter 13: Getting Top Ratings & Avoiding Negative Reviews: Gathering In-App Feedback

by Fuad Kamal

So now your app is live on the Play Store, after months of internal, alpha and beta testing. Your app is hardened and secure, and you've built automated toolchains to rapidly test and update your app. What happens once your software is in the customers' hands?

How do you assess how they feel about the app? How do you collect and respond to feedback? How can you avoid most one-star ratings and ensure your users are happy and have the best possible experience, both with the app and your company? In this chapter, you'll get an inside look at how two large companies accomplished just that and how with a little effort, you can, too.

Responding to Google Play comments in the dashboard

When your app is on Google Play in any form, your users can provide a rating and feedback. This feedback is visible to you in the Play Console under the **Quality** section.

Go to the **Play Console** and open **Quality -> Ratings and reviews -> Ratings**. Here you'll find various statistics and data visualizations for your app's ratings over time. Note that in this section, ratings from both beta and release versions of your app are combined.

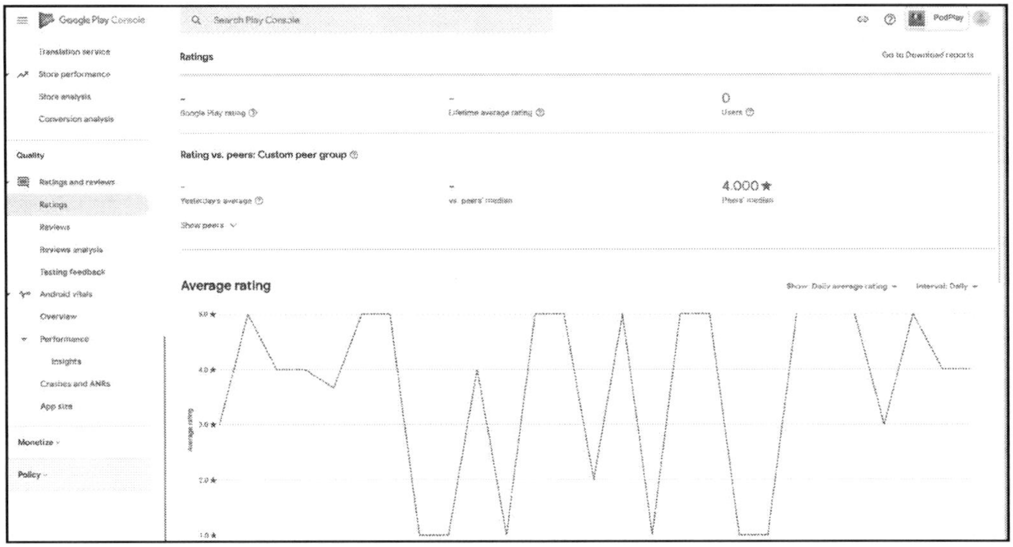

Next, check the **Reviews** section. Here you'll find any reviews for the release version of your app. You may also see a notice reminding you to use the **Google Play In-App Review API**. You'll implement this in Podplay later in this chapter.

Feedback from beta versions of your app appears in the **Testing Feedback** section. You'll find the star rating and user's comments for each review, along with a text box where you can directly reply to the feedback. Your replies will then appear in the Play Store along with the user's review. It's a handy way for developers to provide some sort of response to reviews received in the Play Store.

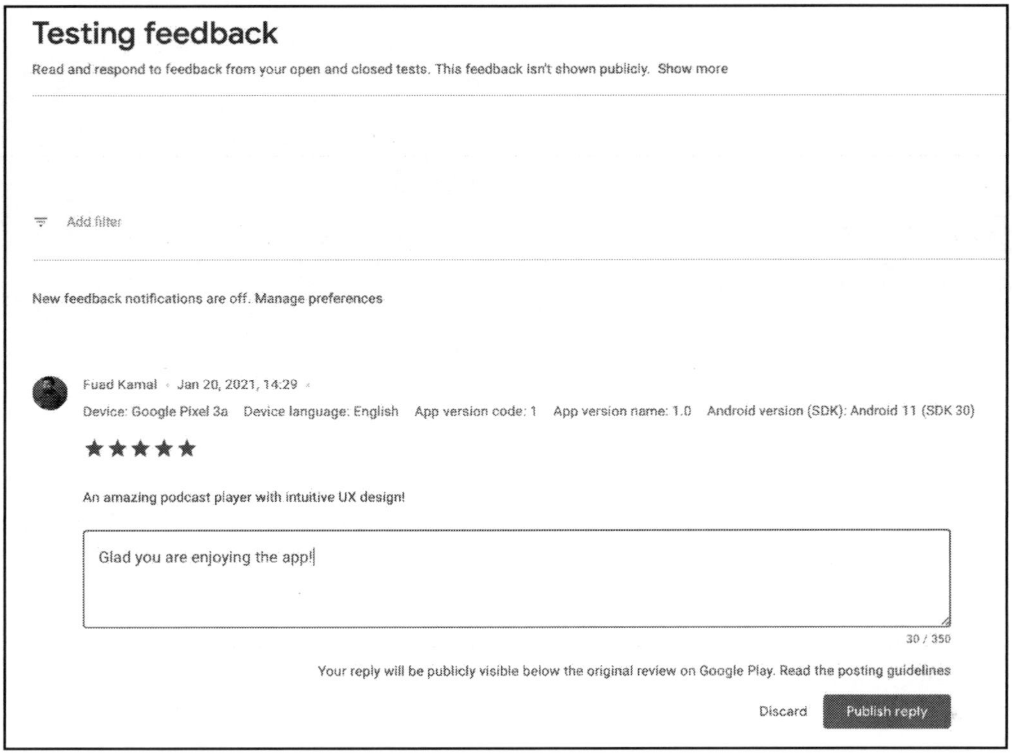

Next, check out the **Notifications** page under the Play Console's **Setup** section. Here you'll find various options to get email notifications, such as a notification when a user updates their review after you've replied to it.

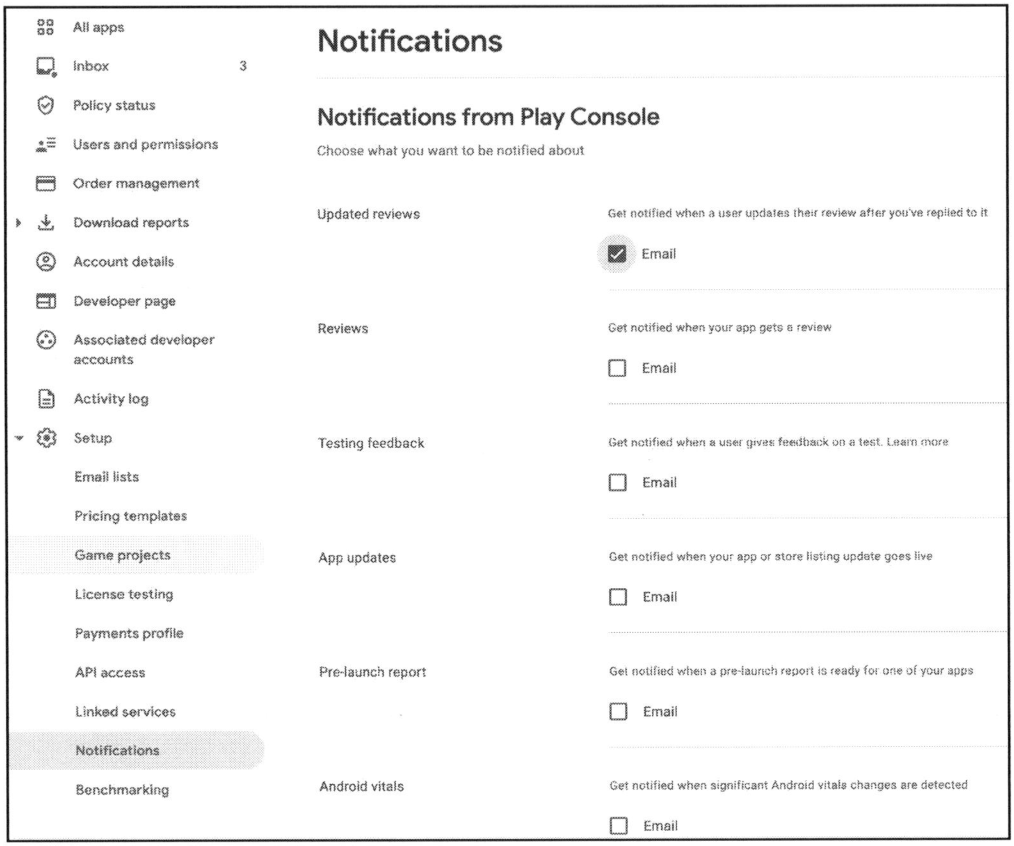

Ratings and reviews can significantly impact the perception of your app and the willingness of new users to download it. Most app developers seem to publish their app and then wait for reviews, good or bad. However, the typical user doesn't make an effort to leave feedback or rate your app on the App Store unless they have a very negative experience. Then, they take the extra effort to go to the Play Store, leave a one-star rating and rant about your app.

Typically these users are frustrated after having a negative experience, and they don't know a more effective way to get the developer's attention to resolve the issue. For example, maybe 70% of your users are happy with your app, but 30% of users have some sort of frustrating experience. Most users with a good experience might not bother to leave a rating or review, while users with a negative experience will make an extra effort to leave a review. The typical net result can be a low one or two-star rating overall on the App Store and a long list of negative reviews, despite most users having a good experience.

However, you can be proactive and guide users to provide feedback directly to you from within your app when they have a negative experience, rather than leaving negative feedback publicly on the Play Store. Likewise, you can encourage users who had a good experience with your app to leave a high star rating and positive review on Google Play.

Case studies: in-app feedback

Earlier in this chapter, you learned the strategy for optimizing your app's ratings and reviews in your favor. That strategy isn't untested theory. More than one company has quickly changed overwhelmingly negative reviews and one-star ratings to positive reviews and four and five-star ratings.

Note that while this book is specific to Android and mainly focused on the Google Play Store experience, the case studies that follow cover *both* iOS and Android apps from these companies. The strategies in this chapter are universally applicable for all platforms. Keep in mind, the app user bases numbered in the *millions* for these companies, but only a small percentage of users left ratings and feedback. Revising their strategies and becoming proactive in how they collected user feedback had a phenomenal impact on both the users' experience and the public perception of the apps.

Target

Target, the eighth largest American retail chain, has been in business since 1962. It has close to 2,000 stores spread across the country. However, their public-facing apps were plagued with one-star reviews and negative ratings. Erik Kerber (https://www.raywenderlich.com/u/kerber), the principal iOS developer at Target, posted the following in the raywenderlich.com slack in July 2017:

> Funny little milestone - 15 months from a stupid line of code to 1 million reviews.
>
> Previously we would typically get 5-20 (typically negative) reviews for every 2-week release. Rewarded for being pests.

They deployed a simple strategy that completely reversed the trend of negative reviews and vastly increased the number of reviews they got. While the code example above is Swift for requesting an App Store review from within an iOS app, the same feature is now available in Android. The iOS framework for this has built-in rules for when and how often the user sees the in-app prompt. Basically, it prevents the user from getting spammed with review requests.

You'll implement this same functionality later in the Podplay Android app. If you want more information on the iOS functionality, you can find the documentation here: https://developer.apple.com/documentation/storekit/skstorereviewcontroller/requesting_app_store_reviews.

Taking a proactive approach of asking users for feedback, rather than waiting for frustrated users to reach out, completely flips the outcome.

Octo Telematics

Octo Telematics, based in Rome, Italy, is the world's leading telematics provider. They produce hardware and apps used by auto insurance companies worldwide to monitor their customers' driving behavior, enabling them to reward good driving behavior with incentives such as discounts on insurance premiums. One of their clients had an app with an overwhelming number of one-star reviews on both the iOS and Android app stores.

Here are some examples of the negative reviews users were leaving, which, if taken in context, amount to bugs that were getting lost in the call centers and never even reaching the developer team:

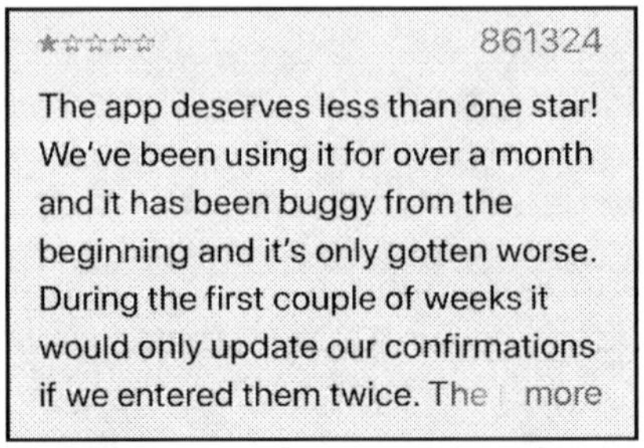

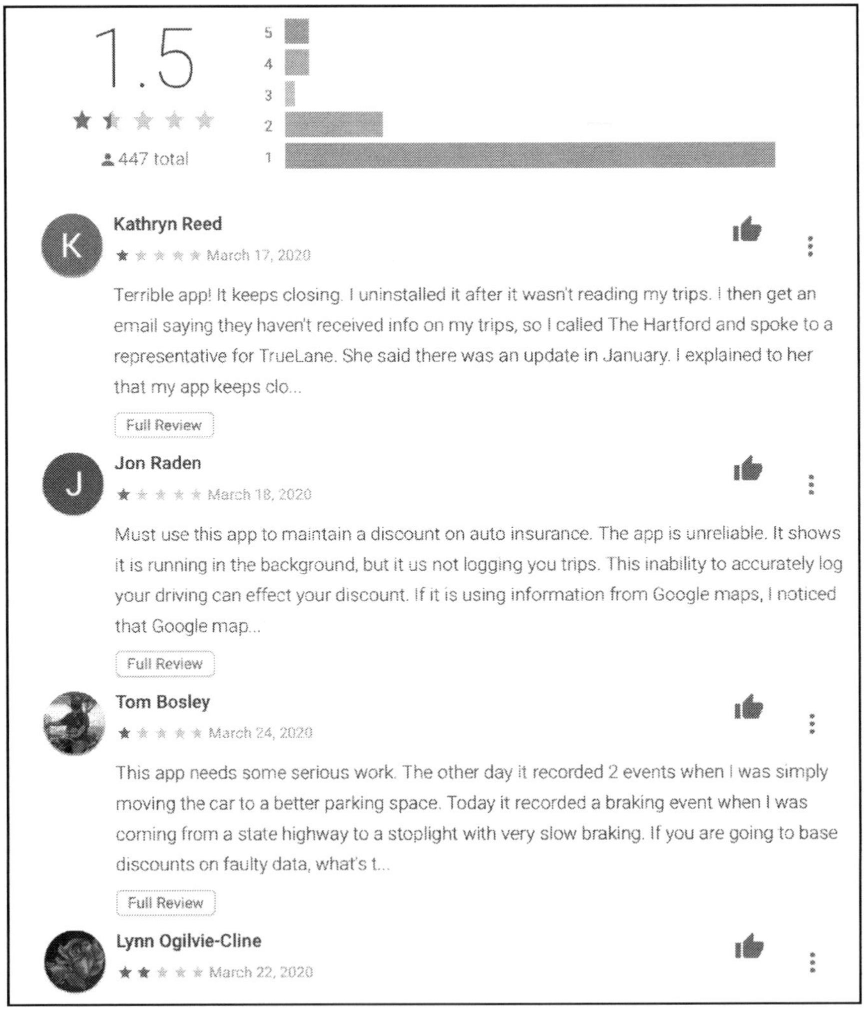

This chapter's author is both a colleague of Erik from Target, via the raywenderlich.com team, and was newly hired as the director of mobile at Octo. So, using a strategy similar to Target's, the mobile team at Octo was able to reverse this negative review trend almost overnight. They took it a bit further, however.

Rather than prompting users to leave ratings and feedback, they additionally directed the users with a negative experience to provide direct feedback to the development team, rather than publicly leaving comments on the App Store. Here's the overall strategy:

1. Prompt the user, in-app, for feedback: How do they like the app?
2. If they love the app, prompt them to leave a rating and review on the respective app store.
3. If they don't love the app, prompt them for **direct feedback**, sent to the developer team.

The direct feedback mechanism uses the JIRA API to create tickets in the development team's JIRA board directly. These tickets further ensure issues are brought front and center and prioritized. When the new version of the app launched with this feature enabled, the iOS App Store ratings went from one star to four stars overall in just a couple of weeks. At the time of writing, it currently sits at 4.7 stars!

This is because Apple implemented a change in their App Store, where new versions of an app get their own rating, rather than the rating being an average of all the versions of the app since its first launch. On the Google Play Store, the app rating is still an average of all versions of the app. While the process took longer, the Android app still increased from 1.5 stars to 3.1 stars overall, and it's still climbing.

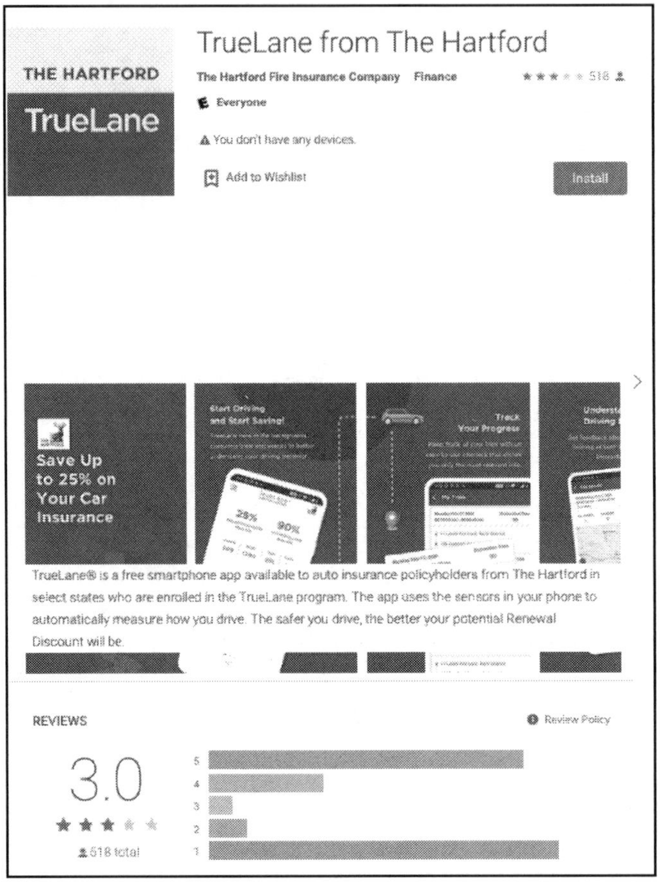

Building an in-app feedback mechanism

Now that you've seen how important it is to properly channel reviews and feedback for your app, you'll learn how to implement it in Podplay. Sending your user out of the app to leave a review in the Play Store can be a disruptive experience. Thankfully, you don't have to do that anymore because Google, and Apple for iOS, now provides in-app review APIs which let users leave feedback and reviews directly from within your app interface.

Creating an in-app review module

To start implementing the in-app review feature, you'll create a new feature module. This module will let you decouple the relevant code from the rest of the code. Decoupling features helps you reuse them across your app or even between multiple projects. In fact, you can even publish the code as a library for other people or organizations to use.

Open the starter project for this chapter. From the menu, choose **File -> New -> New Module**.

From the wizard that appears, choose **Android Library** for the module type:

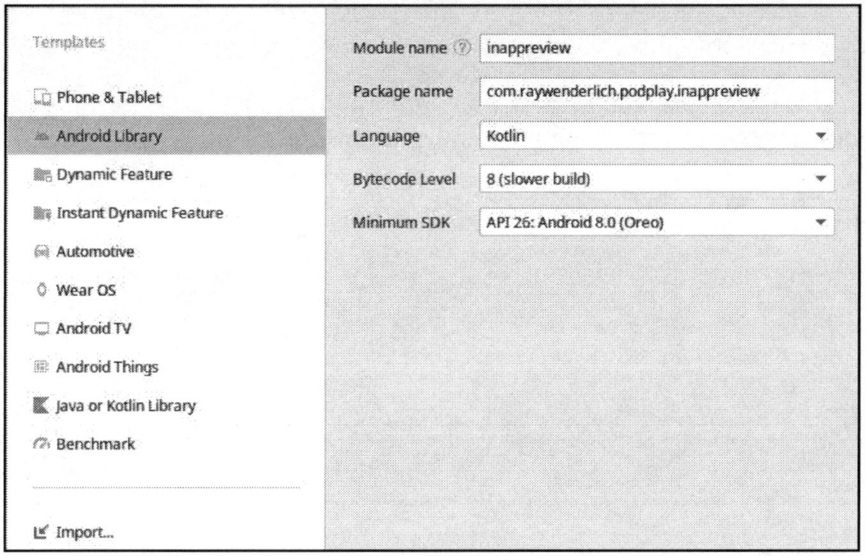

In the next screen, change the name of the module from the default to **inappreview**. Leave the language as **Kotlin** and the Bytecode level at **8**. Change the minimum SDK to match the minimum SDK of the project, which is 26 as of this writing. Click **Finish**, and you'll see a new **inappreview** module in the project.

In your app module's **build.gradle**, add the following to the dependencies section:

```
implementation project(":inappreview")
```

This dependency lets you use the **inappreview** code within the app module. It makes the objects, functions and types you define within the module accessible from your main app code, just as you can with other libraries you add as dependencies to your app Gradle file.

Next, make sure the version numbers for `compileSdkVersion`, `minSdkVersion` and `targetSdkVersion` match in both the app **build.gradle** and module **build.gradle** to prevent any dependency versioning issues. If you want, you can extract the version numbers into variables, so you only need to update them in one place in the future.

Finally, you need to add some dependencies to build this feature.

First, you need the Kotlin dependency and other things, such as styles. Replace the **dependencies** block in the innappreview **build.gradle** with:

```
// 1
implementation "org.jetbrains.kotlin:kotlin-stdlib:
$kotlin_version"
implementation "androidx.core:core-ktx:$coreKtx_version"

//2 - UI
implementation "androidx.appcompat:appcompat:$appCompat_version"
implementation "androidx.constraintlayout:constraintlayout:
$constraintLayout_version"
implementation "androidx.cardview:cardview:$cardView_version"

// 3 - Play Core
api "com.google.android.play:core:$playCore_version"
api "com.google.android.play:core-ktx:$playCoreKtx_version"
```

Here's a code breakdown:

1. Note the use throughout of variables for library version numbers. You can define these variables in the `buildscript` block of your project **build.gradle**. That way, you only need to update version numbers in one place rather than remembering to keep them in sync across multiple Gradle files. The starter project already has version number variables defined. Keep in mind these numbers change frequently: It's usually best to keep your library versions up to date. Also, note the use of double quotes everywhere rather than single quotes. While either notation might be legal in Groovy, using double quotes makes things easier if you ever want to convert your Gradle files to Kotlin instead.

2. You need these to set up the general UI code.
3. The In-App Review API is a part of the **Play Core SDK. The Play Core KTX** library is optional. It provides Kotlin coroutines versions for the asynchronous method calls in the regular Play Core Library and other useful extensions that use the APIs more idiomatic from Kotlin.

Click **Sync Now**. Build and run to check that everything works OK.

Review prompt UI

Next, you need to create the UI for your review prompt.

Start by creating new resource directories within the **inappreview** module for **drawable**, **layout** and **values.** For each, right-click the module package and select **New -> Android Resource Directory**. Then choose the appropriate directory type. Android Studio will then create each of those directories for you under **res.**

You'll use **Databinding** to tie your UI code to your XML layouts. Make sure you enable Databinding:

In the app **build.gradle**, add the following code in the `android{}` block after `compileSdkVersion`:

```
dataBinding {
  enabled = true
}
```

In the inappreview **build.gradle**, add the following code in the `android{}` block:

```
buildFeatures {
  viewBinding true
}
```

The code above enables View Binding in the inappreview module. Click **Sync Now**.

Under **res -> layout** for the **inappreview** module, create a new layout file named **fragment_in_app_review_prompt**. Then replace the contents of the file with:

```
<?xml version="1.0" encoding="utf-8"?>
<androidx.cardview.widget.CardView xmlns:android="http://
schemas.android.com/apk/res/android"
  xmlns:app="http://schemas.android.com/apk/res-auto"
  android:id="@+id/inAppReviewPromptRoot"
  android:layout_width="match_parent"
  android:layout_height="match_parent"
  android:layout_gravity="center"
  android:orientation="vertical"
  app:cardCornerRadius="4dp"
  app:cardElevation="0dp">

  <LinearLayout
    android:layout_width="match_parent"
    android:layout_height="wrap_content"
    android:layout_gravity="center"
    android:orientation="vertical">

    <LinearLayout
      android:layout_width="match_parent"
      android:layout_height="wrap_content"
      android:orientation="horizontal"
      android:paddingTop="@dimen/largeMargin">

      <ImageView
        android:id="@+id/sadFace"
        android:layout_width="@dimen/ratePromptFaceSize"
        android:layout_height="@dimen/ratePromptFaceSize"
        android:layout_marginStart="@dimen/largeMargin"
        android:contentDescription="@string/sad_face"
        android:src="@drawable/sad_face" />

      <ImageView
        android:id="@+id/progressBar"
        android:layout_width="0dp"
        android:layout_height="wrap_content"
        android:layout_marginTop="@dimen/smallMargin"
        android:layout_marginStart="@dimen/promptProgressMargin"
        android:layout_marginEnd="@dimen/promptProgressMargin"
        android:layout_weight="1"
        android:contentDescription="@string/progress_bar"
        android:src="@drawable/progress_black" />

      <ImageView
        android:id="@+id/happyFace"
        android:layout_width="@dimen/ratePromptFaceSize"
        android:layout_height="@dimen/ratePromptFaceSize"
        android:layout_marginEnd="@dimen/largeMargin"
        android:contentDescription="@string/happy_face"
```

```
        android:src="@drawable/happy_face" />

    </LinearLayout>

    <TextView
      android:id="@+id/reviewPromptTitle"
      style="@style/TextAppearance.AppCompat.Headline"
      android:layout_width="match_parent"
      android:layout_height="wrap_content"
      android:layout_margin="@dimen/defaultMargin"
      android:gravity="center_horizontal"
      android:text="@string/inAppReviewTitle"
      android:textColor="@color/charcoal_black"
      android:textSize="@dimen/ratePromptTitleTextSize" />

    <TextView
      android:id="@+id/reviewPromptText"
      android:layout_width="match_parent"
      android:layout_height="wrap_content"
      android:layout_marginStart="@dimen/defaultMargin"
      android:layout_marginEnd="@dimen/defaultMargin"
      android:gravity="center"
      android:text="@string/inAppReviewMessage"
      android:textSize="@dimen/ratePromptMessageTextSize" />

    <TextView
      android:id="@+id/leaveReview"
      android:layout_width="match_parent"
      android:layout_height="@dimen/buttonSize"
      android:layout_marginHorizontal="@dimen/defaultMargin"
      android:layout_marginTop="@dimen/largeMargin"
      android:background="@color/dark_sea_green"
      android:gravity="center"
      android:text="@string/inAppReviewRateNow"
      android:textColor="@color/white"
      android:textSize="@dimen/promptButtonTextSize" />

    <TextView
      android:id="@+id/reviewLater"
      android:layout_width="match_parent"
      android:layout_height="@dimen/buttonSize"
      android:layout_marginHorizontal="@dimen/defaultMargin"
      android:layout_marginTop="@dimen/buttonMarginTop"
      android:layout_marginBottom="@dimen/defaultMargin"
      android:background="?attr/selectableItemBackground"
      android:gravity="center"
      android:text="@string/inAppReviewRateLater"
      android:textSize="@dimen/promptButtonTextSize" />
  </LinearLayout>
</androidx.cardview.widget.CardView>
```

Then copy **drawable** and **values** from the final project into your current project. If you're following along with the provided XML, the UI will look like this:

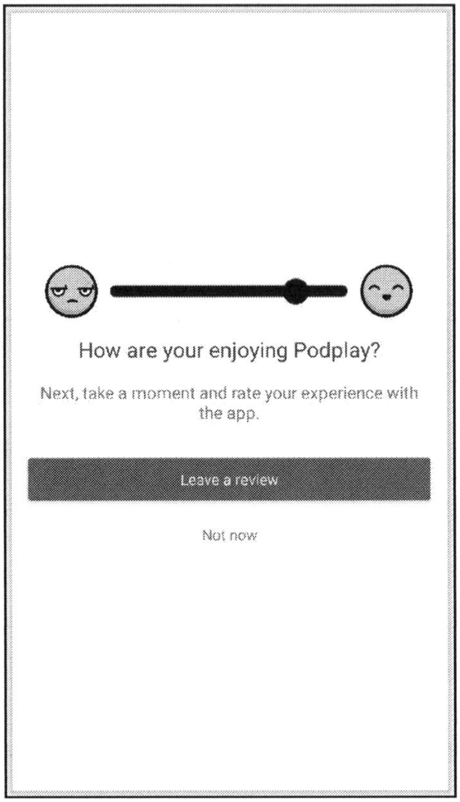

In the inappreview module, create a new package for the Kotlin class corresponding to your layout file and name it **dialog**. Create a new Kotlin class named **InAppReviewPromptDialog** in this module and add:

```
import androidx.fragment.app.DialogFragment

class InAppReviewPromptDialog: DialogFragment() {

  private var binding: FragmentInAppReviewPromptBinding? = null

  override fun onCreateView(
    inflater: LayoutInflater,
    container: ViewGroup?,
    savedInstanceState: Bundle?
  ): View? {
    binding = FragmentInAppReviewPromptBinding.inflate(inflater,
container, false)
```

```
    return binding?.root
  }

  override fun onViewCreated(view: View, savedInstanceState:
Bundle?) {
    super.onViewCreated(view, savedInstanceState)
    initListeners()
    dialog?.setCanceledOnTouchOutside(false)
  }

  private fun initListeners() {
    val binding = binding ?: return

    binding.leaveReview.setOnClickListener
{ onLeaveReviewTapped() }
    binding.reviewLater.setOnClickListener { onRateLaterTapped()
}
  }

  private fun onLeaveReviewTapped() {
    // TODO
    dismissAllowingStateLoss()
  }

  private fun onRateLaterTapped() {
    // TODO
    dismissAllowingStateLoss()
  }

  /**
   * Styles the dialog to have a transparent background and
window insets.
   */
  override fun onStart() {
    super.onStart()
    initStyle()
  }

  private fun initStyle() {
    val back = ColorDrawable(Color.TRANSPARENT)
    dialog?.window?.setBackgroundDrawable(back)
    dialog?.window?.setLayout(
      resources.getDimensionPixelSize(R.dimen.ratePromptWidth),
      resources.getDimensionPixelSize(R.dimen.ratePromptHeight))
  }
}
```

In the code above, you create a `DialogFragment` and set its style. You also set the click listeners for the **Leave a review** and **Not now** buttons.

Build and run again to make sure everything still works fine.

In-app review feature

Now that you've set up the UI, it's time to build out the in-app review feature. You want to show the UI from the previous section after using Podplay for some pre-defined amount of time. The dialog will offer two options: one to rate the app and one to rate it later.

The first option will start the review flow and save the user's selection to preferences, so you don't ask them again. The second option will also save the user's selection to preferences, along with a timestamp for when the event occurred. Then you can again prompt the user after some pre-defined amount of time has passed. In this case, you'll ask them again after a month.

> **Note**: In this exercise you are going to be using a pattern of creating interfaces in implementing them. This is being done to make it easy to integrate this example with **dagger** in the event that you decide to use this in your own application. If you are not using dagger you may want to refactor this o get rid of those interfaces.

Create a new package named **preferences** in the module. Then, add a new interface named **InAppReviewPreferences** in this package. Define the following functions for the interface:

```
// 1
fun hasUserRatedApp(): Boolean

fun setUserRatedApp(hasRated: Boolean)

// 2
fun hasUserChosenRateLater(): Boolean

fun setUserChosenRateLater(hasUserChosenRateLater: Boolean)

// 3
fun getRateLaterTime(): Long

fun setRateLater(time: Long)
```

This interface serves as an abstraction for the logic to store and fetch the data regarding the user's rating choices:

1. Know if the user already rated the app.
2. Know if they instead chose to rate later.
3. Know what "later" means as you'll define a time when to remind them again.

Next, in the same package, add a class named **InAppReviewPreferencesImpl** and replace the contents with:

```
class InAppReviewPreferencesImpl(
  private val sharedPreferences: SharedPreferences
// 1
) : InAppReviewPreferences {

  // 2
    companion object {
        const val KEY_IN_APP_REVIEW_PREFERENCES =
"inAppReviewPreferences"

        private const val KEY_HAS_RATED_APP = "hasRatedApp"
        private const val KEY_CHOSEN_RATE_LATER =
"chosenRateLater"
        private const val KEY_RATE_LATER_TIME = "rateLaterTime"
    }
}
```

In the code above:

1. `InAppReviewPreferencesImpl` implements the interface you defined earlier.
2. You define some constants for storing the user's choices in `SharedPreferences`.

In Android Studio, select **Code** -> **Implement Methods** to fill in the missing interface methods. Then update those methods as follows:

```
override fun hasUserRatedApp(): Boolean =
    sharedPreferences.getBoolean(KEY_HAS_RATED_APP, false)

override fun setUserRatedApp(hasRated: Boolean) =
  sharedPreferences.edit { putBoolean(KEY_HAS_RATED_APP,
hasRated) }

override fun hasUserChosenRateLater(): Boolean =
  sharedPreferences.getBoolean(KEY_CHOSEN_RATE_LATER, false)

override fun setUserChosenRateLater(hasUserChosenRateLater:
Boolean) =
```

```
  sharedPreferences.edit { putBoolean(KEY_CHOSEN_RATE_LATER,
hasUserChosenRateLater) }

override fun getRateLaterTime(): Long =
  sharedPreferences.getLong(KEY_RATE_LATER_TIME,
System.currentTimeMillis())

override fun setRateLater(time: Long) =
  sharedPreferences.edit { putLong(KEY_RATE_LATER_TIME, time) }
```

These functions store and read data to and from shared preferences. Notice you use `edit`, which takes in a lambda function. This extension function is a part of the Core KTX dependency, and you can use it by adding:

```
import androidx.core.content.edit
```

Now that you've implemented the preferences and the date part of the feature, it's time to connect this to your review dialog. Open **InAppReviewPromptDialog** and add:

```
private val preferences: InAppReviewPreferences
```

Instead of initializing an instance of `InAppReviewPreferences` inside `InAppReviewPromptDialog`, you provide it via the constructor.

Next, add the following line to the beginning of `onLeaveReviewTapped()`:

```
preferences.setUserRatedApp(true)
```

When the user taps **Leave Review**, you'll store their choice.

Similiarly, add the following lines to beginning of `onRateLaterTapped`:

```
preferences.setUserChosenRateLater(true)
preferences.setRateLater(getLaterTime())
```

Note the second line will throw an error as you haven't defined `getLaterTime()` yet. This code specifies that the user chose to rate the app later and stores when to prompt them again.

Next, implement `cancel` and `getRateLaterTime()` as follows:

```
private fun getLaterTime(): Long {
  return System.currentTimeMillis() + TimeUnit.DAYS.toMillis(14)
}

override fun onCancel(dialog: DialogInterface) {
```

```
    preferences.setUserChosenRateLater(true)
    preferences.setRateLater(getLaterTime())
    super.onCancel(dialog)
  }
```

> **Note**: When importing the package for `TimeUnit`, choose `java.util.concurrent`.

In the code above, you use `getLaterTime()` to show the ratings dialog after fourteen days. If the user cancels the dialog, you treat it the same as if they chose to "rate later". Alternatively, you could alter the logic of the cancel case or extract these two scenarios into a single function.

Build and run to make sure everything still works as before.

Implementing the in-app review manager

Now that you have almost everything in place regarding project setup and data, it's time to build the in-app review manager. Create a new interface in the **inappreview** module called **InAppReviewManager** and add the following to the body:

```
fun startReview(activity: Activity)

fun isEligibleForReview(): Boolean
```

The code above abstracts two functions:

1. `isEligibleForReview` will check if the app state is ready to show the user an in-app review dialog, and
2. `startReview` will start the review.

Next, add the implementation class for this interface, **InAppReviewManagerImpl**, and add:

```
class InAppReviewManagerImpl(
  private val reviewManager: ReviewManager,
  private val inAppReviewPreferences: InAppReviewPreferences
): InAppReviewManager {

  companion object {
    private const val KEY_REVIEW = "reviewFlow"
  }
```

```
  private var reviewInfo: ReviewInfo? = null

  init {
    if (isEligibleForReview()) {
      reviewManager.requestReviewFlow().addOnCompleteListener {
        if (it.isComplete && it.isSuccessful) {
          this.reviewInfo = it.result
        }
      }
    }
  }

}
```

In the code above, you add a constructor to `InAppReviewManagerImpl` that takes three parameters that are instances of `Context`, `ReviewManager` and `InAppReviewPreferences`. You also add a variable to store an instance of `ReviewInfo`. You first check if it's OK to ask for a review, and if it is, you store information about the review in `reviewInfo`.

Next, add the following code to the same class:

```
override fun isEligibleForReview(): Boolean {
  // 1
  return (!inAppReviewPreferences.hasUserRatedApp() &&
          !inAppReviewPreferences.hasUserChosenRateLater()
          // 2
          || (inAppReviewPreferences.hasUserChosenRateLater() &&
enoughTimePassed()))
}

// 3
private fun enoughTimePassed(): Boolean {
  val rateLaterTimeStamp =
inAppReviewPreferences.getRateLaterTime()

  return abs(rateLaterTimeStamp - System.currentTimeMillis()) >=
TimeUnit.DAYS.toMillis(14)
}
```

Note: When resolving the import for abs, choose `kotlin.math`.

In the code above, you check if:

1. The user hasn't given a rating yet and they haven't chosen to rate later.
2. They've previously chosen to rate later, and enough time has passed since then to prompt them again.

If these conditions are met, your app can ask the user for a review.

3. To check if enough time has passed, you calculate if the difference between the rate later timestamp and the current day is at least two weeks.

Finally, add the following methods to start the review flow:

```
override fun startReview(activity: Activity) {
  val myReviewInfo = reviewInfo
  if (myReviewInfo != null) {
    reviewManager.launchReviewFlow(activity, myReviewInfo)
      .addOnCompleteListener { reviewFlow ->
        onReviewFlowLaunchCompleted(reviewFlow)
      }
  }
}

private fun onReviewFlowLaunchCompleted(reviewFlow: Task<Void>)
{
  if (reviewFlow.isSuccessful) {
    logSuccess()
  }
}

private fun logSuccess() {
  if (BuildConfig.DEBUG) {
    Log.d(KEY_REVIEW, "Review complete!")
  }
}
```

To start the review, you call `reviewManager` to launch `reviewFlow` and pass in which activity you want the flow to be bound to and which information you want to start the flow with. Then you add `CompleteListener` and pass the `reviewFlow` task to `onReviewFlowLaunchCompleted`. If the flow was successful, and you're in a debug build, you log the successful status.

Note that you don't need to do anything with the task or the review info. The manager takes care of everything for you and will launch the flow and show the dialog. The last step is to connect the manager to your UI and the rest of the app.

Connecting the manager to the UI

Finally, you need to connect the manager to the UI. Create an interface named **InAppReviewView** in the `inappreview` module. You'll implement this interface in places you want to expose and use the in-app review feature. Add the following function to this interface:

```
fun showReviewFlow()
```

Next, open **InAppReviewPromptDialog.kt** and add the following code to the constructor:

```
private val inAppReviewManager: InAppReviewManager
```

Then replace the `TODO` comment in `onLeaveReviewTapped()` with the following to start the on review flow when the user taps the review option in the dialog:

```
inAppReviewManager.startReview(requireActivity())
```

Open **PodcastActivity.kt** and add the manager by injection, just as you did above. The manager holds the information to check if the app is eligible to show your review dialog, which is why you need it there. Add the following code to the end of `onCreate()` to set up the view in the `ViewModel`:

```
podcastViewModel.setInAppReviewView(this)
```

You'll get a compilation error since `setInAppReviewView()` doesn't exist yet in the podcast `ViewModel`. Click the error prompt in Android Studio and choose **create member function** to automatically create the corresponding function in the `ViewModel`.

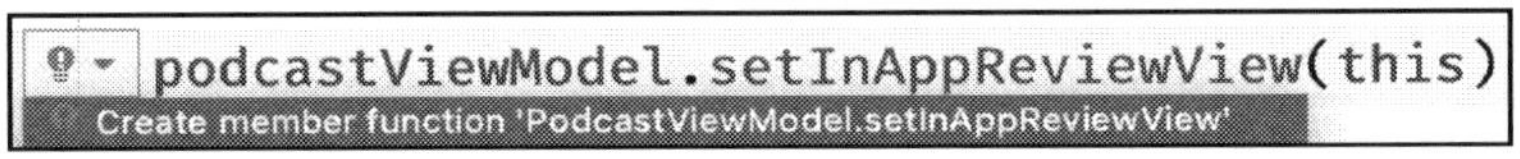

Next, in **PodcastActivity.kt**, implement the **InAppReviewView** interface, so the class signature now looks like this:

```
class PodcastActivity :
    AppCompatActivity(),
    PodcastListAdapterListener,
    OnPodcastDetailsListener,
    InAppReviewView {
```

Then implement `showReviewFlow()`:

```
override fun showReviewFlow() {
}
```

Now, add the following code to the `PodcastViewModel` to add `InAppReviewView`:

```
private lateinit var inAppReview: InAppReviewView
```

And update `setInAppReviewView()`:

```
fun setInAppReviewView(podcastActivity: PodcastActivity) {
  this.inAppReview = podcastActivity
}
```

This sets up the `InAppReviewView`, letting you tell `PodcastActivity` to show your review prompt dialog. Add the following function to `PocastActivity`:

```
private fun checkIfNeedsReviewPrompt() {
  val value = podcastListAdapter.itemCount
  if (value > 3) {
    showReviewFlow()
  }
}
```

The code above checks if there are three or more subscribed podcasts in the podcast list on the screen. You could choose some other criteria for when to show a review prompt, but for this example, assume that if the user has subscribed to three podcasts, they've been using the app enough to have some impression of it.

Next, you need access to instances of `InAppReviewManager` and `InAppReviewPreferences`. First, add the following field declarations in `PodcastActivity` as follows:

```
private lateinit var preferences: InAppReviewPreferences
private lateinit var inAppReviewManager: InAppReviewManager
```

You also need to initialize the field declarations above. Add:

```
private fun setupReviewManager() {
  val sharedPreferences =
getSharedPreferences(InAppReviewPreferencesImpl.KEY_IN_APP_REVIE
W_PREFERENCES, Context.MODE_PRIVATE)
  preferences = InAppReviewPreferencesImpl(sharedPreferences)
  inAppReviewManager = InAppReviewManagerImpl(
    ReviewManagerFactory.create(this),
    preferences
  )
}
```

In the code above, you create new instances of `SharedPreferences` and `ReviewManager` and then use them to create an instance of `InAppReviewPreferencesImpl`.

Inside `onCreate()` right below `updateControls`, add an invocation to `setupReviewManager`.

Now that you have instances of `InAppReviewPreferences` and `InAppReviewManager`, you can create an instance of `InAppReviewPromptDialog`. Add the following code to `showReviewFlow()`:

```
if(inAppReviewManager.isEligibleForReview()) {
  val dialog = InAppReviewPromptDialog(preferences,
inAppReviewManager)
  dialog.show(this.supportFragmentManager, null)
}
```

In the code above, you check if the app is eligible for review. If it is, you create a dialog and show it.

Call `setupReviewManager` inside `onCreate` between `updateControls()` and `setupPodcastListView()`.

Finally, add a call to `checkIfNeedsReviewPrompt()` inside `showSubscribedPodcasts` right after setting the adapter data.

Build and run. Subscribe to four of your favorite podcasts. As soon as you add the fourth podcast, you'll see a review dialog as shown below:

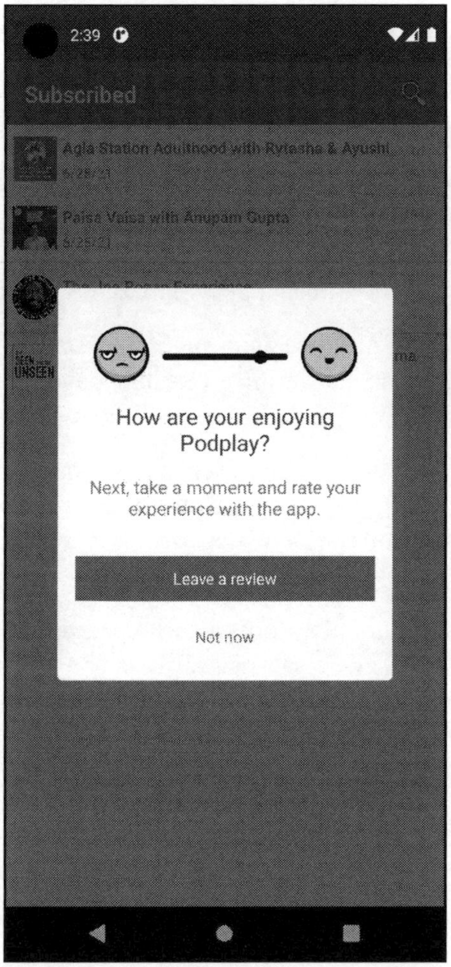

Testing the in-app review feature

In-App Review is tied to the **Play Core API environment**, so you need to do a few things to make it testable and make sure it works. It requires live data from the Play Store or the app you want to publish.

To test In-App Review, you'll need a few different devices or emulators and some fresh Google Play accounts that haven't rated the app yet. Upload your APK for your app with the feature to one of the testing tracks. Fortunately, if you've been following along with this book so far, you're already set up with this!

Testing limitations

Currently, you can only test In-App Review with builds from the Play Store. However, you can test your in-app review integration using an internal testing track or internal app sharing. For rapid iteration, internal app sharing is the way to go. However, note that you can't submit the reviews to the Play Store when using when this method. For that, you need to use the internal test track instead.

With the internal test track, you need to use Google Play accounts that haven't rated the app yet, and you can't request the IAR dialog more than a certain number of times. The actual number depends on some quota set by Google, and it may vary. This quota doesn't apply to the internal app sharing, however.

Also, even if your code works and you get a successful review flow, this isn't a guarantee the user will see the dialog since you may have already hit the quota for the number of allowed requests.

Once you've connected your devices and users as internal testers and download the app through the testing track, you can build and run the app in Android Studio to deploy new versions of the app to the device. However, you need to set up the testing initially.

Finally, keep in mind the points highlighted earlier in the chapter. It's important to know when and how to ask users for a review. If you can use moments of accomplishment or some other milestone that catches the user at a positive time, they may be more likely to take the time to review your app.

Once you have your app and fresh test user accounts set up, test the in-app review feature. Congratulations, and good luck!

Key points

As Rob Napier (@cocoaphony) famously said,

> When thinking about "good enough to ship: "Works 80%" generally doesn't mean works 80% for everyone, so they review you with four stars instead of five. Works 80% usually means "works fine for 80% and is completely broken for 20%, and that 20% write all the reviews."

Remember, users generally don't bother to rate your app until they have a problem. At that point, they'll likely give you a lower rating. Don't just chase after ratings, though. Address the actual problem.

- It's incredibly helpful to engage your users directly to provide positive reviews and intercept users with broken experiences with support.
- You can prompt your users for positive feedback in-app and intercept negative feedback by directly opening a JIRA ticket, bringing your user's frustrations to the developers.
- Google Play provides a dashboard where you can not only monitor your reviews but also respond to them directly.
- Android provides an in-app review API to automate the process of prompting users for reviews.
- Be prudent with the strategies for when to ask for a review.
- Testing the in-app review feature can be hard to set up and a bit tedious as you'll need fresh user accounts, and the process is tied to Google Play.

Where to go from here?

Check out the Android In-App Review video course on raywenderlich.com at https://www.raywenderlich.com/20065814-android-in-app-review/lessons/1

Additionally, suppose you want to take things a step further, like the author did for Octo, and you want to integrate feedback from your users directly into your ticketing system. In that case, you'll want to reference the API for whatever system you use. For JIRA and other Atlassian apps, you can find the API documentation here: https://developer.atlassian.com

To learn more about testing in-app reviews, see the official documentation here: https://developer.android.com/guide/playcore/in-app-review/test

To learn more about creating Android library modules, see the official documentation here: https://developer.android.com/studio/projects/android-library

Chapter 14: Monitoring & Improving App Performance: Android Vitals

By Fuad Kamal

Understanding Android Vitals

The Vitals section of the Play Console contains a tremendous amount of information about the health of your app in the wild. While helpful, all that information might seem overwhelming at first. You might be tempted to put off examining this area or ignore it completely. But even if you ignore Vitals, Google doesn't - and **your app's performance as reported by Vitals directly impacts how easy it is to search for and discover your app or game on the Play Store**.

Vitals reports information like Application Not Responding (ANR), performance benchmarks, battery usage, stability and much more. It collects data from real devices used by your users. As such, you get metrics that you might not otherwise get from internal testing and CI/CD workflows. However, this means the data and the availability of information appearing in Vitals is also subject to certain external factors.

If your app is newly released or you don't have many users, you may not see any data in Vitals. Also, users need to give permission on their devices for developers to collect data, or Vitals won't get any data.

In addition to Vitals, you can also use the Pre Launch Report to get similar data from the Play Console's analysis of your app running on test devices in Firebase Test Lab rather than from real-world devices and users.

However, once your data shows up in Vitals, it can be an excellent and powerful tool. For example, not only can you see how your app is performing, but you can directly see how your app performs compared to your peers and competitors.

Exploring the dashboard

On the Google Play Console, click the **Dashboard** navigation item on the left to see an overview of all the vital information about your app. Take note of the section on Android Vitals where you'll see an overview of the most important metrics from Vitals:

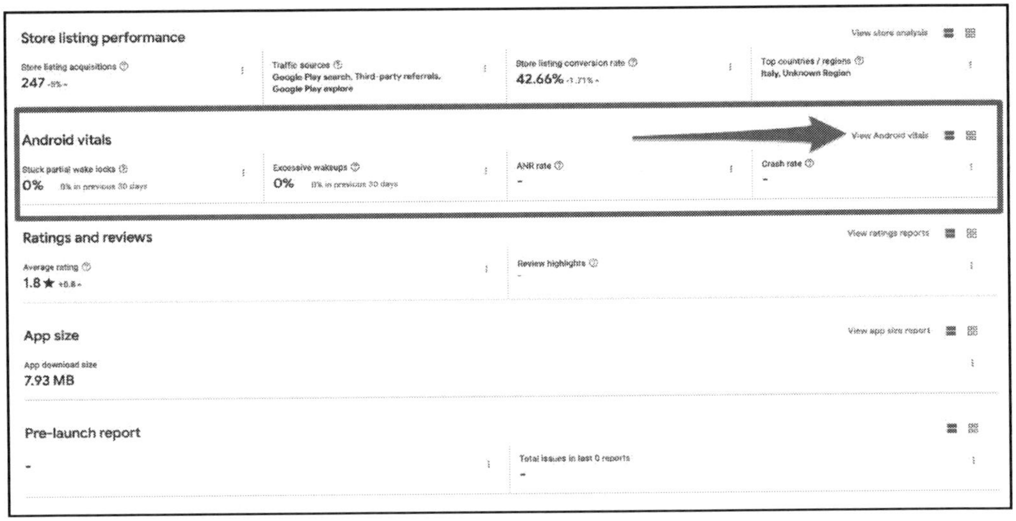

Play Console Dashboard

Click **View Android vitals** to go to the vitals section of the Play Console.

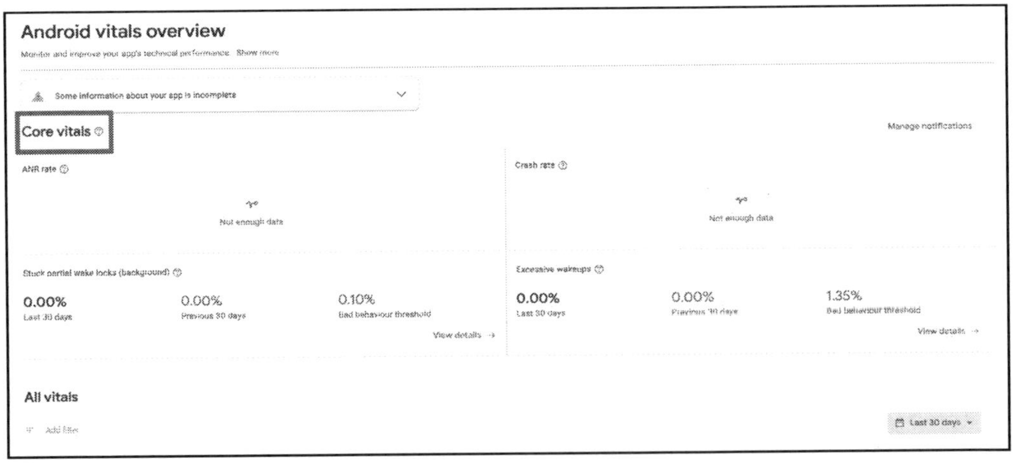

Android vitals

As you can see, under **All vitals**, the number of metrics available in Android vitals is huge. To make it easier, Google identified four **core vital metrics** that have the most significant impact on user experience. You'll find these listed under the top section titled **Core vitals**. They are:

1. ANR rate
2. Crash rate
3. Stuck partial wake locks (background)
4. Excessive wakeups

The first two metrics relate to your app's **stability**, while the last two relate to its **battery usage** and performance. Each metric has a "Bad Behavior Threshold", which is set by Google. If the core vital is over the bad behavior threshold, you get a prominent warning from Google Play, letting you know there's an issue.

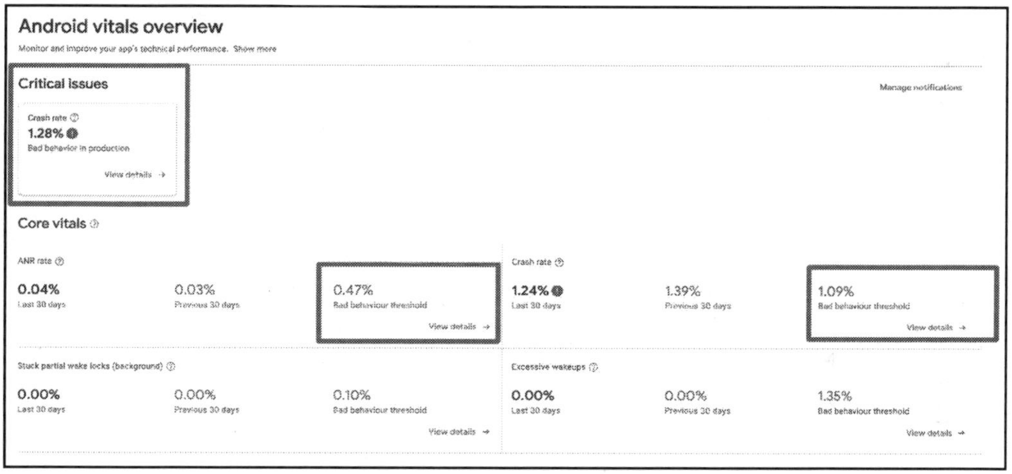

Bad behavior threshold

Click the warning for more detail.

As reported by the core vitals, your app's performance can directly affect how easy it is to search for and discover your app on the Play Store. So if you perform poorly in these areas, users might not be able to discover your app. Therefore it's critical to monitor these behaviors and make sure you stay under the bad behavior thresholds.

There are several filters you can use to drill down into the crash rate.

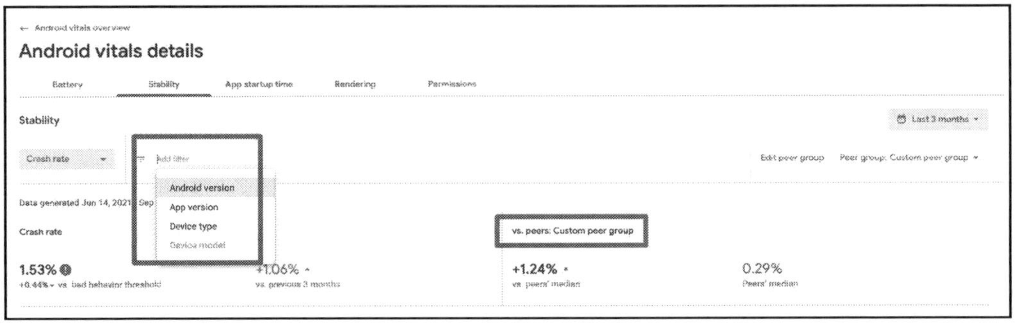

Filters and Peer Groups

In the image above, you'll see that you can filter the crash rate by Android version, app version, device type and device model. You'll learn more about crash rate later. For now, take a look at the section named **vs. peers**.

Peer groups

Peer groups are a unique and powerful Android vitals feature. Here you can compare your app's performance across key metrics with your peer and competitor apps.

This particular example shows **Custom peer group**, a custom group of apps that you define. However, there are various category presets you can compare against.

In this example, the app shown is in the telematics industry. These apps use GPS and other device sensors to report on driving behavior. The app's developers might want to know how their app compares, for example, to other GPS mapping apps or apps in the **Auto & vehicles** categories as shown in the image below:

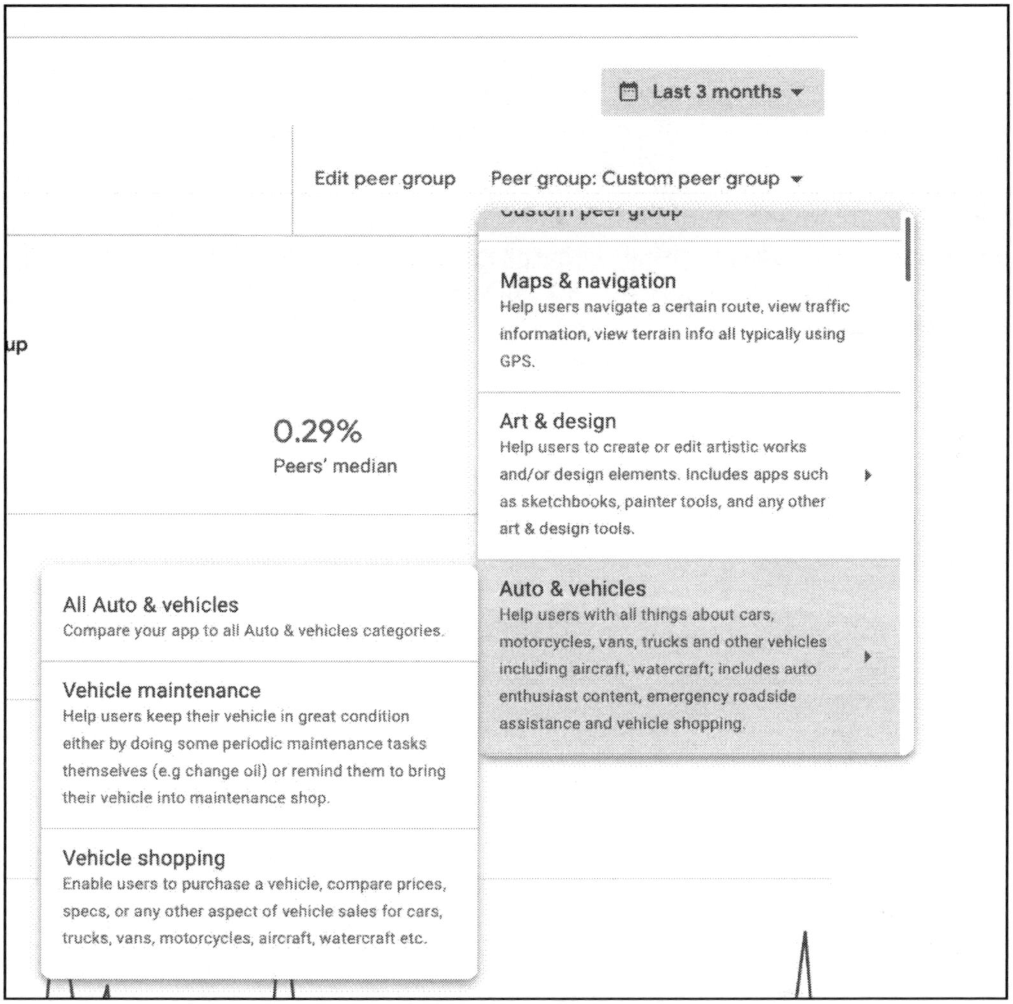

Peer Categories

While your crash threshold might be under the bad behavior benchmark, you can see if it's better or worse than your peer groups.

Vitals is still private: Google designed it carefully so that your competitors can't discern specifics about your Vitals. Still, if you want, you can opt-out of this feature completely so they can't see anything about your app. But then you also can't use the feature anymore to compare yourself against your competitors.

The key is to monitor Android Vitals for any problems and address them early before they get much worse. For example, you can monitor Vitals by signing up for notifications from Android Vitals. With notifications, Google proactively informs you if there are any problems you need to address right away, rather than trying to spot issues yourself manually.

You sign up for Android Vitals notifications the same place you sign up for other notifications in the Play Console. From the Play Console, click **All apps**, then **Setup -> Notifications**. Or, from the Android vitals overview page, click **Manage notifications**:

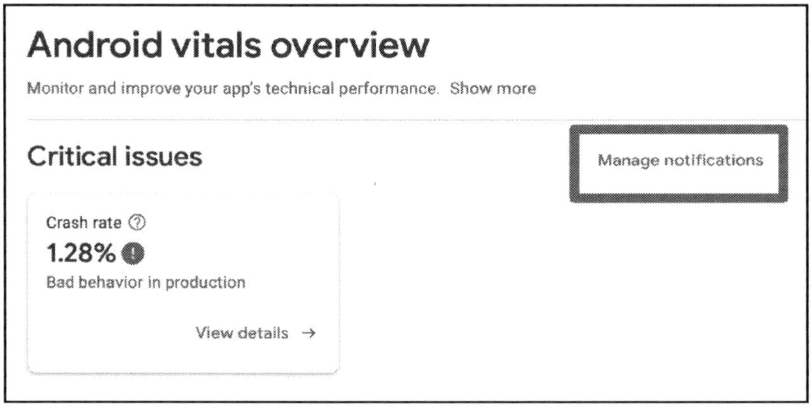

Manage Notifications

Then make sure **Android vitals** is checked:

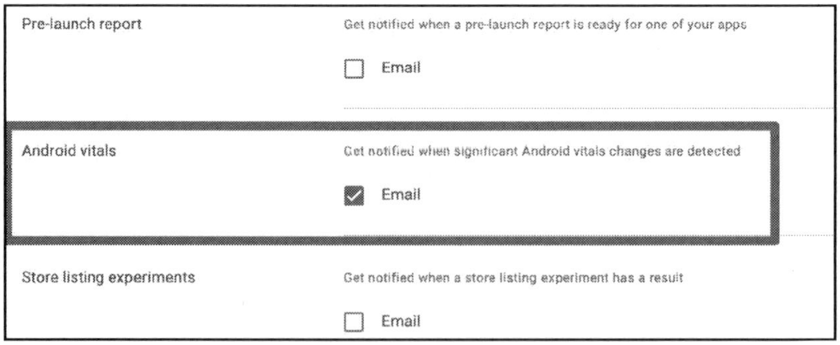

Email Notifications for Android vitals

Crash analytics and reports

Suppose you had a crash rate above the bad behavior threshold. You might use Android vitals to answer questions like these:

1. How long has the crash been going on for?

- If it's not from a recent release, does the crash have to do with a back end issue rather than an issue with the app itself?

2. Is the crash related to a recent version of Android OS?

- You can drill down in vitals to see which versions of Android the crash affected.
- If the crash is Android version-specific, that might give you a clue regarding the root cause of the issue. Perhaps something changed in the behavior of Android?

3. Is the crash related to a specific device or specific hardware issues?

- You can drill down in vitals by device.

4. Is the crash related to a particular app release?

- You can drill down in vitals by release version and pinpoint a particular APK or app bundle involved.

To confirm if a particular release is responsible for causing a crash, drill down in vitals by app version. Then filter on the penultimate version to confirm that version didn't crash as much as the last release. Once you've confirmed that a particular app version is causing a spike in the crash rate, the next step is to view the real-time crash reports.

From the Play Console menu, go to **Android vitals -> Crashes and ANRs**.

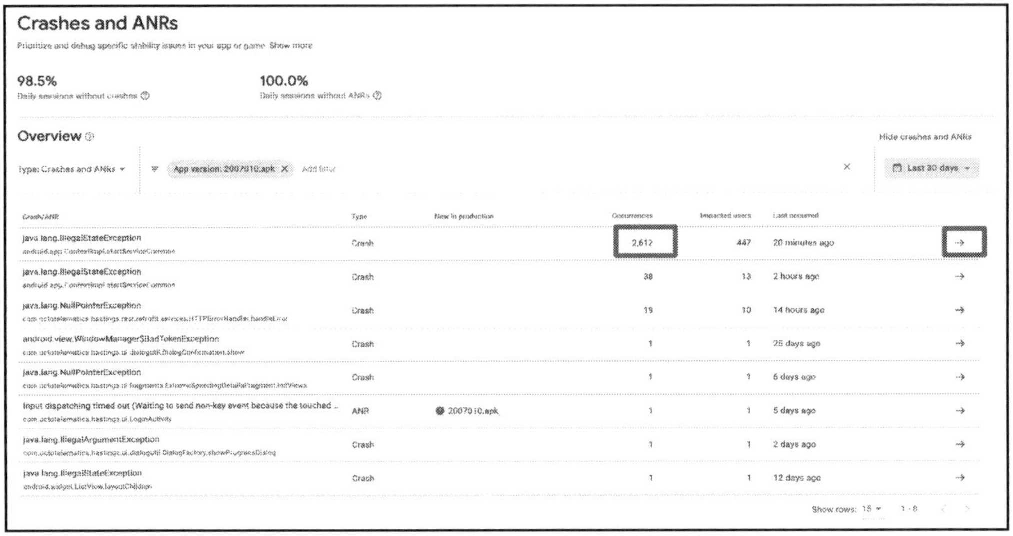

Real time crashes

In the example above, you see a single type of crash that causes most of the crashes for this release version. You can then click the arrow in the rightmost column to see the crash details, view the stack trace of the crash and proceed to debug the issue.

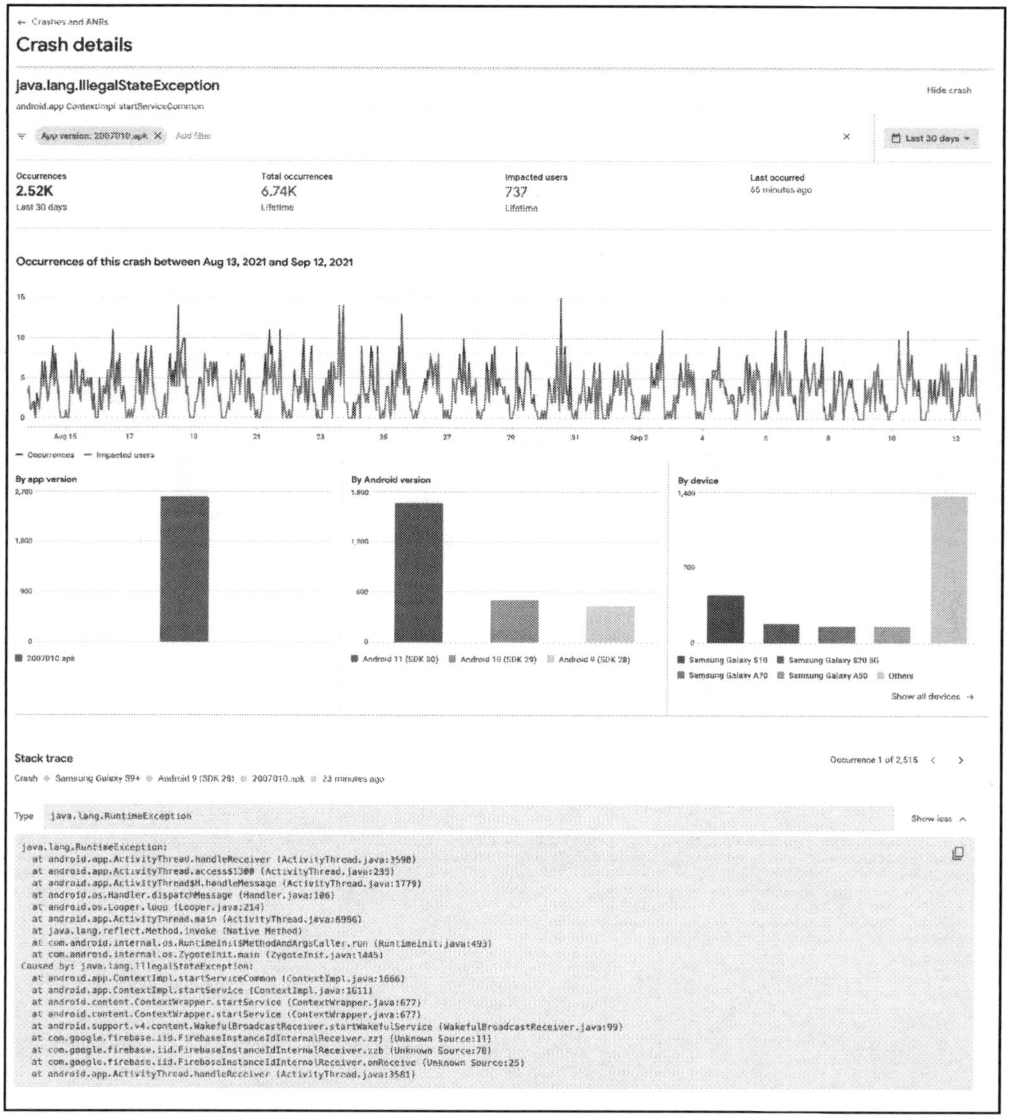

Real time crash details

In the details view, note the **Last occurred** heading. Suppose you thought the crash was a server-side issue, and your back end team had resolved the supposed issue. If the last occurrence of the crash was *after* the supposed fix, you would know that the issue was, in fact, not resolved.

On this page, you'll also see crash details, like the timeline and trends across app version, Android version and device. You can also find the Stack trace similar to the one you get on Firebase Crashlytics.

Reviewing pre-launch reports

The **Pre-launch report**, or **PLR**, is a valuable companion to Android vitals. You'll find it in the release management section of the Play Console. Navigate to **Release -> Testing -> Pre-launch report**. A typical PLR looks like the one shown in the image below:

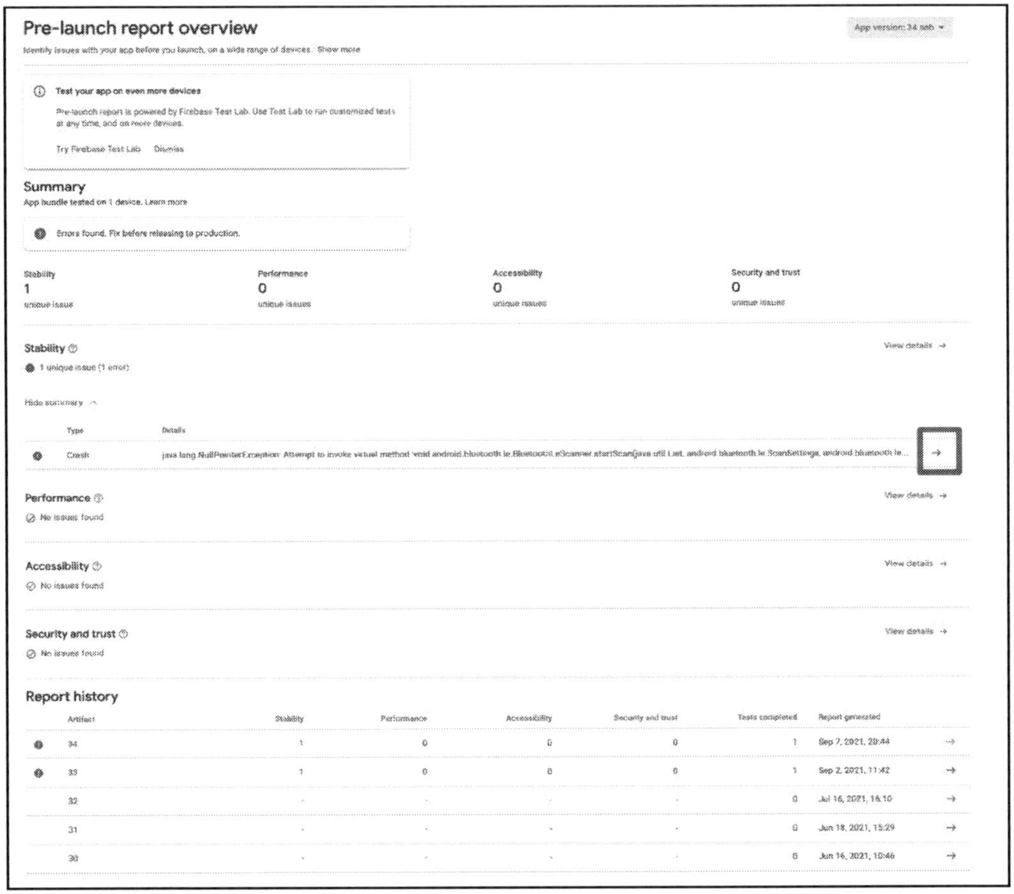

PLR Overview

While Android vitals helps you monitor your app's health after you launch, the pre-launch report helps you check things out before you launch a particular version of your app.

As you explored earlier in this book, you first submit your app to a test track. Even if your app is in production, if you don't have any active test tracks, you may not see any data in the PLR.

Once your app is in a test track, Google runs your app on real devices in the Firebase test lab. Firebase automatically navigates through your app, captures screenshots, crash exceptions and device logs. Google can capture much more metadata in the PLR phase than in Android vitals.

Again, wherever there's a problem, you can click it and get more details. For example, in the screenshot above, clicking the highlighted arrow for the crash shows this detailed stack trace, video and more:

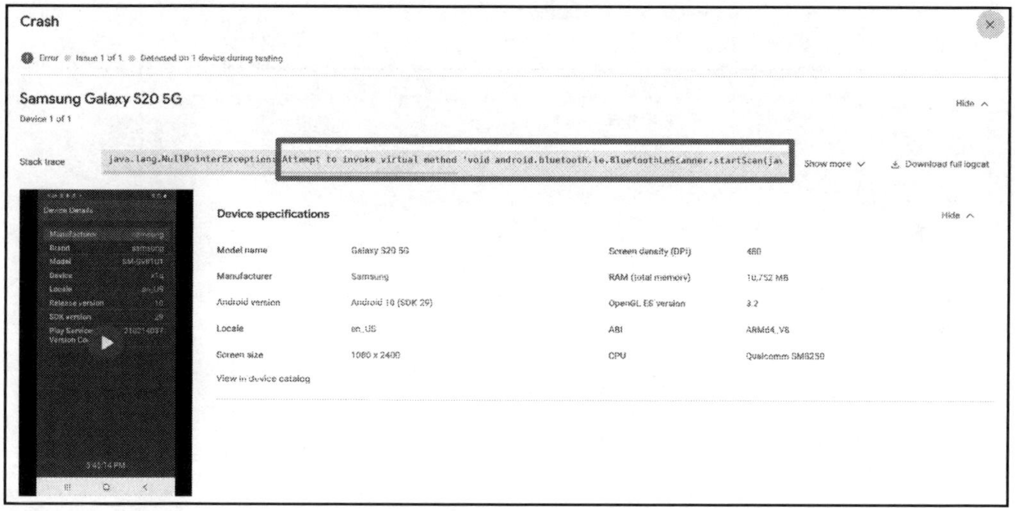

Real time crash details

But unlike Vitals, in PLR for the stack trace, you also get to see the exception message. This type of data is obscured from Vitals due to user privacy concerns. Obscured data includes information about user data, like logcat and credit card information.

Since PLR runs on devices in a test lab that real users don't use there are no privacy restrictions. You can even download the full logcat for a given exception. You can also see a video of the entire test session and see exactly what was going on at the point of the crash. This can be useful even if there are no crashes. For example, you can see how your app renders on different devices your developers might not even have access to.

You can also see screenshots of your app running on different devices and locales.

In Play Console, navigate to **Testing -> Pre-launch report -> Settings**:

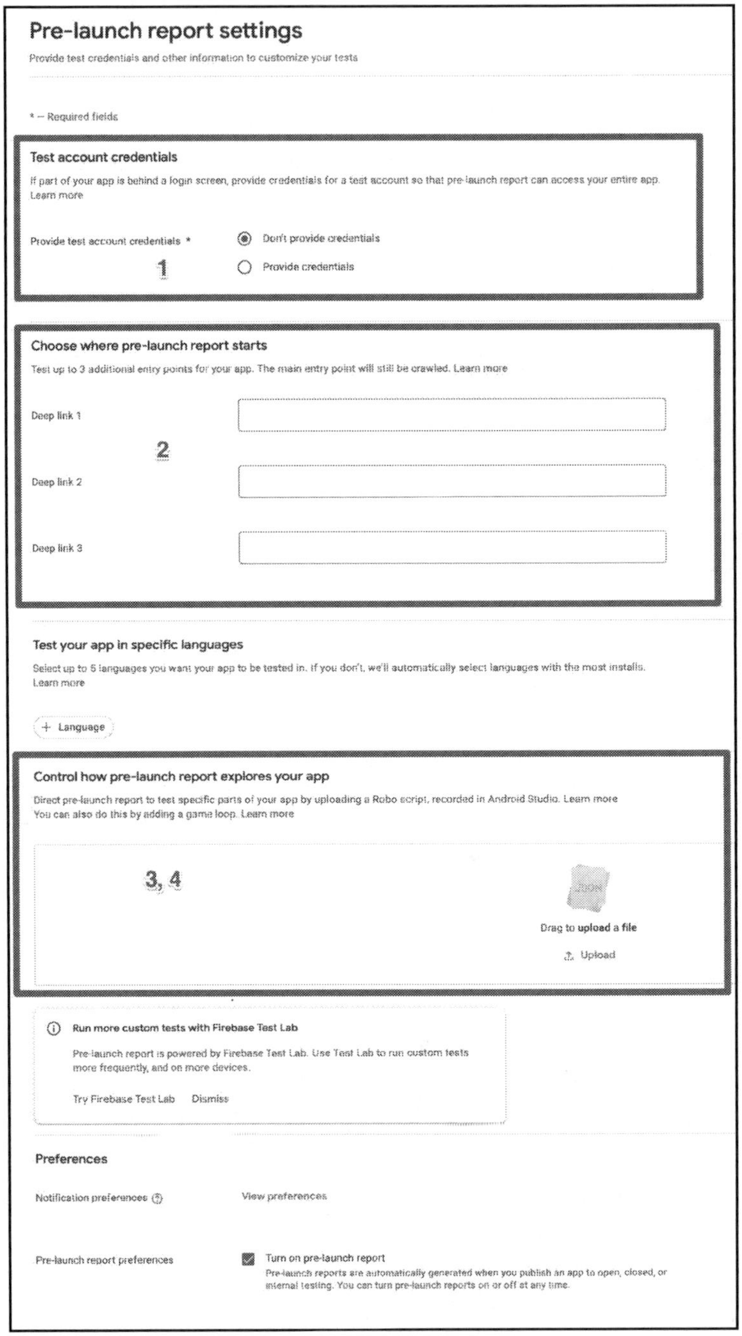

Pre-launch report settings

The PLR crawler is pretty smart when it comes to automatically crawling your app. However, sometimes it needs help to get past certain points. Google has provided four different ways to customize PLR to help it crawl past certain types of choke points:

1. **Providing Test Credentials**: If you have a login screen in your app, the crawler will need a set of test credentials to get past it.
2. **Providing Deep Links**: You can provide up to three different deep links to open your app at particular points and crawl those parts.
3. **Demo Loops**: These are particularly useful for games. You fire off an intent, `com.google.intent.action.TEST_LOOP`. The demo loop executes, and you can check what's happening with key parts of a game or app.
4. **Robo script**: You can provide a custom Robo test script for PLR to execute. For more information on Robo, see https://firebase.google.com/docs/test-lab/android/robo-ux-test.

Using Android vitals to understand your app's power consumption

Well-behaved apps optimize battery consumption by minimizing device radio and CPU usage. Android vitals lets you see the metrics for two common causes of battery drain: **wakeups** and **wake locks**.

Excessive Wakeups

Alarms performing time-based operations that prevent an idle device from sleeping cause **wakeups**.

Wake locks occur when the app has your device working so hard it won't let the device sleep.

For better battery life, use job scheduling APIs to schedule asynchronous tasks and specify conditions to maximize efficiency. This method is suitable for small tasks like clearing a cache and large ones like syncing a database to the cloud.

Understanding your app's performance

The speed at which your app renders impacts user perception of your app performance. Slow render time or frozen frames lead to bad reviews. Apps that have a render time of 16 milliseconds or reach 60 frames per second produce a silky smooth experience for your users. This is the rate at which users can perceive smooth motion within your app.

Render Times

Android vitals lets you see what percentage of users experienced more than 50% of frames with a render time of greater than 16 milliseconds so you can provide a smooth experience across all devices.

Anything greater than a render time of 700 milliseconds is considered a frozen frame, and at this rate, users consider an app to be unresponsive. Avoid slow render times or frozen frames by using frame metrics APIs to measure per interaction frame render times for devices during production.

While the view is somewhat different in PLR, it also provides insight into your app's performance:

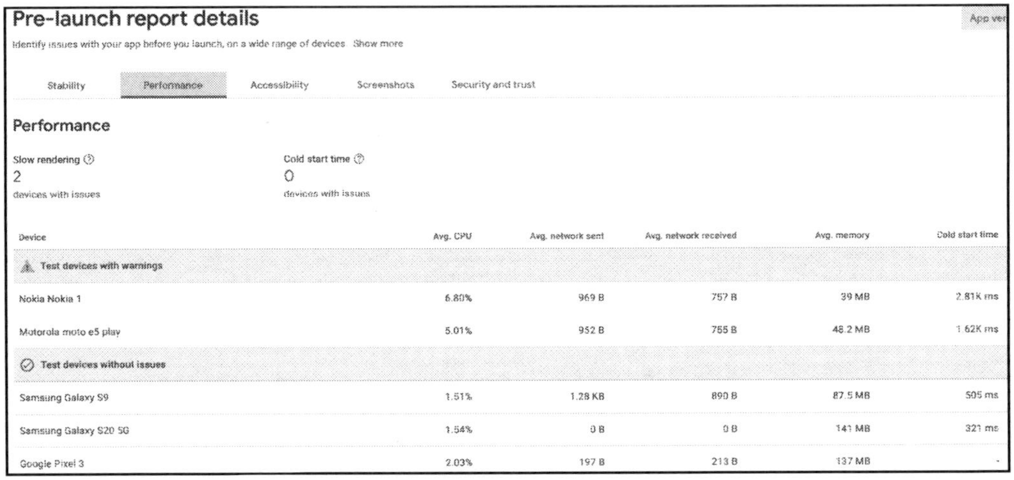

PLR Performance Overview

Click the details for the Nokia handset above, and you'll see a detailed performance report for that device:

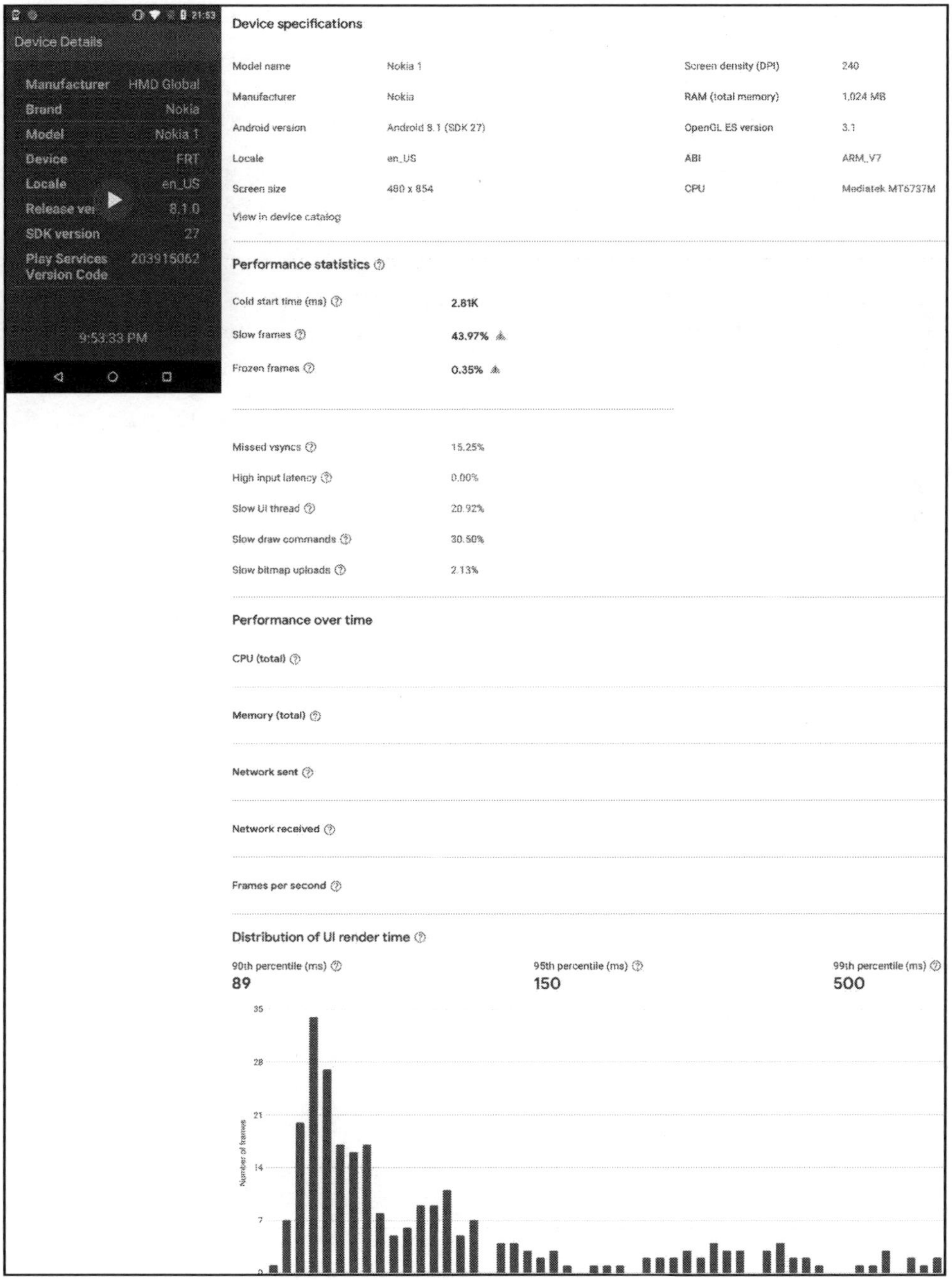

Performance details for Nokia handset

Key points

- Android vitals includes two bad behavior metrics relating to stability, Application Not Responding errors, or ANRs, and crashes. ANRs occur when the app freezes and stops responding to user input for more than five seconds. They're usually caused by deadlocks, slowness in UI threads or background processes.
- When your app crashes, it can be a frustrating experience, impacting retention and leading to bad reviews. The crash rate will show you the percentage of users experiencing crashes in your app.
- One way to address stability issues is to run pre-launch reports, which will test your alpha or beta app on physical devices so you can identify and fix issues before you launch.
- Android vitals provides two bad behavior metrics relating to battery usage: wake locks and excessive wakeups. Background tasks that could be better managed using APIs such as Work Manager cause excessive wakeups. Wake locks typically occur when your app attempts to do too much work at one time in the main thread.
- You can track many other metrics using Android vitals, but those four key metrics are highlighted for you. Use Pre-launch reports for your test track builds to get even more detailed information about your app performance and catch issues before launch.

Where to go from here?

Find out more about Android vitals key metrics and best practices at https://developer.android.com/distribute/best-practices/develop/android-vitals.html.

Learn how you can use WorkManager to schedule tasks in this tutorial on raywenderlich.com: https://www.raywenderlich.com/20689637-scheduling-tasks-with-android-workmanager.

15 Conclusion

Congratulations on completing this book! As you've worked through the chapters, you've learned how to perform a variety of tasks to help you publish and maintain a successful app in the Google Play Store. By now, have a firm understanding of how to publish and distribute a professional, polished app.

Best of all, you can use this book as an awesome reference as you publish your apps in the future.

If you have any questions or comments as you work through this book, please stop by our forums at https://forums.raywenderlich.com and look for the forum category for this particular book.

Thank you again for your purchase. Your continued support is what makes the tutorials, books, videos, conferences and everything else we do at raywenderlich.com possible, and we truly appreciate it!

Wishing you all the best in your continued Android adventures,

Evana, Fuad and Lance

The *Android App Distribution* team

Made in the USA
Monee, IL
05 November 2026

67811054R10190